IDEOLOGY AND FALSE CONSCIOUSNESS

SUNY Series in the Philosophy of the Social Sciences
Edited by Lenore Langsdorf

Ideology and False Consciousness

MARX AND HIS HISTORICAL PROGENITORS

CHRISTOPHER L. PINES

STATE UNIVERSITY OF NEW YORK PRESS • ALBANY

Published by
State University of New York Press, Albany

© 1993 State University of New York

All rights reserved

Printed in the United States of America

No part of this book may be used or reproduced
in any manner whatsoever without written permission
except in the case of brief quotations embodied in
critical articles and reviews.

For information, address State University of New York
Press, State University Plaza, Albany, NY 12246

Production by Cathleen Collins
Marketing by Theresa A. Swierzowski

Library of Congress Cataloging-in-Publication Data

Pines, Christopher L., 1954–
    Ideology and false consciousness : Marx and his historical
progenitors / Christopher L. Pines.
       p. cm. — (SUNY series in the philosophy of social sciences)
    Includes bibliographical references and index.
    ISBN 0-7914-1431-0 (alk. paper)—ISBN 0-7914-1432-9 (pbk. :
alk. paper)
    1. Marx, Karl. 1818–1883. 2. Ideology—History. I. Title.
III. Series.
B3305.M74P48   1993
140—dc20   92–15168
                                                                 CIP

10 9 8 7 6 5 4 3 2 1

Contents

1 Introduction to the Problematic   1

2 Bacon's Theory of Idols and Marx on Ideological Fallacies   17

3 Ideology and the French Enlightenment   29

4 Ideology and Political Class Struggle: Hegel's Philosophy of History and the Political False Consciousness in the Writings of Marx and Engels   65

5 The Hegelian and Feuerbachian Approach to the Alienated Mind   93

6 Alienation and False Consciousness in the Writings of the Young Marx   111

7 Alienation, the Fetishism of Commodities, and Ideology in Capital   127

8 Conclusion   157

Notes   167

Bibliography   227

Index   237

1

Introduction to the Problematic

One of the problems faced in interpreting Marx's concept of ideology is that he himself did not define the term in his writings. Even in the one work where Marx wrote most extensively on ideology, *The German Ideology*, he failed to provide us with a definition of the term. However, in the writings of Engels, Marx's life-long personal friend and political associate, and coauthor with Marx of several works, including *The German Ideology*, we do find a definition of ideology. In a letter to Franz Mehrings (14 July 1898), Engels defined ideology in the following manner:

> Ideology is a process accomplished by the so-called thinker consciously, it is true, but with a false consciousness. The real motive forces impelling him remain unknown to him; otherwise it simply would not be an ideological process. Hence he imagines false or seeming motive forces. Because it is a process of thought he derives its form as well as its content from pure thought, either his own or that of his predecessors. He works with mere thought material, which he accepts without examination as the product of thought, and does not investigate further for a more remote source independent of thought; indeed this is a matter of course to him, because, as all action is mediated by thought, it appears to him to be ultimately based upon thought.[1]

According to the above definition, some of the more prominent characteristics of the ideological false consciousness include the following: (1) human agents are unaware or ignorant of the motive forces impelling their thoughts and actions, i.e., false consciousness entails a lack of real knowledge and an obliviousness to causal influences;[2] (2) what people "imagine" to be the case (what agents perceive to be their real motives in action and the grounds of their beliefs) is not really the case, i.e., ideology entails a set of false or illusory beliefs, even self-deceptions; and (3) human agents possess false consciousness because they interpret their own motives and the source of their ideas in an idealistic way (i.e., "...because all action is mediated by thought, it appears to him to be ultimately based upon thought...")

Now, if Engels's notion of false consciousness defines the classical Marxist conception of ideology, then we should find in the writings of Marx a replication and an approximate facsimile of all or some of the above characteristics. But did Marx have a conception of ideology similar in meaning to Engels's notion of false consciousness?

Some commentators believe he did. For example, in his *The Marxist Conception of Ideology: A Critical Essay*, Martin Seliger argues that Engels's conception of false consciousness defines Marx's conception of ideology as well:

> It seems that Marx himself did not use the phrase 'false consciousness'. This makes no difference as far as his conception of ideological thought is concerned, since instead of 'false' Marx used 'incorrect', 'twisted' 'untrue' and 'abstract' besides nouns like 'illusion', etc. We may thus take 'false consciousness' to denote Marx's view as well.[3]

David Braybrooke seems to concur with Seliger on this point. In his *Encyclopedia of Philosophy* article on "ideology," Braybrooke, like Seliger, argues that for Marx ideology

> signified a false consciousness of social and economic realities, a collective illusion shared by members of a given social class and in history distinctively associated with that class.[4]

However, not all commentators agree with the interpretation that for Marx, ideology signified false consciousness. In a recent book on Marx's conception of ideology, Joe McCarney rejects any attempt to attribute to Marx an "epistemological" conception of ideology. In particular, McCarney rejects the claim that Marx had a conception of ideology as false consciousness.[5]

What McCarney has to say about Engels's definition of ideology as false consciousness is of especial interest. First of all, though McCarney argues that there exists a basic "congruence between [Engels's] treatment of the ideological and that of Marx,"[6] McCarney contends that Engels's definition of ideology is not in congruence with the predominant conception of ideology suggested by their writings. In fact, McCarney believes that the notion of false consciousness is incompatible with Marx's sociological conception of ideology because of its psychological connotations. McCarney remarks:

> It is hard to see how this [definition of ideology as false consciousness] can be taken at anything like face value. Ideology for Marx, and for Engels elsewhere, is an objective social phenomenon grounded in and guaranteed by the existence of classes. Its secret is not to be found in the blindness of individuals to the "motive forces" of their thinking. Where such a suggestion naturally leads is towards the elaboration of theories of ideology along psycho-analytical or existential lines. Within the classical Marxist framework ideology cannot be identified with any kind of self-deception, rationalization or bad faith.[7]

Now, if the notion of false consciousness doesn't define the classical Marxist conception of ideology, then how does McCarney explain Engels's use of the term in defining ideology? According to McCarney, Engels definition should be viewed as

> ...an aberration, an instance of that curious uncertainty of touch [Engels] could sometimes display, even on matters supposedly central to doctrines held jointly with Marx...[8]

Hence, in McCarney's view, Engels usage of the notion of false consciousness was an "aberration" or a passing "whim" of the moment which neither he nor Marx, particularly Marx, were to utilize in the bulk of their writings concerning ideology and the ideological consciousness. Now, McCarney's interpretation of Marx's conception of ideology as well as his disparaging remarks concerning Engels's notion of false consciousness are reflective of a broader contemporary trend in the reinterpretation of the classical Marxist conception of ideology. Like McCarney, what many contemporary theorists would like to do is to expunge any conception of false consciousness from both Marxist and non-Marxist social theory and philosophy.[9]

A review of the most recent and, in some cases, the most influential commentaries on Marx's conception of ideology will bear witness to this almost universal rejection of the notion of false consciousness. For example, David McLellan's book, *Ideology* (Minneapolis: University of Minnesota Press, 1986), summarizes the majority opinion as well as the majority's assessment of Engels's intellectual abilities in the following way:

> The first point to be made is that Marx never used the expression 'false consciousness': the originator of this expression was Engels, whose rather jejune views on ideology...[10]

McLellan also goes on in an Althusserian vein to argue that anyone attempting to attribute a conception of false consciousness to Marx's theories will not be able to find textual support for their interpretation in the later writings of Marx:

> ...any attempt to equate ideology and false consciousness in Marx must rely heavily on *The German Ideology* as opposed to Marx's later writings.[11]

Jorge Larrain has written two books on ideology in recent years to argue, among other things, that the concept of false consciousness is unsound because it is ambiguous, because it fails to convey the sociological nature of Marx's conception of ideology, and finally, because it has implications for the science/ideology distinction which are unacceptable.[12]

On a different though related track, contemporary critics also reject the notion of false consciousness because it entails an epistemological conception of ideology. What contemporary commentators would like to do is to move away from the notion that ideology somehow concerns a problem of knowledge and move towards the notion that ideology is a matter of practical social rationality in which the categories of truth and falsehood do not apply. For example, in his influential essay entitled "Marxism and Humanism," Louis Althusser argues that ideology is important primarily for its noncognitive, social functions.

> ...an ideology...is distinguished from science in that its practico-social function is more important than the theoretical function (function as knowledge).[13]

In a somewhat similar vein, Istvan Meszaros in his recent *Philosophy, Ideology, and Social Science* (New York: St. Martin's Press, 1986) offers as a Marxist definition of ideology the following:

> Ideology, as a specific form of social consciousness, is inseparable from class societies. It is constituted as the inescapable practical consciousness of such societies, concerned with the articulation of rival sets of values and strategies aimed at controlling the social metabolism.[14]

In Meszaros's opinion, Marx himself suggested this practical, sociological conception of ideology in his 1859 preface to his *Contribution to the Critique of Political Economy*. According to Meszaros, in the preface Marx did not distinguish between science and ideology in accordance with a true/false consciousness criterion. Rather, Marx's comparison of ideology with science indicates that he viewed the two as having rationalities serving different kinds of functions— i.e., science as theoretical reason serving cognitive functions and ideology as practical reason serving noncognitive ends.

> It is this practical orientation that defines also they type of rationality appropriate to ideological discourse...to imagine that socialist theory could afford to be 'ideology free'... is in fact a self-disarming strategy...the point is not to oppose science to ideology in a positivistic dichotomy but to establish their practical viable unity.[15]

This contemporary view that the categories of truth and falsehood are irrelevant to the practical, noncognitive nature of ideological rationality is also argued for by Alex Callinicos in his recent book *Marxism and Philosophy* (Oxford: Oxford University Press, 1983). In alluding to Marx's remarks on ideology in the preface to his *Contribution to the Critique of Political Economy*, Callinicos states:

> If we take seriously the 'pragmatic' dimension of ideology, the determination of ideologies by the class struggle, then the question of the truth or falsity of ideologies is besides

the point. What matters is that they are the 'forms in which men become conscious of this conflict and fight it out.'[16]

Thus, we see that there are a number of contemporary objections to the interpretation of Marx as having a conception of false consciousness as well as philosophical objections against the very notion of a false consciousness. To summarize, the main points of the contemporary critique of the interpretation of Marx as having a conception of false consciousness are as follows: (1) the conception of false consciousness is a concept developed by Engels; it is not found in the writings of Marx; (2) Engels's definition of false consciousness has heavy psychological connotations which are incompatible with the sociological conception of ideology as developed by Marx; (3) the very notion of false consciousness is inherently unsound because it is vague and ambiguous, and/or because a "true" or "scientific" consciousness cannot be established in opposition to a "false" consciousness;[17] (4) the concept of false consciousness is an epistemological notion, thereby encouraging the understanding of ideology as primarily an issue of knowledge; however, for Marx, the practical, noncognitive social functions of ideology were more important than the cognitive function of ideology. In addition, as evidenced by his political writings and preface of 1859, Marx departed from his earlier writings on ideology to develop a nonepistemological and sociological conception of ideology in his later writings; (5) as an epistemological notion, false consciousness implies a true consciousness; but the categories of truth and falsehood are irrelevant to the essentially practical, noncognitive nature of ideological rationality; (6) a false consciousness implies a true consciousness and this distinction would imply that Marx distinguished science from ideology in accordance with a true/false criterion. But Marx, according to some commentators, did not distinguish between science and ideology in accordance with a a true/false consciousness dichotomy. Hence, if Marx did not distinguish between science and ideology in accordance with a true/false criterion, then ideology could not have been false consciousness for Marx.

It is my opinion that this contemporary line of interpretation of Marx's conception of ideology is off the mark and not true to the writings of Marx on ideology. First of all, I believe that there does exist a fundamental similarity between the writings of Marx and

Engels on ideology and that the notion of false consciousness essentially defines Marx's conception of ideology. This congruence between Marx's and Engels's conception of ideology as false consciousness is evident: (a) in their writings on scientific methodology in the social sciences (e.g., their calls for social scientists to distinguish between what social agents imagine to be the case about the nature of their societies, their political aims, etc., and what really is the case as known by means of scientific theoretical analysis); (b) in their mutual philosophical concern with opposing and criticizing all idealist forms of understanding from a historical materialist perspective; (c) in their historical and political writings on the political false consciousness of social agents engaged in historical political struggles; (d) in their writings concerning the origins and nature of an alienated, mystified social consciousness; and finally, (d) in their writings in which Marx and Engels identify the common intellectual and historical roots of their conception of false consciousness/ideology.

Furthermore, I contend that there exist significant continuities between Marx's earlier and later writings on ideology which support the interpretation of Marx as having a conception of ideology as false consciousness similar to that of Engels. In particular, I see evidence of strong continuities between the young Marx's analyses of alienated and inverted forms of consciousness with the older Marx's analyses of commodity fetishisms in *Capital*. Hence, I reject the contention that Marx's later writings "break" with his earlier writings on ideology.

My claim that there is textual support for the thesis that Marx and Engels thought alike in their understanding of ideology as entailing the notion of false consciousness will have to be demonstrated in the pages ahead. But before going further, I would like to respond briefly to some of the objections raised by McCarney and others who would reject my interpretation. First of all, it is not clear to me what is necessarily "psychoanalytical" about the notion of false consciousness and why one can't give a sociological interpretation to the notion compatible with the historical materialist outlook of Marx. The idea that people possess false consciousness because they are "blind to the motive force of their thinking," and have illusions about their real motives in action or illusions about the "*a priori*, universality" of their thoughts seems to me to be quite compatible with Marx's claim that people generally are unaware of the social factors influencing their thinking and action, and as a result begin to think falsely about the nature of their social interests in politics or think falsely about the origins and validity of their ideas. For example, Marx's writings suggest that political actors are often socially and historically "unconscious" and as a result are deceived by their own political ideologies into thinking that their political agendas serve universal common interests when in fact they serve particular class interests. In addition, Marx's writings suggest that because people are historically and socially "unconscious" and inclined towards idealist interpretations of their "conscious thoughts"—i.e., people will falsely attribute an *a priori*, eternally valid status to their socially determined and historically relative ideas.

This conception of false consciousness—i.e., that people possess false consciousness because they are "blind to the motive force of their thinking" and have illusions about their real aims in action—is a conception that Marx and Engels most likely inherited from Hegel's notion of "the cunning of Reason." Hegel's notion of "the cunning of Reason" suggests a nonpsychological conception of false consciousness. According to Hegel, history-making agents possess false consciousness because they are unaware of the impersonal, systematic forces determining their thoughts and behavior while at the same time having illusions about their historical interests. This interpretation linking Marx's conception with one of Hegel's conceptions of false consciousness is prominent in the commentaries of George Lichtheim and Erich Fromm, both of whom interpret Marx as having a conception of ideology as false consciousness.

For example, according to Lichtheim in his essay on "The Concept of Ideology,"

> the problem of ideology (in the sense of false consciousness or imperfect consciousness) arises from Hegel because in his view individuals are instruments of history, executers of a process whose meaning is concealed from them...[18]

Fromm, in his book *Beyond the Chains of Illusion*, writes:

> ...Hegel's philosophy of history had a decisive influence on Marx's thought and contained the concept of man serving the aims of history without his knowledge. According to Hegel, it is the 'cunning of reason' which makes man an agent of the absolute idea while he is subjectively driven by his own conscious goals and individual passions.[19]

Hence, I believe that the notion of false consciousness is amendable to a sociological, Marxist interpretation and is not inherently a psychological conception (although, granted, it is difficult to avoid associating the notion with psychoanalysis, given the prominence of the Freudian influence in modern intellectual culture). In fact, while comparisons between Marx's conception of ideology as false consciousness and Freud's idea of rationalization are sometimes drawn by commentators, at the same time most commentators seek to differentiate between Marx's sociological understanding of ideological rationalization and Freud's psychological view. For example, after discussing the similarities between the Marxist approach to ideology with the psychoanalytical view of rationalization, Arnold Hauser points out that the difference between the two theories lies in the fact that for historical materialism, the

> concept of ideology is not based in a personal, empirical psychological theory of motivation, but on the socio-historical forces which express themselves in men's ideas, emotions and actions—often without their knowledge or intention...[20]

In a related vein, John McMurty in his book *The Structure of Marx's World-View* points out that while Marx's

> concept of ideology is closely akin to our everyday concept of rationalization...[the difference] in his case [is that] the articulation and referent of such rationalization is social rather than 'private' or 'individual'...[21]

Since rationalization entails self-deception, in accordance with the above comparison we can talk about a psychological account of personal self-deception and a Marxist sociological account of social group-deception. Thus, while Freud might talk about how individuals can be deceived by their personal psychological rationalizations, Marx in a somewhat different but analogous way could talk about social groups as being deceived by their own social ideologies which rationalize their class interests. Furthermore, by distinguishing between Marxist and Freudian theories, we thus can see how the ideological false consciousness can denote group or collective delusionary thinking about social phenomena as opposed to the psychological conception of idiosyncratic personal delusions.[22]

Now, if we follow the interpretation of Arnold Hauser and others[23] we are led to believe that what Marx and Engels meant by false consciousness is that social agents are deluded or deceived by their own ideologies concerning their real motives in political struggles. But does this definition of false consciousness as a kind of deluded social consciousness or collective self-deception convey what Marx and Engels meant by false consciousness? Two of the problems confronting this book are that I must both demonstrate that Marx like Engels had a conception of ideology as false consciousness and attempt to define what is meant by "false consciousness." One hears the term "false consciousness" bandied about in academic circles, but there has been very little work devoted to analyzing its meaning or meanings. And as the critics Larrain and McLellan have suggested, the vagueness and ambiguity associated with the notion of false consciousness perhaps render the notion unattractive to contemporary eyes.

There is some truth to what Larrain and McLellan argue, and for at least two reasons. First of all, Larrain is correct in his argument that "the expression 'false consciousness' by itself does not specifiy the falsity which ideology entails,"[24] and this is the reason, according to McLellan, why the notion of false consciousness is vague.[25] But Larrain seems to think that for Marx ideology must denote a specific and unique kind of error,[26] which I believe is a dubious assumption. In fact, it is closer to the truth to say that for Marx there are a number of diverse kinds of errors and falsehoods associated with ideology and false consciousness. And because there are a number of errors and falsehoods associated with the ideological consciousness, the notion of false consciousness appears to have more than one meaning in commentaries on Marx.

For example, unlike Arnold Hauser, who links Marx's conception of false consciousness with the error of rationalization, Allen Wood in his book on *Karl Marx* links Marx's conception of false consciousness with the notion of "alienation." According to Wood, Marx inherited a conception of false consciousness as an "alienated consciousness" from his study of Hegel and Feuerbach. In Wood's account,

> both of Marx's predecessors regard alienation as consisting fundamentally in a certain form of acute false conscious-

ness, in a certain error or illusion about oneself, one's humanity or one's relation to ultimate reality...[and] Marx agrees with Hegel and Feuerbach that alienation is closely associated with a certain kind of false consciousness...[27]

The falsehood associated with this "alienated consciousness" appears to be of two kinds, depending on which commentary of Marx one examines. In the first instance, some commentators see the alienated consciousness as false because it "reifies" socially determined thought as a separate "ontological reality" divorced from human, social praxis. As a result of this intellectual reification, human thought becomes lost in a world of its own imaginary abstractions and hence out of touch with reality. This interpretation of Marx's concept of an alienated consciousness is given, for example, by Walter Carlsnaes among others. According to Carlsnaes, for Marx

> an ideological consciousness is 'false' not only in the reified sense of being a 'consciousness' which posits a realm of ideas 'above or beyond' man's praxis, but is also necessarily false since such an imputation rests on the assumption that 'ideas' are not determined by man's material conditions.[28]

Typically, commentators attribute this characterization of the alienated false consciousness to idealist philosophical conceptions and abstract metaphysical thinking, an attribution which they believe Marx intended in his critique of the "illusions of speculative philosophy" as found in *The German Ideology*.[29]

In the second instance, some commentators see the alienated consciousness as false because social agents fail to recognize social reality as a product of their collective labor. From the perspective of this "alienated" or "reified consciousness," according to Carolyn Porter, social reality has the character of a being a reified, alien "thing-in-itself," "operating according to its own immutable laws."[30] In a similar vein, Brian Fay also sees this sense of alienated false consciousness in the writings of Marx. According to Fay, "alienated creatures," for Marx,

> ...do not see themselves in the 'objects' they have created...[they] do not recognize the world they have created as their own world, but rather take it to be something 'just there', something given, something alien and powerful...[31]

Typically, commentators attribute this version of the alienated false consciousness to Marx's analysis of "the fetishism of commodities" in *Capital*.[32] And in contrast to the first version of the alienated false consciousness, this second sense is seen to be indicative of the mind-set of all members in capitalist society, and not just of intellectuals or philosophers. In any case, the above examples suggest that for Marx there may be more than one kind of error or falsity entailed by the notion of false consciousness, as well as different senses of false consciousness.

In fact, the kind of falsity stipulated as being characteristic of Marx's conception of false consciousness may depend, in the final analysis, on which historical and intellectual influence one sees as significant to Marx's conception of ideology. For example, while Allen Wood and others emphasize the influence of the German philosophical tradition (i.e., Hegel and Feuerbach) on Marx's notion of false consciousness, others like Alex Callinicos see the influence of the Baconian and French materialist tradition on Marx. According to Callinicos,

> the concept of ideology [as false consciousness]…has its origins in Bacon's theory of idols, which was taken up by such philosophes as Helvetius and Holbach in their critique of the prejudices…Marx took over and radicalized this analysis by inserting it into his general theory of class struggle.[33]

Callinicos suggests that the notion of false consciousness bequeathed to Marx by the *philosophes* was the notion of a "manipulated" social consciousness—i.e., the lies, deceits and disinformation that propagandists for the ruling class use to manipulate the social consciousness of subordinate groups in the interests of the rulers. In supporting this interpretation of false consciousness, Callinocos refers to Marx's (and Engels's) remarks in *The German Ideology* where Marx (and Engels) contend that "the ideas of the ruling class are in every epoch the ruling ideas" because the ruling class "controls the means of mental production so that the ideas of those who lack the means of mental production are on the whole subject to it." In commenting on this passage, Callinocos concludes:

> This analysis is evidently a development of the Enlightenment critique of religion as a conspiracy of priests and rulers to keep the masses in the dark.[34]

On the other hand, if one were to begin with the influence of Francis Bacon on Marx, one could talk about false consciousness in a Baconian vein as denoting a false understanding and distorted perception of social reality. According to Bacon, the human understanding and perception of reality are falsified and distorted in a number of ways by certain irrational influences and common fallacies which Bacon referred to as "the idols of the mind." Some commentators are apparently intrigued by Bacon's views and suggest that for Marx a socially derived "distorted" perception epitomizes the essential kind of error characteristic of the ideological consciousness. For example, in his introductory text on Marx and Engels, Richard Schmitt writes that

> since the concept of ideology carries with it the connotation of 'distortion', ideology is often characterized, quite generally, as false consciousness.[35]

In a somewhat similar vein, Nicholas Abercrombie in his book entitled *Class, Structure and Knowledge: Problems in the Sociology of Knowledge* specifies the social source of this distortion according to Marx. In Abercrombie's words,

> Many Marxists, when they talk of the way that [class] interests distort systems of beliefs, speak simultaneously of 'false consciousness'. The supposition is, that to the extent that men's interests shape their beliefs, they are falsely conscious.[36]

Finally, in contrast to all of the above, David Rubinstein in his recent book *Marx and Wittgenstein: Social Praxis and Social Explanation* suggests that by false consciousness Marx was referring in an all-inclusive way to the nonscientific, "commonsense" social understanding of people. Rubinstein bases his interpretation on the base/superstructure method of analysis proposed by Marx in his famous 1859 preface. In Rubinstein's view, Marx's base/superstructure model is characteristic of the materialist structuralist tradition in sociology, a tradition which tends to be skeptical if not dismissive of the nonscientific, commonsense social understanding of people.

From the perspective of this tradition, the nonscientific, commonsense social understanding of people could be characterized as a false social consciousness for several reasons, chief of which are the following: (a) the commonsense social mind tends to only grasp the appearances of society as given within the limited social experience of social agents, and appearances can be deceiving; (b) the commonsense social mind is generally ignorant of and unable to perceive the systematic forces and causes underlying social events; and finally, (c) for whatever reason, the commonsense social mind tends to be imbued with various illusions about society.

Since commonsense accounts of society can be so off the mark, it is expected that scientific accounts of society will be radically at odds with commonsense accounts, even employing a categorical scheme different from the categories of common sense. This mistrust of the commonsense social mind and the acceptance of a radical difference between scientific and commonsense accounts of society is evident, in Rubinstein's opinion, in Marx's remarks in his 1859 preface. In Marx's words,

> In considering...[social] transformations the distinction should always be made between the material transformation of the economic conditions of production, which can be determined with the precision of natural science, and the legal, political, religious, aesthetic, or philosophic—in short, ideological—forms in which men become conscious of this conflict and fight it out. Just as our opinion of an individual is not based on what he thinks of himself, so can we not judge such a period of transformation by its own consciousness; on the contrary, this consciousness must rather be explained...

Rubinstein comments as follows on the above remarks of Marx:

> Many aspects of Marx's thought appear to flow from this distinction between objective existence and subjective consciousness: the concept of false consciousness, his theory of social change as initiated by changes in productive relations...[37]

In summary, we see that for those who do interpret Marx as having a conception of ideology as false consciousness, Marx's notion of false consciousness means several different things. According to these commentators, by false consciousness Marx meant:

1. a deluded social consciousness or collective self-deception;
2. an alienated consciousness (sometimes referred to as a reified social consciousness);

4. the manipulated social consciousness of the oppressed;
5. a distorted and false social understanding and perception;
6. the nonscientific, commonsense social consciousness.

For many of the above commentators, Marx's notion of false consciousness (like Engels's) represents an inheritance from previous thinkers influential in the shaping of Marx's (and Engels's) own thoughts on ideology. Furthermore, what's suggested by this intellectual influence on Marx (and Engels) is that the notion of false consciousness itself has a history, with different particular meanings within this history.

In spite of the diverse and often confusing influences Marx's predecessors may have on our attempts to interpret the meaning of Marx's conception of ideology, I submit that an appreciation of this historical and intellectual legacy is crucial for understanding the meaning of Marx's conception of ideology, and, of equal importance, for demonstrating that Marx's conception of ideology is best understood in terms of the notion of false consciousness. In the following pages we will explicate this historical legacy. And in tracing this history, not only will we be uncovering the origins of Marx's (and Engels's) own conception of ideology, but at the same time we will be shedding light on the elusive but captivating notion of false consciousness.

Since I will be retracing the influence of this historical legacy on Marx and Engels, the chapters in this book are organized by the order in which each of the major theorists on ideological false consciousness historically appeared. Hence, in the second chapter we begin with Bacon's theory of the idols and draw comparisons between Marx views on ideological fallacies and Bacon's views. In the third chapter we explore the French Enlightenment's critiques of metaphysics and religion, and show how these critiques influenced Marx's and Engels's views on idealist ideologies and ruling-class ideologies. In the fourth chapter we demonstrate the influence of Hegel's philosophy of history (and French Enlightenment views) on Marx's and Engels's views concerning the political false consciousness. In the fifth chapter we begin with an examination of Hegel's model of the alienated mind and its influence on Feuerbach in his critique of the religious false consciousness. The fifth and sixth chapters go on to demonstrate the influence of Feuerbachian and Hegelian conceptions on the young

Marx's views concerning the alienated false consciousness in politics and economics. Finally, in the seventh chapter we demonstrate how Marx's theory in *Capital* concerning commodity fetishisms and the ideological nature of common sense incorporates views from his earlier writings about the alienated consciousness.

While the chapters are organized in historical order, there is a kind of "dialectical" development depicted in my comparisons. In a sense, each historically successive conception of the ideological consciousness builds on its predecessors; in some cases, the successors criticize and replace the theoretical conceptions of their predecessors, while in other cases the successors add a new dimension to the views of their predecessors. In either case, new and more sophisticated theories concerning the ideological consciousness are developed in this dialectical way involving critique and incorporation.

For example, while Bacon's theory of idols provided a foundation for the *philosophes*' critique of "prejudices," at the same time the *philosophes* added a new social dimension to Bacon's critique of idols. In the hands of the *philosophes*, Bacon's critique was transformed into a critique of dominant social ideologies. In turn, while the French Enlightenment's version of the dominant ideology thesis was to influence both Marx and Engels, at the same time the latter were critical of their French Enlightenment predecessors. As a result, Marx and Engels sought to develop a more systematic class and historical materialist analysis of ideologies as opposed to the conspiratorial views of their eighteenth-century predecessors. Finally, while the Baconian-French Enlightenment tradition provided Marx and Engels with one model for understanding the alienated false consciousness, the Hegelian-Feuerbachian tradition provided them with a different and, in some ways, more sophisticated model.

2

Bacon's Theory of Idols and Marx on Ideological Fallacies

The historical period in which Francis Bacon composed his theory of idols was a period ripe for originating the modern theory of ideology. His theory of idols conforms to the supposition that theories of ideology seem to appear when people begin to question the dominant beliefs of their societies.

According to Bernard Williams, in medieval society

> [the] traditional framework of scholastic teaching had provided a range of patterns for 'legitimating belief': e.g., scripture and the interpretative authority of the church in religious matters...[1]

Medieval scholasticism and its unquestioned faith in the Bible as a source of absolute "revealed truths" higher than all empirical and logical truths dominated the intellectual consciousness of feudal society, and religious conceptions dominated more generally the popular consciousness of the period. With human thought so directed towards the contemplation of religious "realities," it's not surprising that empirical studies of natural "realities" were seldom pursued in the medieval period.

However, with the emergence of new scientific and humanistic modes of thinking, the intellectual authority of this "traditional framework" was to be questioned and eventually rejected by the new, "enlightened" thinkers of sixteenth- and seventeenth-century Europe.

In fact, many other historical factors contributed to a kind of institutional and intellectual "legitimation crisis" in Europe of this period. Excursions into new, exotic geographical realms and the expansion of trade literally had broadened the horizons of Europeans as well as bringing them into contact with alien cultures. This encounter with the "state of nature" and the "uncivilized" natives of the New World was to be instrumental in changing European attitudes and assumptions concerning the relationship between individuals and the social polity. Moreover, with the emergence of new economic practices and capitalist institutions, Europeans began to reevaluate the social utility of feudal-religious proscriptions against usury or profit-taking. Politically, challenges to the feudal way of life were expressed in the critiques of divine right theory of monarchical absolutism and the advocacy of constitutional-republican forms of government. Finally, with the emergence of a nation-state system and market economies, the "waning" of the traditional feudal way of life was ensured. In short, Europe in the sixteenth and seventeenth centuries was a culture in transition, a transition often violent and radical.[2]

Intellectually, some of the signs of this period's "legitimation crisis" were the prevalence of skeptical attitudes in the leading thinkers of the period and a concern with finding new and "indubitable" foundations for human thought. This skepticism and desire for new foundations are perhaps most notable in the reflections of Descartes, who in his "First Meditation" summarized his period's mood in the following way:

> Several years have now elapsed since I first became aware that I had accepted, even from my youth, many false opinions for true, and that consequently what I afterwards based on such principles was highly doubtful; and from that time I was convinced of the necessity of undertaking once in my life to rid myself of all the opinions I had adopted, and of commencing anew the work of building from the foundations, if I desired to establish a firm and abiding superstructure in the sciences.[3]

This climate of opinion characteristic of sixteenth- and seventeenth-century Europe affected Bacon as well. Like so many of his contemporaries, Bacon was critical of the rationalistic, metaphysical and theological orientation of medieval Scholastic thought. In his opinion, medieval Scholasticism was responsible for the misdirection or "alienation" of human thought away from observable nature and towards a study of nonsensible, metaphysical entities. Accordingly, Bacon in his *The Great Instauration* and *New Organon* proposed a new method of knowledge (e.g., the method of induction and experiment) for "reconstructing" all human knowledge and sciences upon proper "foundations."[4] However, before this new method could be practiced, Bacon like many of his contemporaries argued that it was first necessary to expose and eliminate all of the "idols" or errors contaminating the human understanding and thereby preventing a true knowledge of reality.

According to Bacon, the human understanding was "beset" by these "idols."

> The idols and false notions which are now in possession of the human understanding, and have taken deep root therein, not only so beset men's minds that truth can hardly find entrance, but even after entrance is obtained, they will again in the very instauration of the sciences meet and trouble us, unless men being forewarned of the danger fortify themselves as far as may be against their assaults.[5]

Bacon's critique of the idols of the human understanding took the form of an analysis and classification of the various kinds of common fallacies and irrational influences characteristic of the "ideological" understanding. Bacon identified four major types of ideological errors or idols. The first type, the "idols of the tribe," have to do with the naive realist preconception that the human understanding "is the measure of all things," i.e., the fallacy that the way things appear to us in perception is identical to the way things really are. In his critique of naive realism, Bacon argues that "the human understanding is like a false mirror, which, receiving rays irregularly, distorts and discolors the nature of things by mingling its own nature with it."[6]

The second type of ideological influence common to humankind concerns the effects of personal bias in knowledge. According to Bacon, each individual tends to perceive and judge reality in the "light" of his or her own personal experiences and education. As a result, all individual perceptions of reality will be slanted in particular ways, even distorted. Hence, in Bacon's version of Plato's "cave allegory," each person is a prisoner of the "idols" of his or her own "cave."

Perhaps the most important personal ideological biases discussed by Bacon derive from the personal interests and values of individuals. According to Bacon,

> the human understanding is no dry light, but receives an infusion from the will and affections; whence proceed sciences which may be called 'sciences as one would'. For what a man had rather were true he more readily believes.[7]

Bacon's comments suggest that for him only disinterested and perspective-free knowledge can be scientific, whereas ideological accounts of reality are always biased.

The third major type of ideological error analyzed by Bacon concerns the "idols of the Market-Place," Bacon's analysis is of interest for the way it anticipates contemporary philosophical views concerning the nature of language and the influence of language on the human understanding. Bacon rejects the naive and fallacious belief that language is solely a descriptive instrument controlled by the human understanding. According to Bacon, it is also the case that language can shape and structure the understanding; as a result, the reality people know is at times a reality constructed by the categories characteristic of one's language.

Furthermore, Bacon believed that words can create pseudorealities which we mistakenly accept as signifiers for real things. According to Bacon,

> the idols imposed by words on the understanding are of two kinds. Either names of things which do not exist (...fantastic suppositions...to which nothing in reality corresponds), or they are names of things which exist, but yet confused and ill-defined.[8]

The fallacy which Bacon recognizes here is often referred to as the fallacy of reification, a fallacy which Bacon defined in another context in the following way:

> The human understanding is of its own nature prone to abstractions and gives a substance and reality to things which are fleeting...[9]

Finally, the fourth major source of ideological error Bacon identified are the "idols of the Theatre" which arise from the dogmas and falsehoods generated by philosophies and schools of thoughts.

Bacon argued that these idols can be either external or native to human cognition, and socially or psychologically produced.[10] It was Bacon's belief that a knowledge of the origins and influence of these idols on human thought would serve to mitigate their negative epistemological and social effects ("negative" social effects because Bacon believed that these idols hindered the progress of humankind).

In terms of the import of Bacon's theory of idols to the future development of the modern theory of ideology, three features are perhaps most significant. First of all, Bacon bequeathed to his followers an epistemological and pejorative conception of ideology; the "idols" were errors of a collective kind which had to be criticized and eliminated in order to improve the "estate" of humankind. Secondly, Bacon's negative characterization of Scholastic metaphysics was to have great influence on subsequent generations of materialist-oriented thinkers. According to Bacon, Scholastic metaphysics and theology were responsible for giving a false direction to human thought and for the alienation of human thought from natural realities. In order to reorient human thought towards the truth, Bacon proposed the use of new methods of knowledge and a general materialist understanding of things, proposals which were to be enthusiastically adopted by the *philosophes* and, subsequently, by Marx and Engels. Finally, Bacon established the precedent for conceiving the ideological consciousness as a false consciousness. According to Bacon, since the ideological understanding denotes a false understanding and distorted perception of reality, the ideological consciousness can be understood as a false consciousness.

There are some similarities between Marx and Bacon regarding ideology. For example, the genesis of Marx's conception of ideology occurred under similar historical conditions. Like Bacon's historical period, the historical epoch of Marx was marked by a kind of legitimation crisis. In the aftermath of the French Revolution and in the development of the so-called "Industrial Revolution" of the early nineteenth century, the social institutions of the *ancien regime* were no longer viewed as legitimate by many Europeans. Furthermore, the ideologies which justified the social institutions of the *ancien regime* (e.g., the "divine right of kings") were no longer credible to many

Europeans. Hence, the historical age of Marx, like that of Bacon, was ripe for a reevaluation of customary modes of thinking and belief-systems.

In addition, Marx like Bacon identified a number of fallacies and erroneous beliefs which typified the irrationality of the ideological consciousness. These fallacies and false beliefs can be found throughout Marx's writings on ideology, and well match Bacon's impressive list of idols.

In some cases, Marx duplicates some of the idols or fallacies Bacon had already described. For example, in *Capital* Marx criticizes "vulgar" bourgeois economists for mistaking appearances for reality.

> The bourgeois economist, whose limited mentality is unable to separate the form of appearance from the thing which appears within that form...makes it a principle to worship appearances only.[11]

Like Bacon, Marx is critical of those who commit the fallacy of reification in their reasoning. In particular, Marx argues in the *German Ideology* that intellectuals are most susceptible to this type of fallacy. Marx says of the social division between mental and manual labor:

> ...from this moment onwards consciousness can really flatter itself that it is something other than consciousness of existing practice, that it really represents something without representing something real...[12]

In other cases, Marx identifies a new set of idols or fallacies which Bacon had not recognized. For example, as a result of his studies of various class struggles, Marx observed that classes vying for political power tended to represent their particular class interests as "the common interest of all the members of society."[13] In other words, political interests groups tend to commit the fallacy of false absolutization, the fallacy of representing one's own views and interests as "the only rational, universally valid ones." For some commentators, this fallacy of false absolutization essentially defines Marx's conception of ideology.[14]

Another aspect of the fallacy of false absolutization which Marx criticized is the tendency of social agents and intellectuals to view the ideas and assumptions prevailing in their societies as "eternal verities," and as *a priori*, unconditioned products of "pure reason." For example, in a letter to Annenkov (28 December 1846), Marx criticized the French socialist and theorist Joseph Proudhon for commiting this fallacy of false absolutization. According to Marx,

> Proudhon does not state that bourgeois life is for him an eternal verity; he states it indirectly by deifying the categories which express bourgeois relations in the form of thought. He takes the products of bourgeois society for spontaneously arisen eternal beings, endowed with a life of their own...[15]

From Marx's point of view, however, most of the ideas and assumptions which predominate in an historical epoch (e.g., contemporary economic views regarding the principle of competition) are socially relative and true only within the framework of a historically specific kind of society. Of course, the majority of people and many intellectuals are unaware of: (a) the social origins of their ideas; (b) the socially biased character of their ideas; and (c) the historically limited validity of their ideas. Hence, the fallacy of false absolutization entails, among other things, mistaking contingent historical truths for eternal, absolute truths.

Related to the fallacy of false absolutization is the tendency of social agents to view their social institutions as natural and eternally valid institutions, i.e., to believe that the dominant institutions of their societies somehow conform to the "eternal, natural laws" supposedly governing all societies. In particular, Marx singled out bourgeois classical political economists for commiting this fallacy.

According to Marx, bourgeois political economists invariably viewed the social and historically relative economic institutions of capitalism (e.g., wage labor, private property, the market system of production and distribution, competition and the profit motive) as institutions in conformity with "eternal natural laws which are independent of history."[16] The following passage from *Capital* concerning the institution of wage labor encapsulates Marx's critique of the ahistorical and fallacious understanding of bourgeois political economists.

> One thing is clear...Nature does not produce on the one side owners of money or commodities and on the other

side men possessing nothing but their own labor-power. This relation has no natural basis, nor is its social basis one that is common to all historical periods...Capital, therefore, announces from its first appearance a new epoch in the process of social production.[17]

Thus, for Marx, this type of thinking was fallacious because it falsely assumes that social institutions are naturally or divinely ordained, when in fact they are historical creations.

Another type of fallacy Marx discussed in *Capital* involves a kind of fetishistic thinking and conversion. In his discussion of the "fetishism of commodities," Marx remarks how as a result of the commodity form of social production, people tend to attribute human and social qualities to their products while, in turn, treating themselves as marketable objects for sale or hire. For example, in the context of a commodity-producing market economy, products of human labor appear to possess the power to create value much like the value-creative powers of human labor—e.g., the property value of a house fluctuates with its marketability, and monetary savings appear to generate their own interest independent of human labor. On the other hand, people as wage labor are treated as "factors" of production, to be hired, consumed and released contingent on their profitability. Hence, the fallacy resulting from the "fetishism of commodities" consists of erroneously treating persons as objects and objects as persons.[18]

Finally, in many of Marx's discussions on ideology, his writings suggest that one of the common fallacies of ideological reasoning is the fallacy of inversion. The fallacy of inversion refers to the tendency of human agents to mistakenly reverse the proper ontological and causal order of things. For example, in discussing the nature of the "juridical illusion," Marx argues that what is illusory or "ideological" about juridical thinking is that it views society as the product of *a priori* legal constitutions and rules, as opposed to the real truth, which is that legal laws and constitutions are social derivatives serving class interests. Marx commented on this "juridical illusion" and its fallacious, ideological character in one of his footnotes in *Capital*.

> Eden should have asked whose creatures 'the civil institutions' were. From the standpoint he adopts, that of juridical illusion, he does not regard the law as a product of the

material relations of production, but rather the reverse: he sees the relations of production as products of the law. Linguet overthrew Montesquieu's illusory 'esprit des lois' with one word: 'L'esprit des lois, c'est la propriété.[19]

In summary, we see that Marx has his own list of "idols" or ideological fallacies to compare with Bacon's list of idols. However, there are significant differences between Marx and Bacon with regard to their analyses concerning the origins of ideology. Unlike Bacon, Marx was concerned primarily with an analysis of the *social* origins and a sociological analysis of ideological errors and false, illusory beliefs. This is not to say that Bacon was unaware of the social origins of some of the idols common to humankind; however, unlike Marx, the concern with social explanation of idols was not a principal feature of Bacon's theory of idols.

Firstly, in several of his works Marx traced the origins of ideological modes of thinking to the social division of labor (e.g., the division between mental and manual labor, and the class division between various social groups). In the *German Ideology*, Marx argues that the division between mental and manual labor was ultimately the source of reified and idealist ideological modes of thinking. In *Capital*, Marx argues that the social division of labor and market relationships of social agents in capitalism were ultimately responsible for the fetishistic and inverted modes of thinking prevalent in modern society.

Secondly, for Marx biased and partisan modes of thought were often the result of the influence of class interests on thinking. For example, in many of Marx's articles for the *New York Tribune* covering political struggles in the England, France and Germany of his time, Marx subjected the ideologies of political groups to a class analysis in order to uncover the partisan and self-serving character of their ideas.

Finally, aside from the role of class divisions in generating false ideological consciousness, in a more general way alienating social conditions could lead to and support ideological illusions. For example, in Marx's writings on the religious false consciousness, he attributed the origins of religious illusions to social conditions of powerlessness, misery and injustice—social conditions which foster the need for illusionary gratifications and consolations.

Hence, in explaining the origins of ideological reasoning, Marx in contrast to Bacon emphasized the importance of sociological explanations of ideological reasoning. For many commentators, this distinctive feature of Marx's approach to ideology constitutes a significant advance in the development of modern theories on ideology.[20]

Another important difference between Marx and Bacon concerns the science/ideology distinction. Bacon's remarks suggest that science differs from ideology in that scientific accounts of reality are impartial and disinterested, whereas ideological account are biased by the interests and the perspective of individuals. Now, I don't think Marx can or has to concur with Bacon that in order to be scientific theories must be unbiased in the sense of being free of the social perspective and interests of the researcher. However, Marx's remarks are not completely clear on this matter, and sometimes his remarks suggest that he would accept Bacon's views.

For example, in criticizing the theories of Thomas Malthus, Marx's remarks appear to suggest that only bias-free accounts of reality can be scientific. Marx says:

> ...when a man seeks to accommodate science to a viewpoint which is derived not from science itself...but from outside, from alien, external interests, then I call him 'base'...[21]

But if Marx truly meant this (i.e., that science must be bias-free), then Marx was inconsistent and his purportedly "scientific" accounts of capitalism would seem to be invalid by his own criteria. Marx would be contradicting himself because in *Capital* and elsewhere he was quite clear about the fact that he viewed his "critical" theories as being representative of the proletarian class.[22] Furthermore, Marx described his own dialectical method of *Capital* in value terms as a "revolutionary" method designed to be "critical" of society's status quo.[23] Finally, in various letters Marx described himself as being a "loyal champion" of the proletariat.[24] Hence, while Marx was critical of Malthus for being "considerate towards the ruling classes in general...,"[25] Marx also avowed himself to be "considerate" towards the proletariat as their "scientific" representative.[26]

Was Marx being inconsistent? I don't think so, for the following reasons. The problem with Malthus, according to Marx, was that Malthus allowed his social interests and perspective to "falsify" his theoretical conclusions on behalf of the ruling classes. As Marx argues in his *Theories of Surplus Value*:

...Malthus does not sacrifice the particular interests to production but seeks...to sacrifice the demands of production to the particular interests of existing ruling classes or sections of classes. And to this end *he falsifies* his scientific conclusions. This is his scientific baseness.[27]

Moreover, Marx's statements indicate that he believed there was a difference in theory between the truth-values of the bourgeois and proletariat perspectives. In Marx's opinion, the bourgeois standpoint was essentially false and limited in a number of ways, chief of which was its belief in capitalism as the ultimate, natural form of socioeconomic systems.[28] In contrast, the proletariat standpoint correctly viewed society in historical and dialectical terms, and thus included "in its positive understanding of what exists a simultaneous recognition of its negation" (i.e., the inevitable transformation and destruction of capitalist society). Furthermore, Marx and Engels suggested that the proletariat standpoint was an epistemological position derived from an objective study of society, and hence a perspective available to all objectively minded individuals.[29]

While the social perspective of Malthus was considered "falsifying," Marx's own proletariat standpoint was apparently conceived of as a scientifically based "vantage point" for discovering new truths about capitalism while at the same time a "vantage point" for exposing the biases and limitations of his theoretical opponents. And since it is conceivable that some kinds of social perspectives can serve as "vantage points" for discovering new truths about society and for changing our thinking about society at the same time, I don't think Marx has to concur with Bacon's view regarding the necessity for disinterested, perspective-free science.

In summary, in this section we examined the roots of the modern materialist approach to ideology in Bacon's theory of idols. We then examined Marx's own list of ideological fallacies and finally, we examined Marx's distinctive concern with social explanations of ideological rationality.

3

Ideology and the French Enlightenment

SEC. 3–1
THE INFLUENCE OF BACON ON THE PHILOSOPHES AND GENERAL INTRODUCTION TO THE FRENCH ENLIGHTENMENT CONCEPTION OF IDEOLOGY.

Bacon's theory of idols as well as the general materialist outlook of his philosophy were to have a profound influence on the *philosophes* of the eighteenth-century French Enlightenment. Basically, Bacon's critique of idols provided the *philosophes* with a model to follow in their own critique of the metaphysical and religious "prejudices" dominating the thought of their age.[1]

In fact, reverence for Bacon's approach to ideology is evident in various remarks made by individual *philosophes*. For instance, in the following passage from his *System of Nature*, Paul Heinrich Dietrich Holbach's praises Bacon for his insight into the harmful nature of socially prevalent "errors" or "prejudices."

> No error can be advantageous to the human species; it is ever founded on ignorance, or the blindness of his mind. The more importance men shall attach to their prejudices, the more is the fatal consequences of their errors. Thus,

Bacon had great reason for saying that the worst of all things, is deified error.[2]

Like Bacon, the *philosophes* argued that human thought had been given a false direction by metaphysicians and theologians. According to the *philosophes*, under the influence of metaphysics, religion and theology, people had acquired a false understanding of the nature of their own consciousness and ideas as well as the nature of morality, law, economics and political rights. For example, on the basis of metaphysical and religious influences, people were led to think of their consciousness as a spiritual soul dwelling within but independent of the human body, when in fact, according to the *philosophes*, human consciousness was nothing more than "transformed sensation" or reflected matter. In a similar vein, the *philosophes* argued that the traditional religious understanding of morality in terms of sin, evil, and obedience to God's commandments was misguided; in the eyes of the *philosophes*, morality really was a matter of social utility and what was good or bad according to nature.

In short, what people had been taught to believe as real entities—i.e., soul, sin, divine rights, etc.—were nothing more than fictitious ideas produced by a misguided religious and metaphysical imagination.[3] And because the popular and intellectual consciousness of their historical period was dominated by religious and metaphysical ideas, the *philosophes* argued that in effect human thought had become alienated from reality and dwelt in an imaginary, ideological world.

This notion of an alienated ideological consciousness is suggested in various remarks made by Holbach concerning the effects of metaphysical and religious ideas on human thought. For example, in his treatise entitled *The System of Nature*, Holbach contends that

> philosophy, guided by [religious and antinaturalist conceptions], was no longer anything more than imaginary science: it quitted the real world to plunge into the ideal world of metaphysics; it neglected nature to occupy itself with Gods, with spirits, with invisible powers...[Similarly, with the infusion of religious and antinaturalist conceptions in] Morality [it also] became...uncertain...Politics...were perverted by the false ideas which were given to sovereigns of their rights...Jurisprudence and the laws

were subjected to the caprice of religion, who put shackles on the labor, the commerce, the industry, and the activity of nations.⁴

Hence, for the *philosophes*, religious and metaphysical ideas as "ideological" ideas par excellence were nothing more than the erroneous conceits of a "distempered" imagination which, in dominating human thought, produced an alienated ideological consciousness. In accounting for the reasons why people could be misled by their own imagination, two of the major causes cited by the *philosophes* were that people generally were ignorant of nature and inattentive to empirical realities. This type of analysis of the "ideological" imagination was given by Holbach in his *The System of Nature*. According to Holbach,

> Men will always deceive themselves by abandoning experience to follow imaginary systems...All the errors and all the disputes of men, have their foundation in this, that they have renounced experience and the evidence of their senses, to give themselves up to the guidance of notions which they have believed...innate, although in reality they are not more than the effect of a distempered imagination; of prejudices in which they have been instructed from their infancy; with which habit has familarized them; and which authority has obliged them to conserve...⁵

Given the alienated nature of the ideological mind, the *philosophes*, following Bacon's model, argued that human thought could be reconnected to reality by means of an empirical study of natural and observable realities. In effect, what this reorientation of thought meant to both Bacon and the French philosophes was that humanity has to be taught a philosophical worldview which can conduct human thought back to nature and observable realities and away from "the contemplation of chimeras."⁶ For Bacon and the *philosophes*, the only philosophical worldview suitable for opposing the ideological understanding and for reorienting human thought back to reality was materialism.

The materialist outlook constituted a critical philosophy because only materialism was opposed to any belief in the existence of nonsensible, supernatural realities, and as we have seen, belief in the existence of nonsensible, supernatural realities (e.g., God, the soul) was characteristic of both religious thinking and the metaphysical thinking of Scholastics (and as will soon see, of idealist philosophers as well). Moreover, only a materialist philosophy provided a plausible method for distinguishing between objectively grounded abstract ideas or general concepts and false, ideologically grounded "metaphysical ideas."

In regards to this second advantage of materialism for ideological analysis, once again the French philosophes credited Bacon for his path-breaking approach to the analysis of abstract ideas or general concepts. Condillac, in the following passage from his *Essay on the Origin of Human Knowledge,* provides us with an account of the *philosophes'* understanding of Bacon's method for analyzing abstract ideas.

> If the [general] notions we are capable of acquiring are... collections of simple ideas which experience has made us assemble under certain names, it is far more natural to look for ideas in the order in which experience gave them to us than to begin with the definition [as Cartesians do], in order subsequently to deduce the different properties of things.
>
> Thus one sees that we ought to follow in the search for truth the order I have already indicated in speaking of analysis. It consists in re-ascending to the origin of ideas, in tracing their genealogy, and in making different compositions and decompositions of them, in order to compare them...These were my reflections on method when I read for the first time Chancellor Bacon...No one knew better than he the causes of our errors...[7]

In short, what Bacon's "genealogical" method of analysis entailed for the French *philosophes* was an analysis and evaluation of metaphysical, theological, and popular religious ideas in accordance with the empiricist criterion of meaning.[8] In addition, the *philosophes* evaluated socially influential ideas according to their public utility and their compatibility with naturalist moral principles. The *philosophes* believed that if it could be demonstrated that influential philosophical beliefs and social ideals were either empirically groundless or antithetical to the public interest, then such beliefs and ideals should be rejected for their irrational and socially harmful nature.

Perhaps a good summary of the critical project of the French

Enlightenment and its "genealogical" approach to ideology was provided by Holbach in the following passage from his *System of Nature*.

> If man possessed the courage to recur to the source of those opinions which are most deeply engraven on his brain; if he rendered to himself a faithful account of the reasons which make him hold these opinions as sacred; if he coolly examined the basis of his hopes, the foundation of his fears, he would find that it very frequently happens, those objects, or those ideas which move him most powerfully, either have no real existence, are words devoid of meaning, or phantoms engendered by a disordered imagination, modified by ignorance.[9]

This method of analyzing and evaluating ideas in terms of their origins was to have far-reaching effects on the development of Marx's approach to ideology and, generally, to all other materialist-minded thinkers on ideology (e.g., Feuerbach, Mannheim, Freud, Nietzsche, etc.).[10] In fact, it would not be an exaggeration to say that some type of genetic method of analysis essentially defines a materialist approach to ideology as opposed to nonmaterialist approaches, which are concerned more with how ideologies "construct" reality by means of symbols and language.

In the pages that follow, I will examine the utilization of this materialist method by the *philosophes'* in their critique of the dominant metaphysical and ideological "prejudices" of their period. I will then examine the influence of the French Enlightenment critique of ideology on Marx. My examination of the French Enlightenment critique of ideology is divided into two sections: the critique of metaphysics and the critique of religion. I will begin first with a more detailed look at the *philosophes'* critique of metaphysics as exhibited primarily in the writings of Condillac and Holbach. The metaphysics popular at the time of their writings was Cartesian rationalism. In examining this critique, we will see how the *philosophes* opposed their own materialist conceptions to idealist metaphysical conceptions. Subsequently, in section 3–3, I will examine the further development of the materialist critique of idealist ideologies by Marx and Engels. Finally, in section 3–4 of this chapter I will examine the French Enlightenment critique of religion and the influence of this critique on Marx's dominant ideology thesis.

SEC. 3–2

THE FRENCH ENLIGHTENMENT CRITIQUE OF METAPHYSICAL IDEAS

To understand the eighteenth-century materialist critique of metaphysical ideas as ideology, it is necessary to summarize the metaphysical and epistemological position characteristic of Cartesian rationalism in the seventeenth and eighteenth centuries. According to Descartes's rationalist epistemology, the method for acquiring certain knowledge of reality is to proceed deductively from true first principles. To Descartes and his followers, these first principles were understood to be *a priori*, rational truths inherent in the human mind; this is the metaphysical doctrine of innate ideas. Moreover, Descartes and his followers assumed that the mind was an immaterial substance independent of, and unaffected by, the external, material world.

Descartes's conception of method and theory of *a priori* ideas exercised a profound influence on the minds of seventeenth- and eighteenth-century Continental metaphysicians. The *Ethics* of Spinoza was the most rigorous and consistent application of Cartesian principles. Beginning from axioms and definitions understood to be true on the basis of pure reason, Spinoza deduced an intricate system of ideas covering a wide range of topics. Perhaps the culmination of the systematic and deductive ideal of Cartesian metaphysics was realized by Hegel in his *Science of Logic*, published in the early nineteenth century.

After reading these rationalist system builders, one gets the impression that for metaphysicians ideas form a realm of their own, independent of the external world. And, of course, this is what the Cartesian theory of *a priori* ideas argues to be the case. One also gets the impression that for these system builders, knowledge develops solely through an analysis and synthesis of ideas independent of any empirical research.

Now, in opposing the Cartesian metaphysics of their period, the *philosophes'* materialist critique of metaphysics was centered on three main issues. In the first place, the *philosophes* were opposed to the Cartesian doctrine of innate ideas or *a priori* knowledge. Secondly, the *philosophes* were opposed to the idealist conception of mind popular with Cartesians, i.e., belief in the absolute autonomy of the mind vis-à-vis material reality and the immaterial nature of mind. Finally, the *philosophes* were opposed to metaphysics as a suitable method for acquiring knowledge of reality.

Condillac, in his *Treatise on System*, argued that all general ideas are merely complex abstractions derived from experience and formulated as class concepts or categories which designate the common element characterizing a number of particular facts.[11] In rejecting the Cartesian doctrine of *a priori* or innate truths, Condillac essentially sought to demonstrate the materialist view on the origination of necessary truths from experience.

In a somewhat related vein, Holbach argued that necessary truths have their origins in experience and are not native to the human mind. More importantly, in explaining the source of the erroneous idealist conception of *a priori* ideas, Holbach argued that metaphysicians simply were ignorant of the real origins of necessary truths. According to Holbach:

> These pretended inherent ideas of [men's] soul, are the effect of education, of example, of habit, which, by reiterated motion, has taught his brain to associate by ideas, either in a confused or perspicuous manner...In short, [metaphysicians] take those for innate ideas, of which he has forgotten the origin; he no longer recalls to himself the precise epoch or the successive circumstances when these ideas were first consigned to his brain.[12]

Condillac was not content merely with a rejection of the theory of *a priori* ideas. In addition, Condillac rejected the fundamental presupposition of the theory of *a priori* ideas—the Cartesian belief in the autonomy of the human intellect. Along with other *philosophes*, Condillac endeavored to formulate a materialist conception of mind and a materialist view on the origins of consciousness. Within the parameters of Lockean empiricism, Condillac argued in his *Treatise on Sensation* (1754) that all thought was ultimately "transformed sensation" or reflected matter.[13] In a similar spirit, Holbach summarized the basic materialist view concerning the origins of human thought and the material nature of mind in the following way:

> Man's mode of thinking is necessarily determined by his manner of being; it must therefore depend on his natural organization, and the modification his system receives independently of his will.[14]

Finally, the *philosophes* considered the method of rationalist metaphysics as ill-suited for acquiring a true knowledge of reality.

Since rationalist metaphysical methods neglected or rejected empirical studies of reality, the *philosophes* believed that metaphysics was unable to acquire knowledge of ultimate reality, i.e., the system of Nature. And since many of the metaphysical ideas popular with Cartesians and theologicans were, in the opinion of leading *philosophes*, simply empirically groundless forms of the human imagination (e.g., the soul), the *philosophes* rejected metaphysics as an erroneous and imaginary system of thought. In particular, Holbach's critique of Cartesian metaphysics and theology is notable because of his unsparing opposition to all forms of antinaturalist and religious forms of thought.

Although the historical effect of the French Enlightenment critique of Cartesian metaphysics was a rigid distinction between science and metaphysics, I believe it is important to see that one aspect of this antithesis entails the opposition between naturalist-materialist and anti-naturalist-idealist ways of understanding reality and human thought (in addition to being a distinction between truth and error). It was this opposition between a materialist-scientific and an idealist "ideological" mode of understanding which eventually was to have the greatest impact on Marx and Engels in their understanding of the demarcation between nonideological and ideological forms of consciousness.

This French Enlightenment critique of metaphysics also was to influence Destutt de Tracy in his "science of the formation of ideas." Although "ideology" had a predominately neutral connotation for De Tracy, in many ways De Tracy's science of ideology continued the basic program of the French Enlightenment.

Like Condillac, De Tracy embraced Lockean epistemology and the empiricial method for analyzing abstract ideas. In addition, like Condillac, De Tracy was opposed to idealist metaphysical ideas. Using the empiricist criterion of verification, abstract ideas which could not be verified were judged to be groundless by De Tracy, and hence false.[15]

Most importantly, De Tracy shared along with Condillac and the *philosophes* the Baconian aim of "purging" false ideologies from human thought. De Tracy set this purpose for his followers in his inaugural address at his institute for the study of ideas:

> It is above all in setting the moral sciences on a firm and stable basis that you will meet the expectations of Enlightened Europe in the first learned body...It is this motive

which leads me to bring to your attention the science of the formation of ideas.[16]

Hence, by the time of the arrival of Marx and Engels, the study of ideology was firmly set within the context of a materialist approach to the origins and analysis of ideas.

SEC. 3–3

MATERIALISM VS. IDEALISM IN MARX AND ENGELS, AND THE INFLUENCE OF THE EIGHTEENTH-CENTURY CRITIQUE OF METAPHYSICS ON MARX'S CONCEPTION OF IDEOLOGICAL FALSE CONSCIOUSNESS

While it is true that neither Marx nor Engels was a complete and uncritical advocate of the mechanistic and contemplative kind of materialism characteristic of his eighteenth-century predecessors, both men did pay tribute to the path-breaking contribution of their Enlightenment materialist predecessors to the critique of idealist and religious ideologies.[17] Hence, while one has to acknowledge the differences in the kind of materialism distinguishing the philosophy of Marx from the philosophy of his classical predecessors (i.e., Marx's dialectical and historical materialism), at the same time one cannot ignore the importance both Marx and Engels placed on the contributions of their predecessors to the formulation of their own views on ideological false consciousness.

In my opinion the most significant influence of the *philosophes'* materialist critique of idealist metaphysics on Marx and Engels was in disposing them to view idealist modes of thought as essentially ideological forms of consciousness which were to be analyzed and criticized from a materialist perspective. The general materialist method of the *philosophes* concerning the analyses of ideas and forms of human thought in term of their origins also was to have a significant impact on Marx and Engels in their critique of ideological ideas and false consciousness. What needs to be examined in this section is how Marx and Engels pursued and developed further the materialist critique of idealist ideology in a historical materialist form.

In this section I will examine the distinctive character of the historical materialist critique of idealist ideological consciousness and discuss how their critique developed further the materialist project of their Enlightenment predecessors. I will therefore be examining the views of Marx (and Engels) in respect to the following points: (1) their own distinctive historical materialist approach to the origins of human thought and ideological consciousness; (2) the historical materialist critique of idealist interpretations of historically and socially relative forms of thought (i.e., Marx and Engels's version of the *philosophes'* critique of the doctrine of *a priori* ideas); (3) Marx's rejection of the idealist conception of the human intellect as an absolutely autonomous substance and his concern with situating forms of thought on a naturalistic and social basis; and (4) Marx's rejection of idealist metaphysics and idealist methodologies as inadequate for understanding reality, and his characterization of idealist methods of reasoning as an "alienated" and ideological way of thinking.

Basically, the historical materialist approach to human thought in general (and to ideological consciousness in particular) involves investigations into the social determination of modes of consciousness. Marx asserted this basic principle of the historical materialist outlook and methodology in several places in his writings.[18]

Both Marx and Engels believed this principle of the social determination of thought to be justified, given the results of their research and awareness of the influence of social factors on human cognition. In their opinion, sociological analyses of beliefs, collective ways of thinking, and collective errors were warranted because: (a) social conditions are the principal source of ideas, ideals and tacit assumptions;[19] (b) social conditions are the principal determinant in shaping or conditioning the way human agents view reality, and are the principal factor in determining the scope and the limits of the "horizon" of human consciousness;[20] and (c) in some cases, the validity of certain socially influential ideas is contingent on social and historical circumstances.[21]

By giving precedence to the study of objective social being as the key to understanding forms of thought, the principles of historical materialism were therefore consistent with the basic materialist outlook described in the previous section, i.e., belief in the ultimate ontological and causal priority of independent material being and the dependent and derivative status of thought. In this regard, it is worthwhile to note that in his essay entitled "Ludwig Feuerbach and the End of Classical German Philosophy," Engels emphasized the continuity between a materialist outlook in history (i.e., the primacy of social being vis-à-vis forms of social consciousness) with the basic materialist belief in the primacy of being vis-à-vis thought.

According to Engels's argument in his essay "Ludwig Feuerbach and the End of Classical German Philosophy," the philosophical belief in the ultimate ontological and causal priority of the independent material world vis-à-vis human thought was essential to any materialist-minded philosophy, whether mechanistic or dialectical. Engels also argued that materialism and idealism represented the two ultimate and irreducible philosophical frameworks for understanding the relation between being and thought, and for understanding the nature of ultimate reality.[22]

Now, some commentators would oppose the claim that Marx shared the same views as Engels concerning the nature of materialism; in addition, some commentators would be skeptical of the compatibility of a dialectical perspective on the relation between being and thought (i.e., dialectical belief in the mutual interaction between being and thought) with the materialist principle which gives precedence to the ultimate causal and ontological priority of material being (e.g., in the case of historical materialism, the priority of social being vis-à-vis consciousness).[23] I believe, however, that there is evidence to support the claim that Marx had views similar to Engels concerning the nature of materialism,[24] and that like Engels, Marx was interested in opposing idealist forms of thought. Furthermore, in the context of defending historical materialism from the charge of reductionism, Engels did attempt to demonstrate the compatibility between dialectics and the basic materialist outlook—an attempt which some have found persuasive, while others have remained unconvinced.[25] In any case, my concern is merely to emphasize the formal compatibility between historical materialism and the basic materialist principle defined above, and to suggest how historical materialism might be construed as a plausible extention of the basic materialist outlook to the understanding of society and forms of social consciousness.

While the Marxist philosopher may be aware that social being "determines" consciousness, social agents tend to be unaware of the social origins of their ideas and the social limits to the validity of their ideas, according to Marx and Engels. The fact that social agents tend to be ignorant of the social grounds of their beliefs concerning society, morality, politics, religion, etc., as well as to be ignorant of the social and historical limits to the validity of their ideas, constitutes part of the problem of ideological false consciousness as diagnosed by Marx and Engels. One of the ways in which ignorance about the social grounds and the social limits to the validity of one's beliefs contributes to false consciousness, according to Marx and Engels, is the manner in which this ignorance gives support and reinforcement to dogmatic and idealist attitudes on the part of social agents with respect to conventional "commonsense" forms of thought and the "ruling ideas" prevailing in their societies.

Basically, out of ignorance, education, habit and other social factors,[26] social agents tend to "idealize" the dominant assumptions, ideas and categories characteristic of their historical cultures and social groups, thereby attributing to their socially relative beliefs the status of being absolutely valid and rational *a priori*. For example, in the capitalist epoch it is widely assumed that human nature is "naturally" selfish and competitive, and that the profit motive is socially beneficial. However, in the feudal society which preceded capitalism, profit-taking on economic transactions was universally condemned as usury by members in this society. Members of feudal societies had stronger group self-identities (e.g., the various corporate "estates" of feudal society) than the "individualistic" self-identity characteristic of social agents in contemporary capitalist societies. In spite of the conflicting character of the two social belief-systems, members of each of the societies likely would insist that their respective dominant social conceptions are the only true and rationally valid ones.

In accepting what was false to be true—i.e., social and historically contingent ideas to be eternally valid, *a priori* truths—these people demonstrated false consciousness, according to Marx and Engels. They showed false consciousness, according to Marx and Engels, because they failed to perceive the socially and historically relative nature of their social conceptions, and because they failed to discern the social and historical limits to the validity of the ideas characteristic of their cultures and social groups. In a related way, social agents demonstrated false consciousness, according to Marx and Engels, if they failed to perceive the socially partisan and socially biased character of their beliefs.[27]

In the following passage from his critical essay on the writings of Joseph Proudhon, Marx draws a connection between false consciousness and ignorance of the social grounds of ideas. According to Marx, Proudhon, like most other social agents

...has not perceived that economic categories are only abstract expressions of these actual relations and only remain true while these relations exist. He therefore falls into the error of the bourgeois economists, who regard the economic categories as eternal and not as historical laws.[28]

Now, one of the characteristic ways in which this social false consciousness manifests itself, according to Marx and Engels, is in the treatment of social categories and ideas by intellectuals. Basically, Marx and Engels argue that intellectuals tend to interpret and transform the "ruling ideas" of their historical cultures into metaphysical "pre-existing, eternal ideas." However, because the "ruling ideas" of societies are neither "eternally valid" nor "products" of pure reason, idealist interpretations of social categories by intellectuals are false.

We can find evidence of Marx's and Engels's critique of the idealist false consciousness of intellectuals in many of their writings. For example, in writing on the tendency of lawyers and jurists to understand the legal codes of their societies in an idealistic way, Engels makes the following relevant remarks concerning the ideological character of idealist interpretation of the legal principles of societies.

The reflection of economic relations as legal principles is necessarily also a topsy-turvy one: it goes on without the person who is acting being conscious of it; the jurist imagines he is operating with *a priori* propositions, whereas they are really only economic reflexes; so everything is upside down. And it seems to me obvious that this inversion...so long as it remains unrecognised, forms what we call ideological conception...[29]

Interestingly, prior to the above passage Engels argued that it was inevitable that jurists and legal scholars would lose sight of the connection between their legal principles and social reality. According to Engels, with the codification and systematization of legal ideas, legal principles were bound to acquire the appearance of having an *a priori* rational status.[30] In his other writings, Engels argued that idealist interpretations of other forms of social consciousness (e.g., morality, philosophy, etc.) also were inevitable for the same kind of reasons.[31] Engels argued that with the inevitable rationalization of forms of social consciousness (in addition to the social division between mental and manual labor, see below), it was understandable that intellectuals were disposed to make metaphysical-like interpretations of social forms of thought.

In the case of Marx, an excellent illustration of his critique of the idealist false consciousness of intellectuals can be found in his commentaries on the writings of Joseph Proudhon, a nineteenth-century French socialist best known for his book *What is Property?* In a letter to P. V. Annenkov (28 December 1846), Marx criticized Proudhon for treating the principal categories of nineteenth-century bourgeois political economy as if "they were eternal verities" (e.g., the principle of "competition" as a natural and eternal law of economics).

> Proudhon does not state directly that bourgeois life is for him an eternal verity; he states it indirectly by deifying the categories which express bourgeois relations in the form of thought. He takes the products of bourgeois society for spontaneously arisen eternal beings, endowed with a life of their own, as soon as they present themselves to his mind in the form of categories...[32]

I think the above passage makes it quite clear how Marx's critique of idealist conceptions as a kind of false consciousness is essentially similar to Engels's views as well as displaying the continuity of Marx's critique of idealist conceptions concerning the origins and status of ideas with the *philosophes'* critique of metaphysics. According to Marx, two things make Proudhon's consciousness a false consciousness: (1) Proudhon is unaware of the social origins of his ideas and yet he presumes that these socially generated ideas are spontaneous, *a priori* products of pure reason; and (2) because of his ignorance of the social determinants of his ideas, and his "idealist" construal of these ideas, Proudhon falsely believes that the dominant ideas of bourgeois society are eternally valid, when in fact they have a limited historical and social validity.

Interestingly, twenty years after the above letter, Marx continued to criticize the false consciousness of Proudhon in similar terms. The following passage from Marx's letter to J. B. Schweitzer (24 January 1865) is of interest because it encapsulates Marx's own version of the eighteenth-century critique of the idealist theory of *a priori* ideas.

> [Proudhon] shares the illusions of speculative philosophy in his treatment of the economic categories;...instead of conceiving them as the theoretical expression of historical relations of production, corresponding to a particular stage of development in material production, he transforms them by his twaddle into pre-existing ideas...[33]

Hence, Marx judged idealist views concerning the origins and validity of first principles to be illustrative of the false consciousness of intellectuals. Finally, in an excellent summation of their views concerning the idealist tendencies of intellectuals, Engels wrote that intellectuals have a false consciousness because they treat socially generated and historically valid ideas as if they were "independent entities, developing independently and subject to their own laws."[34]

Now, one way by which Marx and Engels tried to expose and dispel the false idealist conceptions of social agents and intellectuals was by means of a historical materialist *genetic* analysis of influential social beliefs and ideas. Here too the approach of Marx and Engels was roughly consistent with, and hence comparable to, the *philosophes'* critique of metaphysical and erroneous ideas, a critique which also valued the use of genetic analyses in order to expose the origins of ideological ideas.

However, those factors which Marx and Engels believed to be relevant in accounting for the formation of ideological false consciousness were not always similar to those cited by the *philosophes* in their accounts of the origins of false consciousness. Generally, philosophers of the Enlightenment accounted for the origins of ideological "prejudices" in terms of such factors as human ignorance, an overly active human imagination and human credulity. However, explanations in terms of these factors alone were are not fully adequate to account for the persistent and widespread nature of idealist forms of false consciousness in law, politics, religion, philosophy, art, and in the general practical consciousness of social actors.

The advance Marx and Engels made over their eighteenth-century predecessors was in a consideration of the influence of objective structural features of societies in the formation of idealist forms of false consciousness and idealist interpretation of socially influential ideas. For example, in *The German Ideology*, Marx and Engels discussed how the social division between mental and manual labor contributed to idealist forms of thought, including the formation of religious ideologies.[35] According to their social structural analysis, the practical social position of intellectuals as "mental laborers" and their exclusive preoccupation with ideas make intellectuals lose touch with material social realities and eventually the connection between the system of their ideas and material social realities. With the rationalization of social and practical ideas over time, and with the development of theoretical traditions, the rationalization and systematization of ideas add the finishing touches to the false appearance of ideas as absolutely independent vis-à-vis social and material circumstances. Hence, while the social division between mental and manual labor is not a direct cause of idealist forms of consciousness, it is one of the underlying factors of the formation and support of idealist false consciousness, according to Marx and Engels.

Though Marx and the *philosophes* do differ somewhat in their explanations concerning the origins of idealist forms of thought and metaphysical ideas, we should not overlook the fact that Marx attempted to develop further the eighteenth-century materialist critique of idealist metaphysical ideas as part of his general critique of ideological ideas and false consciousness. This basic materialist program shared by Marx with his eighteenth-century predecessors also is evident in regards to the two remaining points chosen for comparing Marx's critique of ideology with that of the *philosophes*: Marx's rejection of idealist theories asserting belief in the essential independence or absolute autonomy of the human intellect, and Marx's repudiation of traditional metaphysics as a unique method of knowledge distinct from the empirical sciences.

Marx's rejection of the idealist conception of the human intellect as an absolutely autonomous faculty of judgment and his rejection of the idealist conception of human consciousness as a private, personal consciousness are evident in several passages in *The German Ideology*. In this text, Marx and Engels argue that human consciousness is a social product, and that all modes of thought have a practical and social basis. As practically and socially conditioned, human rationality is not, therefore, an absolutely unconditioned faculty of judgment possessing it own stock of innate ideas. Hence, in opposing idealist conceptions of human consciousness and reason Marx and Engels advocated the interpretation of thought according to the principles of historical materialism. In this respect Marx and Engels were essentially carrying forward the materialist program for a "naturalistic" interpretation of thought as pursued by their eighteenth-century materialist predecessors. In the spirit of their materialist predecessors, Marx and Engels express their opposition to idealist interpretations of thought in the following way:

> neither thoughts nor language in themselves form a realm of their own,...they are only manifestations of actual life...Morality, religion, metaphysics, all the rest of ideology and their corresponding forms of consciousness, thus no longer retain the semblance of independence.[36]

Finally, like the *philosophes*, Marx and Engels looked upon the materialist outlook and methodology as a corrective to the idealist metaphysical ideas and methodologies which prevailed in their era of "German ideology." Their critique of German Hegelian metaphysics is comparable to the *philosophes'* critique of Cartesian metaphysics in that like the *philosophes*, Marx and Engels rejected metaphysics (and idealist methodologies in particular) as unsuitable and inadequate methods for knowing reality. Marx and Engels argued that the empirical method of investigation and the naturalist outlook of modern science were far more suitable and reliable for acquiring real knowledge than the nonempirical and "speculative" methods of metaphysics. In this way, Marx and Engels concurred with the judgment of the *philosophes* that the traditional methods of metaphysics were not adequate for a real, "positive" knowledge of reality. According to Marx and Engels,

> where speculation ends...there real, positive science begins: the representation of the practical activity, of the practical process of the development of men...When reality is depicted, philosophy as an independent branch of knowledge loses its medium of existence. At best it can only be taken by a summing-up of the most general results, abstractions which arise from the observation of the historical development of men.[37]

It is worthwhile to note in the above passage that neither Marx nor Engels denied philosophy a role in the process of knowledge; like the *philosophes*, what they rejected was the presumption of idealist philosophers that rationalist metaphysics could compete with the empirically-oriented sciences in the acquisition of knowledge of reality.

However, unlike the *philosophes*, Marx and Engels were not dogmatic in their opposition to idealist metaphysics. According to the perspective of the French *philosophes*, idealist metaphysics were absolutely irrational and imaginary systems of thought. Marx and Engels were far more sensitive to the hidden cognitive and rational possibilities concealed within the mystified ideological forms of idealist philosophies. This nondogmatic attitude on the part of Marx and Engels is evident, for example, in their relationship to Hegel's idealist philosophy. Marx appropriated and transformed Hegel's dialectical method as well as some Hegelian conceptions (e.g., alienation) for use in his own scientific theories and methods for investigating and explaining capitalism.[38]

And while there might be some rational content to idealist metaphysics, nonetheless Marx and Engels rejected the idealist outlook in knowledge due to its overall false and "alienated" ideological character. In particular, Marx and Engels were critical of idealist approaches to the study of history and social reality. Following the principles of the French Enlightenment and Feuerbach, Marx and Engels opposed their own historical materialist understanding of history and social reality to ideological understanding of idealism.

According to Marx and Engels, what made the idealist outlook in knowledge an ideological outlook was that the idealist outlook was both an alienated and inverted perspective on reality, in addition to being an epistemologically inadequate method. First of all, the idealist outlook was an "alienated" ideological perspective because it was a perspective ignorant of fundamental material and social realities and secondly, it was a perspective lost in a world of speculative and metaphysical abstractions. As the young Marx was to say, idealist thinking is a kind of "alienated thinking [because it is] a thinking which disregards nature and actual man..."[39] Marx and Engels argued that the idealist outlook is an "inverted" ideological perspective because idealism in their opinion essentially reverses the proper ontological and causal order of things. Perhaps the most prominent example of this alienated and inverted way of thinking in the culture of their age was Hegel's philosophy of history.

In part, Marx and Engels's debate with idealist historians in *The German Ideology* involved philosophical questions concerning the ultimate ontological and causal foundations of history. According to Hegel, social organizations were ultimately manifestations of Mind or patterns of thought; and historians should study the ideas characteristic of a historical epoch (e.g., the historical forms of consciousness, or, in Marx's terminology, "the ruling ideas" prevailing in a society or culture) and the changes in societal belief-systems over time in order to understand the rationality of history. In the Hegelian scheme, therefore the study of history in essence amounted to a study of the evolution of ideas and forms of thought; ideas were believed to be the ultimate determining force in history, and Mind was the ultimate ontological basis of societies.

In some ways, the *Verstehen* method in the social sciences as advocated by Max Weber and members of the hermeneutical (e.g., Charles Taylor) and phenomenological (Alfred Schutz) tradition represents a variation on the basic idealist approach to the study of society as found in Hegel's philosophy of history. Like Hegel, proponents of the *Verstehen* methodology in the social sciences give prominence to the study of the consciousness of social participants for understanding the nature of societies. Why should social scientists give primacy to the study of the consciousness of social participants? Because societies are essentially created patterns of subjective and inter-subjective meanings constituted by the intentional and symbolic actions of rational agents. To understand societies on the basis of this method, therefore, requires an interpretation and explication of the "common-sense meanings" and collective "self-understandings" which are constitutive of societies and which are presumed by social participants in their social interactions with each other. It, therefore, is arguable that proponents of the *Verstehen* methodology in the social sciences also believe, like Hegel, that societies are essentially manifestations of mind or ideas.[40]

According to Marx, the idealist outlook and method in the social sciences is an "alienated" ideological perspective primarily because it excludes any consideration of the material and natural foundations of societies. To argue (or imply) as idealists do that social systems are essentially independent of nature, and therefore essentially determined by the consciousness of social participants, ignores how societies are themselves constrained by external natural forces and how societies have developed and evolved in response to the imperatives of the material and natural needs of its members. Marx says that because human beings "need to eat, drink, etc. in order to live," one of the fundamental and necessary requirements of all societies is the production of the material means to satisfy the needs of human beings. But this "necessity" to labor for the sake of human survival is a universal and eternal necessity imposed by Nature and not by the minds of human beings, according to Marx. In this vein, the following remarks by Marx from *Capital* are appropriate. According to Marx, the labor process

> ...is the universal condition for the metabolic interaction between man and nature, the everlasting nature-imposed condition of human existence, and it is therefore independent of every form of that existence, or rather it is common to all forms of society in which human beings live.[41]

Hence, in opposition to idealism, Marx cites the importance of the natural and material foundations of societies. More specifically, the technical and economic organizations which societies have evolved in order to cope with natural contingencies and fulfill the natural requirements of its members (e.g., the historical mode of production of a society) are emphasized by Marx as the basic foundations of societies.

In his second criticism of idealist theories of history and society, Marx argues that idealists fail to consider how the minds and volitions of social actors are themselves constrained and determined by the independent economic and class structure of their societies. Human agents make history, according to Marx, but under conditions which they have not freely chosen and which exist independent of their will.[42] Hence, every social agent is confronted by an objective social reality with properties of its own (e.g., division of labor, class structure, etc.) which "exert a controlling influence on the beliefs and actions of social members."[43] From Marx's materialist perspective, therefore, social reality is not simply reducible to the ideas in the minds of social agents (or in the case of Hegel, the World-Historical Spirit), nor is it the case for Marx that social systems are patterned according to the ideas in the minds of social agents; rather, in Marx's view, the ideas in the minds of social agents are patterned in accordance with the system of their social relations, a system which exists independent of their minds as an objective reality with distinct properties of its own.

Furthermore, Marx argues that idealist methodologies are epistemologically inadequate in other ways. In the first place, if social being "determines" consciousness, then idealists are in error in giving prominence to the study of social consciousness for understanding social reality; by doing so, they confuse causes with effects, and effects with causes. Hence, from Marx's perspective, idealist accounts in the social sciences are responsible for fostering inverted or "upside-down" explanations of history and society, and this upside-down view of reality is what Marx and Engels frequently characterize as an ideological perspective or false consciousness.

Marx and Engels also reject giving primacy to the study of the social consciousness of historical participants as the primary datum of the social sciences because the social consciousness of historical participants is not reliable. Marx and Engels argue that the social consciousness of historical participants is not reliable for two reasons: (a) social participants seldom have a true or adequate understanding of their societies, and the conceptual scheme which they are accustomed to using for understanding their societies tends to be at variance with the realities of their societies;[44] (b) for the most part, the principles social agents utilize for justifying their social/political actions cannot be relied upon for scientific inquiries because social agents are often deceived or even dishonest about their real motives in social/political struggles.[45]

In short, because the social image in the minds of historical participants often fails to correspond with the real nature of their societies, historical and sociological accounts relying upon the "ideological self-images" of societies as "both the *explanans* and the *explanandum* of social inquiry"[46] are doomed to giving superficial, even false "ideological" accounts of their subject matter, according to Marx and Engels. Hence, from the materialist perspective of Marx and Engels, idealist methodologies are intellectually bogus because they do not go beyond the "ideological" facades or "appearances" of societies in order to get to the real essence of their subject matter. Or, as they say in *The German Ideology*:

> Whilst in ordinary life every shopkeeper is very well able to distinguish between what somebody professes to be and what he really is, our historians have not yet won even this trivial insight. They take every epoch at its word and believe that everything it says and imagines about itself is true.[47]

In conclusion, like their materialist Enlightenment precedessors, Marx and Engels were concerned with "purging" the sciences (in their case, the social sciences) of their idealist ideological errors and reconstituting the study of social reality on a materialist, empirical basis. In this way, like the *philosophes*, Marx and Engels used the opposition between materialism and idealism as a basis for distinguishing scientific from ideological forms of understanding in the study of history and social reality.

In this section we have examined how Marx and Engels developed further the materialist critique of idealism as ideology. We have seen that in criticizing idealist forms of understanding as a type of false consciousness, the critiques of Marx and Engels were strikingly similar. For both men, social agents were false conscious because: (a) they "idealize" and "absolutize" the "ruling ideas" of their societies, thereby attributing a false "eternal" validity to their social and historically relative ideas; and (b) the social agents are ignorant of the social and historical grounds of their ideas and ignorant of the historical and social limits to the validity of their ideas. Finally, we have examined how for Marx and Engels the distinction between materialist and idealist forms of understanding provided a basis for distinguishing between scientific and ideological approaches in the social sciences. We have seen that like the *philosophes,* Marx viewed the idealist outlook in theory as an "alienated" ideological consciousness.

SEC. 3-4
THE FRENCH ENLIGHTENMENT CRITIQUE OF RELIGION AND THE DOMINANT IDEOLOGY THESIS

In this section, we will be examining how the French Enlightenment critique of religion laid the foundations for the "dominant ideology thesis." According to the dominant ideology thesis, certain ideas dominate the social consciousness of people. When these ideas "are believed widely enough and strongly enough,"[48] they constitute the prevailing or dominant social ideology (ideologies) of a society. These ideologies are invariably the "ideas of the ruling class," either because the ruling class or their "propagandists" impose their ideas on subordinate groups, or else because these ideas function in various ways to serve the interests of the rulers (i.e., by "legitimating" the social status quo which rulers are interested in preserving, etc.). Furthermore, by dominating the social consciousness of subordinate groups, these ideologies prevent the oppressed from comprehending the class realities of their societies and prevent them from understanding their real class interests. In a word, the dominant social ideology prevents the oppressed from becoming "class conscious." The dominant ideologies of a society are invariably false, either because such ideologies assert certain things to be true which in fact are not, or else because these ideologies prevent people from having a true understanding of their societies, class interests, etc.

Through an exploration of the writings of Paul Heinrich Dietrich Holbach and Claude Helvetius, we will see how their critique of religion laid the foundations for a social theory concerning dominant social ideologies. In turn, we will examine the influence of this critique by Holbach and Helvetius on Marx, and the differences between the theories of Marx and the *philosophes* concerning the origins and nature of dominant social ideologies. Finally, we will examine Marx's own critique of the dominant social ideologies of capitalism as found in his writings in *Capital*.

To begin: according to Holbach, if ideas could not be empirically verified, they should be dismissed as meaningless illusions, the products of human imagination. In his judgment, theological and religious ideas are "chimeras" because they are empirically groundless notions.

> There is a science that has for its object only things incomprehensible. Contrary to all other sciences, it treats only of what cannot fall under our senses…This science is called theology, and this theology is a continual insult to the reason of man…[Furthermore] the principles of every religion are founded upon the idea of God. Now, it is impossible to have true ideas of a being, who acts upon none of our senses. All our ideas are representations of sensible objects. What then can represent to us the idea of God, which is evidently without an object?…Can an idea without an archetype be any thing but a chimera?[49]

Not only are religious beliefs empirically groundless, but in addition, religious beliefs are morally harmful and antithetical to the real interests and happiness of humankind, according to Holbach.

Whoever has seriously meditated on religion and its supernatural morality; whoever has carefully weighed their advantages and disadvantages, will be fully convinced that both are injurious to the interests of man, or directly opposite to his nature.[50]

Thus, from Holbach's materialist perspective, religious beliefs are emprically groundless and morally disadvantageous. What then explains popular belief in such purportedly "irrational" ideas?

Following the principles of explanations favored by the English and French materialists of his era, Holbach argues that human ignorance and fears have served to render human beings credulous, and therefore more susceptible to belief in the irrational ideas of religion.

Ignorance and fear are the two great hinges of all religion. The uncertainty in which man finds himself in relation to his God, is precisely the motive that attaches him to his religion. Man is fearful in the dark—in moral, as well as physical darkness. His fear becomes habitual, and habit makes it natural.[51]

However, Holbach argued that psychological theories of religious beliefs cannot comprehend how religious ideologies serve important social and political functions in societies. What needs to be shown, according to Holbach, is how popular belief in religious illusions is encouraged by ruling elites in order to serve their particular social interests.[52] In pursuing this sociological type of investigation, Holbach lays the groundworks of the dominant ideology thesis.

According to Holbach, priests and the political rulers had formed an alliance with each other in order to serve their own vested social interests at the expense of the interests of the majority and the public good. Priests and rulers had utilized religious ideas in order to maintain the populace in a state of ignorance and mystification, and to legitimate their social standing and political authority in the eyes of the majority. In the following passage from his *System of Nature*, Holbach gives his account on the French Enlightenment's view concerning the conspiratoral origins of dominant social ideologies.

Ambition, imposture, and tyranny, have formed a league, to avail themselves of [popular religious ideas]...to the end that they may blind the people, and bend them beneath their yoke. The monarch makes use of it, to give a divine lustre to his person, the sanction of Heaven to his rights... The priest uses it, to give currency to his pretensions, to the end that he may, with impunity, gratify his avarice, pride, and independence...[53]

As we see from this passage, one of the ideological functions fulfilled by the widely believed theory concerning the divine right of kings was to legitimate the authority of rulers. In criticizing this ideology, Holbach, like other social critics of his period, advocated the liberal social contract theory.[54]

Another popular religious belief which Holbach criticized for its social and political "ideological" functions was the Christian doctrine on the heavenly afterlife. According to Holbach, the doctrine of the future life

...has been of the greatest utility to those who have given religions to nations and made themselves its ministers: it was the foundation of their power; the source of their wealth; the permanent cause of that blindness...which it was their interest to nourish in the human race...[55]

While religious beliefs like the doctrine of the future life and the divine right of kings served to rationalize and legitimate the social standing and authority of priests and rulers, at the same time such "ideologies" (or "prejudices," according to Holbach's terminology) also functioned to obfuscate the social understanding of their subjects. Holbach argued that religious ideologies encouraged the oppressed to view their own social misery and inferior social status as being divinely ordained as opposed to being humanly created. In addition, religious ideologies encouraged the oppressed to view the social status and political power of their social superiors as also being divinely ordained as opposed to being humanly created. Finally, such ideologies prevented the majority from becoming aware of their "true" rational interests and the public good.

Prejudices...have blinded man upon the true nature of government...they have believed that their sovereigns were Gods disguised, who received with their birth, the right of commanding the rest of mankind...and that they were not accountable for the misery they engendered...[people have]

lived in misfortune, because they...believe [God] condemned them to be miserable...[56]

Oppressed by the double yoke of spiritual and temporal powers, it has been impossible for the people to know their happiness...Men have had no other Morality, than what their legislators and priests brought down from the unknown regions of heaven...It is only by showing them the truth that they will perceive their true interests and the real motives that ought to incline them to do good...But everything conspires to blind them, and to confirm them in their error...[57]

We see from the above passage that in Holbach's view, the majority are unable to perceive their true social interests because of the manipulation of their social consciousness by members of the ruling elite. Furthermore, Holbach argues above that the majority are more susceptible to manipulation and deception because of the state of ignorance in which they are kept by ruling elites who control public institutions responsible for education, the legislation of laws, and the dissemination of public opinion.

In short, Holbach's writings allude to a sociological conception of false consciousness. According to Holbach, social agents are ignorant and deceived about their real interests, they have a false understanding as to the real nature of their societies, and they are ignorant about the social functions of their beliefs. By means of deception, manipulation and their commanding position in society, political elites utilize false ideological ideas like "the divine right of kings" to foster a false social consciousness. And they do so, in Holbach's opinion, because a socially ignorant and false-thinking majority is essential to the preservation of their unjust social regimes.

One of the novel developments of Holbach's critique of religion was to encourage investigations into the social and political functions of false and socially influential ideas like religious ideas. In this sociological conception of ideology as developed by Holbach, certain ideas are ideological not only because they are false, but because of their social and political functions. Those ideas used for legitimating tyrannical political authority and domination by a self-interested, greedy power elites are characterized as "prejudicial" or ideological ideas by Holbach. Because theories like the divine right of kings and the doctrine on the heavenly afterlife could be used for rationalizing and justifying social domination, Holbach's writings suggest a conception of ideology as the disguised rationalizations of partisan class interests. Finally, Holbach's writings demonstrate the intimate link between false consciousness and ideology.

Using similar kinds of arguments, Claude Helvetius, a fellow *philosophe* and acquaintance of Holbach, also argued that popular acceptance of false and irrational beliefs like religious ideas is due to the manipulation of social consciousness by ruling elites intent on deceiving subordinate social groups. According to Helvetius, members of the ruling elite (e.g., princes and priests) are able to impose their own "ideology" on subordinate social groups because they alone have the power to shape public opinion and resolve political disputes in a manner which serves their private interests. The following remarks from Helvetius's *Treatise on Man* are pertinent:

> Opinion, we are told, is the queen of the world...almost all questions in morality and politics are resolved by the strong and not by the rational; and that if opinion rules the world, it is at least the powerful that rule opinion.[58]

Furthermore, Helvetius argues that rulers and priests have an interest in deceiving their subjects because the particular interests of ruler are not always compatible with the interests of their subjects and the public good. Because of this conflict of interests, Helvetius argues that it was necessary for monarchs and priests to "rationalize" or misrepresent and disguise their real interests in order to "conceal from the people the true principles of morality."[59]

> ...the public interest, which is that of the majority, among whom the principles of sound morality ought to find support, [is] not always...agreeable to the interest of those most in power...[in fact, it is often the case that the] interests [of rulers are] contrary to the general good...[As a result, rulers have recognized that] their power had no other foundation than the ignorance and weakness of mankind: they have therefore imposed silence on whosoever, by discovering to the people the true principles of morality, would have opened their eyes with respect to their misfortunes and all their rights.[60]

In order to reveal the incompatibility between the public good and the "idealized" partisan interests of rulers, Helvetius prescribes a method of analysis which requires the social critic to treat the ideas of the ruling class as a "rationalization" or mask for dissembling their self-serving interests:

> it would be sufficient for this purpose [i.e., ideological analysis] to remove the obstacles placed against...progress by the two kinds of men [i.e., political tyrants and religious fanatics]...the only means of succeeding in this, is to pull off their masks, and...show that the protectors of ignorance are the most cruel enemies of humanity.[61]

Helvetius's method for "pulling off the masks of imposture" was to profoundly influence Marx and Engels.[62]

Finally, like Holbach, Helvetius was particularly critical of the role of the clergy and the Church's domination of education in the genesis and reproduction of a religiously oriented false social consciousness. According to Helvetius,

> ...the name of virtue should be given to such actions only, as are useful to the public, and conformable with the general interest. [But] has [not] theology constantly kept the people from knowledge of this sort of virtue? and has it [not] always obscured in them the ideas of it? It is the effect of the interest of theology; and it is in conformity to this interest, that the priest has everywhere solicited the exclusive privilege of public instruction.[63]

Now, these ideas of Holbach and Helvetius were instrumental to the development of the "dominant ideology thesis" popular in contemporary "power elite" sociological theories and Marxist-inspired theories on ideology.[64] According to the *philosophe* version of the "dominant ideology thesis," political leaders and priests need to deceive their subjects because their partisan class interests are antithetical to the interests of the majority and the public good. In order to protect their vested social interests and political authority, members of the ruling elite have joined together in an ongoing intentional conspiracy to impose a false consciousness on their subjects through the promotion and public indoctrination of false ideological beliefs or "prejudices." These false and influential "social" ideologies, therefore, are the intellectual "masks" or "disguises" utilized by the ruling elite for rationalizing and legitimating their social status and authority; at the same time, they are social ideas employed by the ruling elite to deceive their subjects. The inability of members of subordinate social groups to perceive their real interests and understand the true nature of their societies is thus due to the domination of their social consciousness by ruling class ideologies.

MARX'S DOMINANT IDEOLOGY THESIS

Marx incorporates many aspects of the French Enlightenment version of the dominant ideology thesis. Like the *philosophes*, Marx argues that ruling class ideologies misguide the social consciousness of oppressed classes, cause oppressed groups to misperceive their rational class interests, and impede the development in oppressed groups of a true understanding of social realities.[65] And like the *philosophes*, Marx argues that ruling social groups invariably misrepresent their particular class interests as if they were the common interest and the interest of the majority.[66] Finally, like the *philosophes*, Marx (and Engels) argue that

> the ideas of the ruling class are in every epoch the ruling ideas, i.e. the class which is the ruling material force of society, is at the same time its ruling intellectual force. The class which has the means of material production at its disposal, has control at the same time over the means of mental production, so that thereby, generally speaking, the ideas of those who lack the means of mental production are subject to it.[67]

However, there are some important differences between Marx's version and the French Enlightenment version of the dominant ideology thesis. First of all, Marx argues that the ideological misrepresentation of particular interests as general interests by ruling classes is not always a deliberate and conscious misrepresentation on their part. In some cases, ruling classes and dominant social groups vying for political power also are unaware of the ideological nature of their ideas, according to Marx.

More importantly, Marx (and Engels) argue that theoretical

explanations of the origins of dominant ideological conceptions (and hence, false social consciousness) in terms of ruling class conspiracies to deceive are not fully adequate for explaining the pervasive influence of the "ideas" of ruling classes in societies. The pervasive influence and widespread social acceptance of the "ideas" of the ruling class can only be due to the fact that these "ruling ideas" and "ideological forms of social understanding" have a systematic origin, according to Marx (and Engels). Hence, instead of explaining the origins of false social consciousness in terms of ruling class conspiracies to deceive, Marx argues that false consciousness and dominant social ideologies have to be explained in terms of their systematic social origins.

This nonconspiratorial, structuralist conception of the origins of the "ruling ideas" of societies, and hence, false social consciousness, is evident in the following passage from *The German Ideology*.

> The ruling ideas are nothing more than the ideal expression of the dominant material relationships, the dominant material relationships grasped as ideas; hence of the relationships which make the one class the ruling one, therefore, the ideas of its dominance.[68]

Hence, from the point of view of Marx and Engels, the basic conceptions informing ruling class ideologies are ideas which arise "naturally" in societies as the immediate, empirical appearances of the dominant institutional and class relationships prevailing in societies.[69]

Of course, Marx did not reject the notion that rulings classes and their agents sometimes conspire to deceive subordinate groups.[70] Furthermore, Marx was well aware of the fact that ruling classes, more than oppressed groups, possess the material, social means for imposing their social views on the majority, and the passage just quoted shows Marx's view concerning how economic control confers ideological control in societies. However, for Marx theoretical explanations in terms of ruling class conspiracies to deceive are not adequate for revealing the deeper systematic and primary social roots of dominant ideological conceptions and ideological forms of social understanding.[71] In the final analysis, for Marx social appearances were themselves deceiving.

One of the theoretical virtues of Marx's theory is that Marx could explain how both ruling and subordinate classes could be subject to similar social illusions and therefore possess false consciousness. This is not something his eighteenth-century predecessors could accomplish, given their theory of a deceiving ruling class and a deceived oppressed class.

According to Marx, the empirical appearances reflected in the ideology of the ruling class are social images which both members of ruling and oppressed social groups directly encounter and experience in the course of their daily practical interactions with each other. While these images convey the "appearances" of the institutional and class relationships of society to the minds of social agents, they do not represent the real essence of their social and class relationships. At least in capitalist societies, the reality of capitalism is represented in a radically inverted way by its phenomenal forms of appearances, according to Marx. In any case, because of the false and deceiving nature of social appearances, Marx argues that both ruling and subordinate groups are subject to false consciousness.[72]

Since the basic conceptions of dominant social ideologies are spontaneous and empirically given social conceptions reflecting the "surface" of social reality, Marx argues that it is quite "natural" for both ruling and subordinate classes to view these ideological conceptions as veridical representations of their societies. Since ideological forms of social understanding have a systematic basis (e.g., in the mode of production of societies), Marx argues that it is natural and inevitable for social agents to view the general ideological frameworks of their societies as *prima facie* rational and valid forms of social understanding. The following passage from Marx's *Capital* is relevant:

> It is also quite natural...that the actual agents of production themselves feel completely at home in these estranged and irrational forms...for these are precisely the configurations of appearance in which they move, and with which they are daily involved...These forms of appearances are reproduced directly and spontaneously as current and usual modes of thought...they are forms of thought which are socially valid, and therefore objective, for the relations of production belonging to this historically determined mode of social production.[73]

As we have said, both Marx and Engels argued that social agents will tend to view the dominant assumptions of their societies on such matters as human nature and values as "eternal truths." For example, according to Marx and Engels, social agents in capitalist societies tend to believe that all human beings are "naturally" selfish and that competitive market relationship between people are "natural" forms of productive relationships true for all societies.[74] In terms of moral-political values, Marx and Engels argued that social agents in capitalist societies invariably believe in the fundamental "moral equality" of all human beings and the "natural rights" of individuals to legal and political equality in the state.[75] And again, what disposes people in capitalist societies to presume the eternal validity of these beliefs is that these beliefs are the customary or "ruling ideas" of their societies.

Hence, for Marx, in contrast to the *philosophes*, people possess false consciousness not because they ignore experience but rather because they give too much credence to the empirical appearances of their societies.[76] Because there is some objective content to ruling class ideologies, Marx rejected the *philosophes'* notion that "ruling class ideologies" are simply a bunch of "lies" and "groundless conceits."

Now, while the basic principles of the historical materialist and realist approach to the analysis of dominant social ideologies were formulated in the text of *The German Ideology*, it wasn't until his work *Capital* that Marx was to apply these principles to the analysis of a dominant social ideology in a systematic and cogent way.[77] What Marx achieved in *Capital* was a demonstration of the objective, social conditions which made possible the ideological domination of the collective social consciousness in capitalism by the ideology of the bourgeoisie.

According to the ideological standpoint of the bourgeoisie, the profit-oriented, market economy of capitalism fosters an economically just society—a society where the equal rights of individuals are respected, and a society most conducive to the flourishing of personal liberty for all. Now, according to Marx's analysis, what accounts for the socially influential nature and plausibility of these beliefs is that the market relationships between social classes in capitalism do convey the appearance of personal freedom, equality and justice. In other words, these "ruling ideas" characteristic of the ideology of the bourgeoisie are derived ultimately from the social appearances which arise from one of the dominant social institutions in capitalist societies, i.e., the market relationships which mediate the interactions between the wage-earning working class and the capital-owning bourgeoisie.

The following passage from *Capital* makes evident Marx's views on the socioeconomic origins of bourgeois ideology.

> [T]he sphere of...commodity exchange, within whose boundaries the sale and purchase of labor-power goes on, is in fact a very Eden of the innate rights of man. It is the exclusive realm of Freedom, Equality, Property, and Bentham. Freedom, because both buyer and seller of a commodity...are determined only by their own free will... Equality, because each enters into relation with the other,... and they exchange equivalent for equivalent. Property, because each disposes only of what is his own. And Bentham, because each looks only to his own advantage. The only force bringing them together, and putting them into relation with each other, is the selfishness, the gain and the private interest of each.[78]

As this passage makes evident, Marx was quite willing to grant that at the level of empirical appearances, there is some partial truth to the ideological claims of the bourgeoisie. Let me try to explicate what Marx viewed as the partially true content contained within the market-based ideologies of the bourgeoisie.

When capitalists contract with workers in the labor market for employment purposes, capitalists pay workers wages or money in exchange for use of the latter's labor-power. To workers and capitalists, the payment of wages makes it appear as if the value of the workers's productivity has been paid in full. Hence, the wages paid to workers seem to be just.

Since both workers and capitalists seem to have exchanged equivalent amounts of value—i.e., the value of the workers' labor-power being equivalent to the money or wages paid by capitalists—both workers and capitalists appear to have equally benefited from their transaction. Finally, because they each freely agreed to enter into a transaction with each other, their market relationship appears to them as uncoerced and hence, as a matter of a free, personal choice.

However, Marx argues that this is only how things appear on the surface of things as a result of the commodity form of the capital-worker relationship. According to Marx, by making a class relationship of domination and exploitation appear as a fair and just relationship between free and equal individuals, the wage or market form of the capitalist-worker relationship conceals the real essence of their relationship and presents their relationship in a false and inverted way.

To begin with, their relationship is not really just, because workers are not paid for the full value of their productive labor. According to Marx, workers always produce more value than what they are paid for. What wages actually provide for is the average subsistence needs of workers. However, in the average daily labor-time it takes for workers to labor for their subsistence, there still remains additional labor-time left in the day for workers to produce additional value. This additional "surplus-labor time" provides the source of the unpaid "surplus value" appropriated by the capitalist, and hence the source of capitalist profits. Marx argued that the wage-form or money-relation between capitalist and workers conceals this exploitation while representing an injustice in an inverted way as justice.

> [T]he wage-form...extinguishes every trace of the division of the working day into necessary labor and surplus labor, into paid and unpaid labor. All labor appears as paid labor...[hence] the money-relation conceals the uncompensated labor of the wage-labor.[79]

Furthermore, Marx argues that the market relationship between capitalist and workers conceals the ultimate dependence of workers on capitalists for their means of subsistence and the capitalists' domination of workers by virtue of their ownership and control of the means of production. The fact that workers are "free" to choose for whom they want to work and where they want to work does not change the reality that they are dependent on others for work and hence for the means of their own subsistence.

> The dull compulsion of economic relations sets the seal on the domination of the capitalist order over the worker. Direct extra-economic force is still of course used, but only in exceptional cases. In the ordinary run of things...it is possible to rely on his [the worker's] dependence on capital, which springs from the conditions of production themselves...[80]

> ...the appearance of independence is maintained by a constant change in the person of the individual employer, and by the legal fiction of a contract...[81]

For all of these reasons, workers and capitalists are unequal in status, power and wealth. As one commentator aptly noted regarding the mystifications arising from the commodity form of the relationship between workers and capitalists:

> By restricting their vision to the wage-labor transaction itself...they are able to enlist the ideals of freedom and equality to justify the wage-labor relation and ultimately the whole set of social relations built upon it. But this feat of tunnel vision is a rather fragile accomplishment. Once we look beyond the transaction itself, we see that the exchange is not free because of the profound inequalities of the respective position of the worker and the capitalist.[82]

In a similar vein, Marx himself concluded that the commodity form of the relationship between workers and capitalists is a "mere semblance" or "show" which conceals the real content of their relationship while representing it in an inverted, upside-down manner.

> [T]the relation of exchange between capitalist and worker becomes a mere semblance belonging only to the process of circulation, it becomes a mere form, which is alien to the content of the transaction itself, and merely mystifies it. The constant sale and purchase of labor-power is the form; the content is the constant appropriation by the capitalist, without equivalent, of a portion of the labor of others...[83]

Hence, according to Marx's class and structural analysis of capitalism, the ideological claims of the bourgeosie are partially true at the level of empirical appearances, but from the standpoint of the social system as a whole these ideological claims are essentially false. On the other hand, while these ideological claims can be refuted on analysis, however, this does not negate their practical and compelling influence on the minds of social agents in capitalism, according to Marx. Why? Because as Marx argues, the compelling force of bourgeois ideological claims in capitalism is due ultimately to the fact that they are the socially determined forms of thought which correspond to the empirical appearances of the dominant social institutions of capitalism (e.g., wage-labor, market transactions, private property, etc.). While one can rationally criticize these ideologies at the level of thought, criticism alone cannot destroy the false appearances and social false consciousness arising from the institutions of capitalism. To do this, according to Marx, would require radical transformations in the institutions of society.[84]

Though it may be natural for human beings to be taken in by societal appearances, it is not inevitable that they should remain their intellectual captives.[85] Human beings do have the intellectual capacity to get beyond appearances to apprehend the truth. But there has to be a desire or "interest" on the part of social agents to get beyond the appearances of their societies in order to know the hidden truth of their societies. In most cases, according to Marx, members of the ruling class are not really interested in a critical and comprehensive knowledge of the political and economic realities of their societies, because such knowledge is not advantageous to their practical class interests. They are more interested in social mystification than in the real truth.[86]

In this section we have examined the eighteenth-century critique of religion and demonstrated how this critique evolved the sociological thesis of a dominant ruling class ideology and the concomitant notion of social false consciousness. We then traced the influence of the *philosophes'* dominant ideology thesis on Marx, and the differences between Marx's formulation of the dominant ideology thesis and that of his eighteenth-century forebears. Finally, we examined Marx analyses in *Capital* concerning the market-based social ideologies of capitalism, and the social false consciousness which results from the market transactions between the bourgeoisie and the working class.

4

Ideology and Political Class Struggle: Hegel's Philosophy of History and the Political False Consciousness in the Writings of Marx and Engels

SEC. 4–1
INTRODUCTION

In the last chapter we discovered that for Marx the socioeconomic mode of production prevailing in an historical epoch is the source of distinctive social beliefs, categories of social understanding, and shared illusions constituting the dominant ideologies of a society. According to Marx, these dominant ideological forms of thought represent something like the "common sense" of a society; they are the given, customary conceptions through which social agents comprehend their social experience, and the normative ideals which social agents utilize for articulating their moral and political claims on one another. Since these dominant ideological conceptions are historically and socially determined, it follows that societies with different modes of production will have different ideological social mentalities, belief-systems and "ruling ideas."[1]

For example, in the slave-owning societies of classical antiquity, a master-slave social mentality prevailed; accordingly, it was assumed by the leading social theorists of the period that people were by nature morally and politically unequal. It was then argued that the domination of the majority by a minority master class was justified according to natural principles.[2] In contrast, in modern market societies where different kinds of human labor are made equivalent by means of universal monetary measures,[3] it is widely believed that all persons are morally and politically equal; as a result, only democratic majority rule can be justified in accordance with this society's "self-evident truths" (cf. the U.S. Declaration of Independence: "We hold these truths to be self-evident").

In medieval feudal society, religious forms of thought and religious ideological conceptions dominated the social consciousness of its members. Monarchs ruled by "divine right" and the social hierarchy symbolized the "great chain of being."[4] In terms of the socioeconomic basis of the religious form of social consciousness of medieval Europe, the following remarks of Engels are relevant:

> [T]his theological welding was not only in ideas, it existed in reality...[The Catholic] Church, which, owning about a third of the land in every country, occupied a position of tremendous power in the feudal organization...Besides, the clergy was the only educated class. It was therefore natural that Church dogma was the starting point and basis of all thought.[5]

Marx and Engels argued that because of the systematic influence of dominant social ideologies, it is inevitable for members from different social classes and sections of classes to formulate their political and social conflicts with each other in terms of the prevailing ideological forms of thought available to them. In other words, social agents for the most part will utilize the conceptions and categories characteristic of the dominant social ideologies of their time to give expression to their particular class interests and political aims until new ideological forms of thought and conceptions arise to challenge and supersede the older, dominant social ideologies.[6] Hence, for the most part the ideological dimension of the political struggle between classes and class fractions will take place within the conceptual forms of the prevailing social ideologies, according to Marx and Engels.[7]

While the meaning of certain dominant ideological conceptions may be the same for all in a society, some of the "ruling ideas" of a society are subject to more specific interpretations along class lines because dominant ideological categories tend to be very abstract in their nature, according to Marx and Engels. For example, in contemporary Western societies where the categories of liberty, equality and democracy dominate, these concepts by themselves are simply too general or vague in their meaning to denote anything specific.[8] If these concepts are to mean anything, they must be given a specific denotation by political groups interested in advancing their own social agendas. Thus, for radicals interested in advancing a socialist agenda, "democracy" might mean "workers' control" or "participatory democracy." For conservatives interested in protecting private property rights, democracy might mean a market-oriented "representative democracy" or "laissez-faire government."

In their writings, Marx and Engels both gave examples of different class interpretations of dominant ideological conceptions. For example, Marx observed that members of the ruling class tended to utilize religious ideas in politically and culturally conservative ways to rationalize and legitimate the inequalities of their societes.[9] He also observed that oppressed groups sometimes utilized religious ideas in a politically and culturally radical fashion to protest against the inequalities of their societies. As he said in his introduction to the critique of Hegel's *Philosophy of Right*,

> The wretchedness of religion is at once an expression of
> and a protest against real wretchedness. Religion is the sigh
> of the oppressed creature...[10]

In a similar vein but in reference to modern "juridical"-egalitarian ideologies, Engels argued that the idea of "equality" in capitalism had both a bourgeois and proletarian connotation.[11] According to Engels, "equality" for bourgeois liberal theorists was essentially legal and political equality in the liberal democratic state. For socialist and proletariat theorists, however, "equality" included the more radical demands for social and economic equality.

In short, the political writings of Marx and Engels provide many observations and analyses of how different social classes and class factions utilize the dominant ideological conceptions of their societies in order to express their class interests and further their social-political aims.

Now, in the hands of recent interpreters of Marx's conception of ideology, Marx's writings on the different political usages of social ideologies by social classes have been used to deny any identification of Marx's conception of ideology with Engels's conception of false consciousness. From the perspective of these contemporary commentators what Marx's political writings suggest is a nonepistemological, functionalist conception of ideology in which the categories of truth and falsity do not apply.

Perhaps a good definition of what is meant by a nonepistemological, functionalist conception of ideology is provided by Nicholas Emler. He defines "ideology" in the following way:

> I take an ideology to be a set of beliefs, characteristic of a social group, which 'explains' its culture, its position and relation to other groups, and which rationalizes its values, priorities, and social arrangements. These beliefs may, according to some external criterion, be true or false...But what makes a set of beliefs an ideology is its function—promoting a particular way of life or set of social arrangements or political programme.[12]

In reference to the interpretation of Marx's conception of ideology, Istvan Meszaros provides us with a good example of the nonepistemological, functionalist interpretation in his recent book entitled *Philosophy, Ideology and Social Science*. According to Meszaros, by ideological consciousness Marx meant a political-class consciousness concerned with "the articulation of rival set of values and strategies aimed at controlling the social metabolism."[13]

Joe McCarney, in his recent book *The Real World of Ideology*, also follows this nonepistemological, functionalist reading of Marx. According to McCarney,

> the thesis of this essay is that the role of ideas in the class struggle constitutes the substance of Marx's conception of ideology. To say this is to imply a systematic indifference on his part to other sorts of consideration; an indifference that extends to the cognitive status of the forms of consciousness that fall within the ideological realm. For Marx, it may be said, ideology is not an epistemological category.[14]

Chantel Mouffe utilizes Gramsci's interpretation of Marx's prefatory remarks to his 1859 *Contribution to a Critique of Political Economy* as a textual basis for rejecting an epistemological reading of

Marx's conception of ideology and for supporting the sociological-functionalist interpretation. According to Mouffe, since class ideologies are practically efficacious, it is inconceivable how an interpretation of the ideological consciousness as false consciousness could be defended. Accordingly, Mouffe advocates a Gramscian interpretation of Marx's conception of ideology. In Mouffe's own words:

> According to Gramsci, the starting point of all research on ideology must be Marx's assertion that 'men gain consciousness of their tasks on the ideological terrain of the superstructures' so that the latter, he declares, must be considered as 'operating realities which possess efficacy' [and not as illusory epiphenomena].[15]

Finally, based on his review of recent Marxist theorists on ideology, Alex Callinicos also advocates the rejection of epistemological interpretations of ideology as denoting false consciousness. According to Callinicos,

> if we take seriously the 'pragmatic' dimension of ideology, the determination of ideologies by the class struggle, then the question of the truth or falsity of ideologies is beside the point. What matters is that they are the 'forms in which men become conscious of this conflict and fight it out'...What I propose is that we dispense with the notion that ideologies are imaginary representations, false beliefs, illusions: ideology is, on Therborn's definition, 'that aspect of the human condition under which human beings live their lives as conscious actors in a world that makes sense to them to various degrees'.[16]

Hence, in the eyes of some contemporary commentators, what was important for Marx was understanding how ideologies function in the class struggle and how different social classes utilize ideologies in order to advance the self-interests of their class. They contend that epistemological considerations of ideologies were irrelevant since for Marx "the defining characteristic for a consciousness to be ideological [was] its significance, utility in the class struggle."[17] For some of these theorists it is difficult to envision how ideologies could be false since they are practically efficacious in the class struggle.

For my part, I disagree with all of these claims. While I agree with these theorists that one of the defining characteristics of an ideology is its social significance with respect to class inequalities, I understand this to be a necessary but not a sufficient condition for defining ideology. I would add as another necessary defining condition that the ideas must be false in some way to count as an ideological idea according to Marx.

But if ideologies are false, how then can they be practically efficacious? I would argue that false ideas can be practically efficacious only up to a point. For example, an illusion might serve to inspire the passions of a group or serve to draw together a fragmented, demoralized nation. However, I'm doubtful that such shared illusions could succeed in realizing the long-term well-being of a people. Of course, the extent of the practical efficacy of any illusion is really an empirical issue requiring historical research and even psychological research. But what has history already told us about the social utility of such collective illusions as the militarist-nationalist ideology of Nazism or the witch hysteria of early modern Europe?

Even Marx recognized that ideological illusions could be efficacious to some degree. In the opening to *The Eighteenth Brumaire of Louis Bonaparte*, Marx commented on how the "illusions and self-deceptions" of the French and English bourgeois revolutionaries helped to inspire and sustain their revolutionary morale. Nonetheless, Marx criticized these bourgeois ideologies as an example of ruling-class ideologies which falsely pretended to be in the general interest when in fact they served particular sectional interests.

While it is likely that ideologies may have some short-term instrumental or emotional value for social groups, it is very likely that ideologies will express class interests in a false or distorted fashion. For example, in the case of ruling classes the falsity of their ideologies might consist in the fact that particular interests are misrepresented as the general interest. In the case of oppressed groups, their ideologies might prevent them from having a clear and true comprehension of their real class interests, and hence their ideological consciousness could result in distracting them from their proper political aims. Hence, ideologies are more likely to mislead and deceive than to provide any long-term benefit to the oppressed. And if social agents are misled or deceived by their ideologies, what does this say about their consciousness?

The general point I take Marx to be making in his political writings is that the ideologies used in class struggles (whether ruling-class ideologies or the ideologies of the oppressed) are epistemologically flawed in some manner. The fact that bourgeois liberal-democratic ideologies may have served "progressive historical interrests" at one point in history (i.e., against feudal ideologies) still does not negate certain falsehoods inherent in those ideologies. Nor does it refute the fact that as an ideology it imposes certain limits on the social understanding of political actors which prevents them from having a true understanding of their political struggles.[18]

It seems to me that the functionalist view gives up too much, therefore, when it rejects a pejorative conception of ideology as false consciousness and when it rejects any epistemological concern with the cognitive content of ideologies. If "ideology" simply comes to mean the worldview or political programme of a social group, are we to assume then that all ideologies are equally valid because only their functional value for a group matters, and not their truth or falsity? Surely partisans advocating nonracist or nonsexist "ideologies" believe that there is something unreasonable and untrue about the ideology of their opponents while their own positions are reasonable and true. I doubt, for example, that feminists mean to say that the problem with sexist ideologies is that they "articulate values and social strategies" different from feminist values and social strategies. The ideological idea that men are morally or intellectually superior to women is a false idea, no matter what value one wishes to attach to this idea. Hence, I would submit that no reasonable person can honestly believe that the cognitive content of ideologies is irrelevant; furthermore, since it is assumed that there is more to ideological critique than simply comparing one's own social perspective with that of another, I would submit that social theorists must believe that they have access to objective and rational criteria in order to criticize their opponents' "ideologies."

If ideologies are false, then it follows that a true social consciousness can be distinguished from a false ideological consciousness. But skeptics argue that there is no way a true social consciousness can be distinguished from a false consciousness in social theory, because objective knowledge is not possible in social theory.[19] Social theories, according to one version of the skeptical position, represent the biased perspective of partisan social groups.[20] If all social theories are ideologically biased (by embodying the partisan social perspective of their authors), one theory cannot be more objective or more true than another theory.

For some, this version of the skeptical argument against a theory of false consciousness has its roots in the views on the sociology of knowledge advanced by Karl Mannheim.[21] While it is true that Mannheim at times expresses this kind of skepticism,[22] I would argue that Mannheim was not always consistent in his views concerning the biasing effects of social conditions on human cognition. In fact, in a somewhat ironic reversal to the opening skepticism of his *Ideology and Utopia: An Introduction to the Sociology of Knowledge*, Mannheim argues in the text that in some cases the social perspective of certain groups can serve as a "vantage point" for discovering objective truths about society unseen from the perspective of other social groups. According to Mannheim,

> ...the fact that our thinking is determined by our social position is not necessarily a source of error. On the contrary, it is often the path to political insight...[How so? because] the social interests of a given group make the members of that group sensitive to certain aspects of life to which those in another position do not respond.[23]

It would follow that if the social position and interests of certain groups provides them with a "vantage point" for acquiring more objective knowledge of society and, at the same time, a "vantage point" for exposing and criticizing the ideological limitations and biases of rival social groups, then a true scientific consciousness can be distinguished from a false ideological consciousness in social theory.[24] From this it would follow that Marx could justifiably argue that his proletariat standpoint in social theory represents a truer and therefore nonideological perspective on social reality in contrast to the false ideological standpoint of bourgeois theorists whom he criticizes.

Finally, and of most importance, I submit that the nonepistemological, functionalist interpretation of Marx is simply not true to the political writings of Marx on the ideological consciousness in politics. It also fails to appreciate the historical influence of Hegel and the French Enlightenment on Marx's thought. As I have tried to demonstrate in the previous chapter, there does exist a basic congruence between Marx's conception of the ideological consciousness and Engels's notion of false consciousness. In my opinion, this congruence is evident as well in their writings on the ideological dimension of political and historical class struggles.

The interpretation of Marx's (and Engels's) conception of ideology in terms of a notion of false consciousness makes sense given the French Enlightenment influence on Marx's thought. In fact, many of the themes Marx and Engels inherited from their French Enlightenment predecessors reappear in their writings on the ideological dimension of political class struggles. For example, the view of the French Enlightement that political elites use ideologies to "mask" and "idealize" their particular class interests as the general interest can be found in the writings of Marx and Engels. The view of the French Enlightenment that the social consciousness of oppressed groups are misguided by the ideologies of the ruling class and that oppressed groups fail to perceive their real interests also appears in their writings.

Furthermore, the influence of Hegel's philosophy of history on Marx's and Engels's notion of political false consciousness is also ignored by functionalist interpreters. Since we have not yet discussed this Hegelian influence on Marx and Engels, in the next section we will begin with an examination of how Hegel's philosophy of history suggests a certain distinctive kind of false consciousness.

SEC. 4-2
HEGEL'S "CUNNING OF REASON" AND FALSE CONSCIOUSNESS

One of the features of the French Enlightenment's dominant ideology thesis was the view that lurking behind lofty, idealistic phrases were self-interested motives. According to the *philosophes*, political elites "conspired" to create ideologies which would rationalize and disguise their self-interested motives and help them to deceive and manipulate their subordinates. Hence, on this view, political elites were well aware of the deceptive nature of their ideologies.

Hegel, however, introduced a radically new step in the theory of ideological false consciousness when he suggested that even the great political rulers of history—the Caesars and Napoleons—were themselves deceived by their ideologies and ignorant of the real motives behind their political thoughts and actions.

According to Hegel's philosophy of history, historical actors were agents or instruments of a historical process which transcended their conscious minds yet motivated their passions and ideas. On this view, all human agents, including political elites, are unaware of their real motives in action as well as being profoundly ignorant of the broader historical significance of their political acts. In Hegel's account of this pervasive historical unconsciousness, the following passage from his lectures on *Reason in History* is of importance:

> The first glance at history convinces us that the actions of men spring from their needs...[that] passions...and interests are the sole springs of action and the main efficient cause...But one may indeed question whether those manifestations of vitality on the part of individuals and peoples in which they seek and satisfy their own purposes are, at the same time, the means and tools of a higher and broader purpose of what they know nothing, which they realize unconsciously.[25]

This notion that historical actors could be the unconscious agents of a transcendent purpose which they realize in the pursuit of their self-interests was a notion Hegel described as "the cunning of Reason."

> [T]his may be called the cunning of Reason—that it sets the passions to work for itself, while that through which it develops pays the penalty and suffers the loss.[26]

Hegel's "cunning of Reason" suggests the following reasons why historical actors possessed false consciousness: (1) historical agents were unaware or ignorant of the real motive forces behind their thoughts and actions; (2) historical agents were ignorant of the broader historical significance of their actions; and (3) the conscious motives which human agents imagined to be their real motives were in fact only their ideological or imaginary motives, because behind their conscious motives were broader historical motives which determined their thoughts and actions; that is, historical actors had false consciousness because they had illusions about their real motives in political action.

While this sense of false consciousness represents the dominant theme in Hegel's notion of the "cunning of Reason," it is only proper to note that Hegel's remarks concerning the ideological consciousness of historical actors were not always compatible with each other.

Shlomo Avineri has argued that Hegel was inconsistent in his remarks concerning the extent to which historical agents possessed false consciousness. According to Avineri,

> what is intriguing is that Hegel seems unsure of himself about the extent to which the world-historical individuals were aware of the historical significance of what they were doing.[27]

The inconsistency in Hegel's thinking about historical-political false consciousness is perhaps most evident in the following passage from his *Reason in History*. According to Hegel, "World-historical Individuals," i.e., the Caesars and Napoleons,

> had no consciousness of the general Idea they were unfolding, while prosecuting those aims of theirs...But at the same time they were thinking men, who had an insight into the requirements of the time—what was ripe for development.[28]

But while Hegel's remarks concerning the historical false consciousness may not completely cohere with each other, in my opinion the general tenor of his remarks sufficiently conveys the sense of false consciousness I have described above.

More importantly, the import of Hegel's philosophy of history for a conception of the ideological false consciousness was not lost sight of by Engels. In his essay "Ludwig Feuerbach and the End of Classical German Philosophy," Engels credited Hegel's philosophy of history more than that of the French Enlightenment because of Hegel's advanced awareness of the presence of historical forces lurking behind human consciousness.

In criticizing the French Enlightenment, Engels argued that the *philosophes* were not sufficiently aware of the systematic historical and class forces impelling human passions and consciousness. Engels praised the *philosophes* for their astute recognition of the reality of self-interest lurking behind ideological phrases, but he criticized them for failing to analyze the historical and class origins of political self-interests. As Engels was to remark in his essay,

> ...the old materialism becomes untrue to itself because it takes the ideal driving forces which operate there as ultimate causes, instead of investigating what is behind them,

what are the driving forces of these driving forces. The inconsistency does not lie in the fact that ideal driving forces are recognized, but in the investigation not being carried further back behind these into their motive causes.[29]

Engels goes on to credit Hegel's philosophy of history for pursuing an historical analysis of political self-interests:

On the other hand, the philosophy of history...particularly by Hegel, recognizes that the ostensible and also the really operating motives of men who act in history are by no means the ultimate causes of historical events; that behind these motives are other motive powers, which have to be discovered.[30]

According to Engels, the problem with Hegel's philosophy of history, and more particularly with Hegel's notion of "the cunning of Reason," is that Hegel

...does not seek these powers in history itself, it imports them rather from outside, from philosophy...into history.[31]

What Engels is criticizing here is Hegel's belief in the reality of a "mysterious" transcendent Reason or spiritual Mind which manipulates and utilizes human passions for its own purposes. Engels and Marx both criticized Hegel's conception of history in their work *The Holy Family*. In their opinion, Hegel's Universal Reason was nothing more than an alienated and reified conception of human powers.[32]

In spite of the metaphysical nature of Hegel's conceptions, I would argue that the notion of historical false consciousness suggested by Hegel's philosophy of history had a considerable influence on both Marx and Engels in their understanding of the political false consciousness of history-making agents. In fact, elements of Hegel's notion of historical false consciousness are suggested in Engels's definition of ideology as false consciousness (cf. Engels's letter to Mehring). For Hegel historical actors possess false consciousness because they are ignorant of the real driving forces compelling their thoughts and actions. In a somewhat similar vein, Engels's definition contends that people possess false consciousness because: (a) they are ignorant of the motive forces of their thinking (thus Engels says, "he works with mere thought material, which he accepts without examination as the product of thought, and does not investigate further for a more remote source independent of thought"); (b) they have illusions and misconceptions about their real motives (Engels says, "the real motive forces impelling him remain unknown to him...Hence he imagines false or seeming motive forces"); and (c) people interpret their own motives and the sources of their ideas in an idealistic way ("...because all action is mediated by thought, it appears to him to be ultimately based upon thought").

Now, I contend that these general attributes of Engels's definition of false consciousness reappear in some form or another in his and Marx's writings on the ideological class struggle in politics and history. According to Marx and Engels, the class struggle in politics and history is conducted with a false consciousness because political actors misinterpret their real class motives in an idealistic and illusory way, and present their partisan sectional interests as disinterested moral and political universal ideals. Political actors are either ignorant of the broader social and historical significance of their political controversies; they have an inadequate, even deluded, understanding of the historical and class dynamics involved in their political struggles; or they are both ignorant and deluded. Finally, both Marx and Engels criticized idealist interpretations of political class struggles by historians and other social analysts as indicative of an "ideological" understanding of history and politics.

By demonstrating how these general attributes of Engels's definition of false consciousness reappear in his and Marx's writings on the political false consciousness in historical class struggles, I will be indirectly demonstrating the Hegelian influence on Marx's and Engels's conception of the political false consciousness in historical class struggle. This will provide further proof of why contemporary commentators are wrong to reject the interpretation of Marx's conception of ideology in terms of Engels's notion of false consciousness.

SEC.4–3
THE WRITINGS OF ENGELS ON FALSE CONSCIOUSNESS, HISTORY AND POLITICAL CLASS STRUGGLES

In his essay entitled "Ludwig Feuerbach and the End of Classical German Philosophy" (1888), Engels doesn't explicitly mention the concept of false consciousness; however, in discussing the relationship between historical laws of society and human consciousness, Engels analyzes this relationship in terms very similar to the conceptual elements he stipulated in his letter to Mehring regarding the notion of false consciousness. As in the letter to Mehring, "Ludwig Feuerbach and the End of Classical German Philosophy" distinguishes between the conscious motives of human actors and "the real ultimate driving forces of history" lying behind these motives:

> In the history of society...the actors are all endowed with consciousness,...nothing happens without a conscious purpose, without intended aims. But this distinction, important as it is for historical investigation...cannot alter the fact that the course of history is governed by inner general laws...[What's important, therefore, is the necessity to investigate] what driving forces...stand behind these motives? what are the historical causes which transform themselves into these motives in the brain of the actors?[33]

Engels contends that for the most part, human actors are not conscious of the historical forces determining their actions and thoughts. At the same time, Engels argues that these "driving causes" of history "are reflected clearly or unclearly, directly or in an ideological, even glorified form" in the consciousness of human actors.[34] By differentiating between a clear, undistorted understanding of the historical determinants of human activity and thought, and a mystified, "ideological" understanding of these forces, Engels's distinction suggests the same conception of ideology as false consciousness defined in his letter to Mehring.

Now, what are the historical determinants which are not fully and adequately cognized by political actors? According to Engels, political actors do not fully or clearly comprehend the class interests underlying their actions and thought processes. In fact, they misinterpret their class interests in an "indirect" and "ideological" way as moral principles or lofty political ideals. In his letter to Conrad Schmidt (27 October 1890), Engels discusses how class interests are comprehended in an ideological way by political actors as political ideals:

> Just as the movement of the industrial market is generally...reflected in the money market—and naturally

inverted,—so in the struggle of opposing classes which existed beforehand is reflected in the struggle between government and opposition...also invertedly...[and] indirectly, not as a class struggle but as a struggle for political principles.[35]

Of course, social agents and political actors may *imagine* they act *only* from pure disinterested motives and *solely* for the sake of lofty ideals. But the political ideals and principles of political actors are in truth only the "ideological forms" of their real motives, according to Engels and Marx.[36] In effect, the political ideologies of classes function to disguise and hide from social agents their real motives or class interests in political struggles. Consequently, Marx and Engels argued that social agents have false consciousness because, for the most part, the social agents themselves are ignorant of (and even deceived as to) their real motives in the political struggle. Moreover, social agents fail to comprehend and misinterpret the historical-class significance of their political struggles. That is to say, they understand their political conflict not as a class conflict involving opposing social interests, but as a struggle between conflicting political ideals. Following the method of ideological analysis established by Helvetius and Hegel, Engels and Marx argues that it was the task of historians and political analysts to reveal and raise to a self-conscious level the hidden and underlying historical and partisan class interests implicit in political controversies. Of course, unlike Helvetius and Hegel, Marx and Engels utilized a class analysis for revealing the class interests hidden behind ideological disguises.

An excellent illustration of Engels's analysis of the social false consciousness of political actors in historical struggles and the superficial nature of idealist historical accounts can be found in his work *The Peasant War in Germany* (1850).

According to the interpretation of the Protestant Reformation by idealist historians, the causes of the Reformation can be traced ultimately to a difference in the religious beliefs of the contending parties concerning the nature and aims of the "Christian" community. Various individuals of the nascent German middle class and many members of the peasantry believed that the religious equality and communitarianism of the original Christian church represented the true religious and social ideals of a Christian commonwealth;

members of the aristocracy and higher Church hierarchy, however, believed that the principles of absolute authority and hierarchy as embodied in the Roman Catholic church represented the basic religious and social ideal of Christian society. Theologically, this conflict took the form of a debate between those like Luther who believed that personal faith, without the mediation of the clerical hierarchy, was sufficient for Christian salvation and those who believed that the authority and hierarchy of the church was a necessary means to personal salvation. Both sides sought to justify their political aims and social agendas on the basis of the Bible and the writings of the early church fathers.

As a historical materialist, Engels's objective was to demonstrate that

> the political and religious theories were not the causes...[of the] so-called religious wars of the 16th century [but in fact] very positive material class-interests were at play...[And] if the class struggles of that time appear to bear religious earmarks, if the interests, requirements and demands of the various classes hid themselves behind a religious screen, it little changes the actual situation, and is to be explained by conditions of the time.[37]

As in his essay on Ludwig Feuerbach, we can see in this quotation how Engels gives prominence to the role of class interests in historical struggles. It also reveals some things about Engels's view regarding the nature of ideologies and the cognitive status of the ideological consciousness, and explanations for the particular form ideologies take in specific historical periods.

Engels says the religious ideologies of the Reformation served as "screens" for "hiding" the interests of the various contending social groups. He says the revolutionary and communist aspirations of the peasantry were expressed in an indirect manner by means of "the [ideological] cloak of Christian forms."[38] The notion that ideologies somehow hide class interest behind various intellectual guises suggests the phenomenon of rationalization, a phenomenon often characteristic of the political false consciousness.

Furthermore, in discussing the radical ideologies of the peasantry, Engels mentions how these ideologies had the effect of distorting the aspirations and falsifying the social conceptions held by members of the peasant class. He says that drawing on the millenarian tradition of Christianity, peasants represented their revolutionary and egalitarian aims of overthrowing and abolishing the hierarchical class system of feudal society as a desire for the "Millennium" (the Last Judgment) and as a desire for the restoration of the communalism and social egalitarianism of the original Christian covenant. In conceptualizing the relations between themselves and their class oppressors, peasants represented their feudal class relationships as religious-moral relations between the holy "righteous" class (i.e., themselves) and the ungodly "devilish" class (i.e., the feudal lords and Church officials). From the "ideological" point of view of the peasants, the purpose of their political struggles was to rearrange society so as to better conform with the "will of God"(as opposed to rearranging society so as to better conform with the interest of the majority and the common good).

Of course, by radicalizing and unifying the oppressed peasantry, such ideological aspirations and social misconceptions were practically efficacious to a degree. Nonetheless, by representing their class struggle as a religious struggle, such ideological representations created a false consciousness in the rebellious peasants, particularly in the leadership of the Peasant Rebellion. As Engels argued, one of the reasons why their rebellion failed was that the peasants and their leaders failed to comprehend their real interests due to their religious ideological understanding of their class struggle. Because of their false consciousness, the peasants and their leaders attempted to realize their "imaginary interests" at the expense of their real rational interests.

In Engels's opinion, Thomas Münzer is an example illustrative of the political liability of an ideological false consciousness. In Engels's view, Münzer's ignorance of the social and historical dynamics operating in the Reformation and his religious-chiliastic delusions, were responsible for his misguided leadership of the peasant movement. According to Engels, sixteenth-century Germany was ripe for the overthrow of feudalism and the political ascendency of the nascent bourgeoisie; it was not ready, however, for the kind of revolutionary programs advanced by the more radical elements of the peasant movement. Furthermore, what was clearly impossible was any attempt to realize a history-ending apocalypse. Hence, if Münzer had had a clearer, nonideological consciousness of the historical and social forces present in his epoch, he would have seen that the real interests of the peasantry would have been best served by an alliance with the reformist German middle class against the feudal and Church aristocracy. But outraged by the injustice and impiety of his society, and motivated by an irrational belief in the approach of the Last Judgment, Münzer would not accept an alliance with any group which did not share the same intense religious feelings and radical chiliastic aspirations as himself. Münzer's ideological beliefs and decisions led to the political isolation of the peasantry, and their ultimate defeat.

Interestingly, Engels does not fault Münzer for his false consciousness. Instead, Engels justifies Münzer's false consciousness on the basis that he was socially determined to express the political aspirations of his class in mystical-religious, ideological forms.

According to Engels, because the Church was the dominant intellectual force and educational institution in feudal society (as well as a dominant economic force in the Middle Ages), all intellectual and social forms of consciousness were dominated by religious and theological ideas.[39] Since all intellectual and social forms of consciousness were dominated by religious and theological ideas, it was inevitable that the political class struggle would be expressed in religious terms. Engels says in his "Ludwig Feuerbach and the End of Classical German Philosophy":

> The Middle Ages had attached to theology all the other forms of ideology—philosophy, politics, jurisprudence—and made them subdivisions of theology. It thereby constrained every social and political movement to take on a theological form. The sentiments of the masses were fed with religion to the exclusion of all else; it was therefore necessary to put forward their own interest in a religious guise in order to produce a great tempest...[40]

While all of the various classes engaged in the Peasant Rebellion utilized the religious "ruling ideas" of their epoch, the use of religious ideologies by the peasantry ultimately was against their real interests.

Engels's analysis of the ideological class struggle at the time of the Protestant Reformation gives a good illustration of how class struggles are conducted with a false consciousness. It also shows the influence of Hegel's philosophy of history on his formulation of the political false consciousness. Engels points out that the peasants really believed they were fighting to bring about the "kingdom of God" on earth and that they had divine sanction for their political actions. In truth, however, their religious ideologies concealed from them the class basis of their actions, mystified their understanding of the social dynamics in their historical epoch, and prevented them from comprehending their real interests. In Engels's analysis of the role of Thomas Münzer, we see how Münzer fits Engels's definition of false consciousness. According to Engels, the elements of Münzer's false consciousness were his ignorance of the broader social and historical forces in his period and his religiously "deluded" understanding of the classes and political aims involved in the rebellion.

SEC. 4-4
FALSE CONSCIOUSNESS AND POLITICAL CLASS STRUGGLES IN THE WRITINGS OF MARX

Illustrations of Marx's class analyses of political ideologies can be found in several of his writings. In his journalistic articles for the *New York Daily Tribune*. Marx's analyses of the Tory-Whig political dispute in the British elections of the early 1850s are of use for understanding his method of analysis. However, perhaps the most useful works for examining Marx's analyses of the social false consciousness of political actors are his articles published in the *Neue rheinische Zeitung*, which cover the European revolutions of the 1848, and his work entitled *The Eighteenth Brumaire of Louis Bonaparte*, which covers the political and parliamentary struggles in France preceding the coup d'etat of Louis Bonaparte. I will begin my examination with Marx's *The Eighteenth Brumaire of Louis Bonaparte*.

According to Marx, the parliamentary political struggles in France between 1848 and the 1850s can be viewed, at one level of analysis, as a "simple struggle between Republicans and Royalists."[41] The Republicans sought to establish a liberal democracy in France in the wake of the 1848 revolution. The Royalists, on the other hand, were concerned with restoring some form of monarchical government to France.

The Republican and Royalist groups each were political coalitions composed of a variety of smaller political factions. The Republicans consisted of an alliance between social democrats, workers, and petty-bourgeois groups. The Royalists consisted of an alliance between two factions held together only by their common opposition to the more radical elements of the Republican coalition. These two Royalist factions were the Legitimists and the Orleanists. The Legitimists desired to restore a member from the House of Bourbon to the throne, whereas the Orleanists desired to restore a member from the House of Orleans.

Ostensibly, the Republicans advocated liberal democractic principles and the defense of "the eternal rights of man,"[42] an ideology inherited from the French Revolution of 1789. The Royalists, on the other hand, were united in their "common hatred" of Republican ideals. Hence, the conflict between the ideals of constitutional liberal democracy and of traditional hereditary monarchy. However, in Marx's opinion, any political analysis which remains at this level—i.e., interpreting the political conflict in France of 1848 as a conflict about different political ideals—would be "superficial." As he says, "Looking at the situation and the parties more closely...this superficial appearance veils the class struggle..."[43]

Marx himself engaged in a class analysis of the ideologies and membership of the warring Republican and Royalists coalitions. In his view, a class analysis of political events and ideologies was more profound than, say, the *Verstehen* method of analysis employed by idealist historians or social scientists.

What Marx had to say concerning the internal factionalism of the Royalist side of the parliamentary conflict affects the interpretation of his notion of ideology. As we have said, the Royalist coalition was divided between the Legitimist and Orleanist factions. Although both were in favor of a monarchical form of government, their political loyalties were to different aristocratic houses. In refusing to compromise with the other faction, each justified its refusal on the basis of its traditional political loyalties. As a result of their divisions, Louis Bonaparte was able to succeed in his political aspirations.

From his historical materialist point of view, however, Marx analyzed the causes of the difference between the Legitimists and the Orleanists or the political expression of class interests. According to Marx,

> what kept the two sections apart...was not any so-called principles, it was their material conditions of existence,

two different kinds of property...the Legitimate Monarchy was merely the political expression of the hereditary rule of the lords of the soil, as the July Monarchy was only the political expression of the usurping rule of the bourgeois parvenus.[44]

He identifies these particular class interests as the "rivalry between landed property and capital." For Marx, their political ideologies "veiled" their common and particular class interests. As members of the big property-owning classes (e.g., land-owners, industrialists, bankers), the *general* royalist ideology of the Legitimists and the Orleanists expressed their common class opposition to the radical political and social programs advocated by the more radical Republican groups and socialist parties. But their *particular* version of monarchy, Legitimist or Orleanist, expressed their particular property interests and opposition to each other. Thus, like Engels's analyses of the religious ideologies popular in the Protestant Reformation, Marx analyzed political ideologies as the "rationalized," distorted expression of class interests.

What Marx had to say about the self-awareness of the Legitimist and Orleanist members is of particular significance. In the following passage, Marx begins by referring to the social origins and content of ideologies:

Upon the different forms of property, upon the social conditions of existence rises an entire superstructure of distinct and characteristically formed sentiments, illusions, modes of thought and views of life. The entire class creates and forms them out its material foundations and out of the corresponding social relations. The single individual who derives them through tradition and education may imagine that they form the real motives and the starting point of his activity...[45]

"But to imagine that one's political actions are motivated solely for the sake of political and moral ideals," to finish out Marx's thought, "is to be deluded and ignorant of the real grounds of one's political commitments." What Marx suggests in the passage above is that members of the Orleanist and Legitimist factions possessed false consciousness. Their ideological differences helped to disguise and conceal from them the class basis of their political differences. By criticizing the deluded, idealist consciousness of political actors, Marx's political analysis evokes Engels's definition of false consciousness.

Now, it is clear from other passages in *The Eighteenth Brumaire* that Marx believed that political actors are more or less self-deceived by their own ideologies, and that for the most part, political actors are unaware of the class basis and partisan nature of their political-ideological commitments. One of the distinctive ways in which this ideological self-deception manifests itself in politics, according to Marx, is the way sections of the ruling and middle classes present their own sectional class interests as if their sectional interests were really the interest of the majority and for the common good.[46] The fact that most members of the ruling and middles classes genuinely believe that their self-serving ideological deceits really are in the interest of the majority and for the common good is pointed out by Marx in speaking of the French petty-bourgeoisie:

> ...one must not form the narrow-minded notion that the petty-bourgeoisie, on principle, wishes to enforce an egoistic class interest. Rather, it believes that the special conditions of its emancipation are the general conditions under which modern society can alone be saved...Just as little must one imagine that the democratic representatives are all shopkeepers or enthusiastic champions of shopkeepers...What makes them representatives of the petty bourgeoisie is the fact that in their minds they do not go beyond the limits which the latter do not go beyond in life, that they are consequently driven theoretically to the same tasks and solutions to which material interest and social position practically drive the latter. This is in general the relationship of the political and literary representatives of a class to the class that they represent.[47]

For Marx, then, members of the ruling and middle classes can be self-deceived and therefore blind to the self-serving nature of their ideological rationalizations because of the effects of social circumstances and practical class interests on their understanding.[48] Not only does it serve their interests to believe in the correctness and public utility of their ideological views, but the ruling and middle classes sincerely believe in their views because of the influence of "education," "tradition" and the limiting nature of their social experiences. For Marx members of the ruling and middles classes can possess false consciousness and therefore can be ignorant of the way their ideologies "dissemble" their real motives.[49]

The problem with the political consciousness and ideological commitments of the French proletariat in the period between 1830 and 1848, in Marx's judgment, was that the majority of the French proletariat were dominated ideologically by the "republican-democratic" ideology of the bourgeoisie. According to Marx, when the French proletariat should have been struggling to abolish the political rule of the bourgeoisie and liberal democracy in order to establish a classless society and socialist state, the majority of the French proletariat in the political revolutions of the early nineteenth century were allying themselves with sections of the bourgeoisie in order to establish liberal democracy. While such alliances made sense in the French Revolution of 1789, which was wedged against feudal absolutism, it no longer was in the rational interests of the proletariat to continue such alliances in the changed social circumstances of the early nineteenth century, according to Marx. In their ideological commitment to the "republican-democratic" ideology, Marx argued, the French proletariat was failing to perceive its real interests.

Marx argued that this commitment to the "republican-democratic" ideology was responsible for the proletariat's inadequate and sometimes "deluded" understanding of the class dynamics present in the political struggles of that epoch. Thus, in Marx's judgement, the political defeat of the French working class in the 1848 revolutions was the result in part of their own false consciousness. Marx summarized the false consciousness of the French proletariat in this period by saying,

> the workers in Lyon thought they were only pursuing political ends and were only soldiers of the republic, whereas in reality they were soldiers of socialism. Their political understanding obscured for them the roots of social misery, falsified their insight into their true aims, and belied their social instinct.[50]

Now, exactly how was this commitment on the part of the French proletariat to liberal democracy responsible for their false consciousness? In the first place, the categories characteristic of democratic ideology were not conducive to a class understanding of social agents and a class understanding of the political struggles within the state, according to Marx. For example, within the framework of liberal democratic ideology, the proletariat and the petty bourgeoisie were not distinguished as different classes with separate interests; instead, they were conceived of as "the people" and thought to have the "same" social and political interests. Secondly, Marx argued, the democratic ideology exaggerated the amount of political power possessed by "the people," thereby fostering illusions in the minds of the proletariat and their leaders concerning the extent of their real power. In turn, this democratic "faith" in the "power" and patriotic sentiments of the people deterred the political leaders of the proletariat from any factual analysis of the real political situation between the classes, it also disposed them to underestimate the power of their class opponents. These points on the political false consciousness of the French republican-democrats are evident in the following remarks by Marx:

> the democrats concede that a privileged class confronts them, but they, along with all the rest of the surrounding nation, form the *people*. What they represent are the people's rights; what interests them are the people's interests. Accordingly, when a struggle is impending, they do not need to examine the interests and positions of the different classes. They do not need to consider their own resources too critically. They have merely to give the signal and the people, with all its inexhaustible resources, will fall upon the oppressors.[51]

In the third place, Marx argued, the democratic-republican ideology instilled the French proletariat and their parliamentary representatives with a utopian faith in the social and political possibilities of liberal democracy. According to Marx, the French proletariat and their middle class political allies believed that with the establishment of the republican-democratic state, political rule by a privileged minority would be eliminated and the "people" (or *citoyens*) would rule. In Marx's opinion, however, under the republican-democratic form of government, the bourgeoisie would be the real rulers, not "the people."

Finally, the French proletariat and their middle class political allies believed, according to Marx, that liberal democracy would eliminate class differences and conflict by establishing the preeminence of national solidarity and national interests. But in Marx's judgment, it was false to believe that patriotism and the liberal democratic state could resolve the class antagonisms between the bourgeoisie and the proletariat; their conflicts were inevitable due to the opposing nature of their class interests. What belief in liberal democracy really achieves, according to Marx, is a kind of collective repression of the fact of class differences and antagonisms. It fosters a kind of collective delusion regarding an imagined social solidarity in the nation-state. Here Marx discusses the democractic delusions of the parliamentary representatives of sections of the French proletariat and middle classes:

> The Reforme knows no better way of changing and abolishing these contradictions [between the bourgeoisie and the proletariat] than to disregard their real basis...and...withdraw into the hazy blue heaven of republican ideology... this pleasant abstraction from class antagonisms, the sentimental equalization of contradictory class interests, this fantastic elevation above the class struggle...was the special catch-cry of the February Revolutions [of 1848].[52]

Hence, in Marx's judgment, the majority of the French proletariat in the 1830 and 1848 French revolutions possessed false consciousness because: (a) they had an inadequate and sometimes "deluded" understanding of the class dynamics of their period; (b) they did not have an adequate and true understanding of their real class interests; and (c) their ideologies prevented them from having a true and adequate understanding of their political situation and real class interests, i.e., a true class consciousness.

In several respects Marx's analysis of the political false consciousness of the French proletariat is comparable to Engels's analysis of the false consciousness of the German peasantry. Like Engels, Marx argued that while the ideologies of the oppressed give expression to their class interests, their ideologies ultimately do not serve their real interests. According to Marx's analysis of the ideological consciousness of the French proletariat, the French proletariat expressed their real interest in a classless society (and hence, the abolition of social inequalities) in a distorted and "vague" way as a desire for democracy and rule by "the people" or "the majority." This view of Marx concerning the proletariat's ideological understanding of their interests is evident in the following passage:

> ...the cry of 'social republic' with which the revolution of February was ushered in by the Paris proletariat, did but express a vague aspiration after a Republic that was not only to supersede the monarchical form of class-rule, but class-rule itself.[53]

Marx argued that their democratic ideological understanding of their social interests worked against the French proletariat because it prevented them from understanding their real rational interests. Engels made a similar point in discussing the false consciousness of Thomas Münzer. Moreover, like Engels, Marx argued that the dominant ideological conceptions utilized by the oppressed for understanding their political and social relationships were inadequate and self-defeating because they prevented a true class consciousness of their social relationships and the political struggle. Just as Engels discussed false consciousness, so Marx argued that the political defeat of the French proletariat in the 1848 revolution was partly the result of false consciousness.

Engels said one reason that social agents and political actors possess false consciousness is that they are ignorant of the larger social and historical significance of their political struggles. In his political writings, Marx also criticized the socially myopic political consciousness of political actors. For example, in discussing the political struggle in Germany in the post-1830 era, Marx argued that members of the rival political parties were not aware of the larger social significance of their political disagreements, and hence were not fully aware of what they were fighting for. From the perspective of the engaged participants, the basic disagreement between the parties for the National Assembly and the parties for the Crown was whether or not Germany should adopt a policy of political centralization or federalism.[54] According to Marx, however,

> what took place here was not a political conflict within the framework of *one* society, but a conflict between two societies, a social conflict, which assumed a political form.[55]

In Marx's view, members of the opposing political parties were unaware of the fact that "the Crown represented feudal aristocratic society, just as the National Assembly represented modern bourgeois society."[56]

Marx was particularly critical of the members of the Berlin National Assembly for their social ignorance and deluded understanding of their class interests. As a result of their illusions about German society and the possibility of radical political reforms in the Germany of 1840s, the democrats of the Berlin National Assembly fell victim to the political counterrevolution in Germany. Marx wrote in his "Trial of the Rhenish Democrats" concerning the false consciousness of the National Assembly members,

> the Berlin National Assembly clearly nursed extravagant illusions and did not understand [their] own position and [their] conditions of existence [because they erroneously believed] that an amicable arrangement and reconciliation with the Crown was still possible and worked towards it.[57]

In opposing the political views of the German democrats in the Berlin National Assembly, Marx argued that the social interests of the Crown and republican reformists were not reconcilable. In trying to alert the radical democrats to the impossibility of any peaceful reconciliation with the monarchists, Marx's remarks are illuminating with respect to his conception of ideology:

> ...we ask the so-called Radical-Democratic Party not to confuse the starting-point of the struggle...with the goal... The final act of constitution cannot be decreed, it coincides with the movement we have to go through. It is therefore not a question of putting into practice this or that view, this or that political idea, but of understanding the course of development.[58]

Here we see Marx encouraging the radical-democrats to overcome their tunnel-vision view of the political conflict and become aware of the broader historical-class context of their political conflict with the Crown and of their real interests in the struggle (i.e., to overthrow the feudal society of Germany and create political conditions suitable for the emerging society of capitalism).

In summary, on the basis of Marx's political writings we have seen how Marx's conception of the ideological consciousness of political and social actors concurs with Engels's definition of false consciousness. In the case of both Marx and Engels, we have demonstrated how they understood the political struggles between social classes and sections of classes as a struggle conducted with a false consciousness. We have seen evidence of the influence of both the French Enlightenment and Hegel's philosophy of history on Marx and Engels in their interpretation of the political class struggle as a struggle conducted with a false consciousness. For example, we have noted the similarities between the historical materialist class analysis of ideologies with Helvetius's method of unmasking ideals, and the influence of the French Enlightenment view regarding how dominant ideologies misguide the oppressed. Furthermore, we have seen the influence of Hegel's notion of the historical false consciousness on Marx's and Engel's formulation of the political false consciousness. Finally, we have analyzed the reasons of Marx and Engels as to why the oppressed are unable to perceive their real interests.

In conclusion, I see no justification for the claims made by some contemporary commentators concerning some alleged difference between Marx's concept of the ideological consciousness in political class struggles and Engels's definition of false consciousness. I do not believe that Marx's political writings support the contention of some contemporary commentators that Marx rejected the relevance of epistemological categories to an evaluation of political ideologies and an evaluation of the social awareness of political actors.

5

The Hegelian and Feuerbachian Approach to the Alienated Mind

SEC. 5–1
INTRODUCTION TO THE HEGELIAN MODEL OF THE ALIENATED MIND

In examining the Baconian and French Enlightenment materialist tradition on ideology, we saw that one of the ways in which this tradition construed false consciousness was in terms of an *alienated* consciousness. According to Bacon and the *philosophes*, human thought had become alienated from reality as a result of its domination by metaphysical and religious beliefs. Perhaps for this tradition the "otherworldly" religious consciousness was the paradigmatic example of the alienated consciousness because of its ignorance and indifference to natural realities and preoccupation with illusory, supernatural "chimeras."

While this was one version of the false alienated consciousness, Hegel, the nineteenth-century German *idealist* philosopher, developed a different model for conceptualizing the alienated mind. According to Hegel, the World Spirit or Absolute Mind *unknowingly* symbolizes its own spiritual essence in an *alien* and *reified* form in the process of objectifying itself in the external world. Spirit has false consciousness, according to Hegel, because Spirit fails to recognize its own essence in its creations; however, for Hegel this false consciousness is unavoidable because of the "alien" appearance of "objectified" Spirit (even though external "objectivity" is really the "reified" essence of Spirit, according to Hegel).

> Although this world has come into being through individuality, it is for self-consciousness immediately an alienated world which has the form of a fixed and solid reality over against it...the Spirit whose self is an absolutely discrete unit has its content confronting it as an equally hard unyielding reality, and here the world has the character of being something external, the negative of self-consciousness. This world is, however, a spiritual entity...its existence is the work of self-consciousness, but it is also an alien reality already present and given, a reality which has a being of its own and in which it does not recognize itself.[1]

This Hegelian model for understanding the alienated false consciousness was to exercise a profound influence on subsequent German philosophers, including Feuerbach and Marx. According to the Hegelian model, the subject possesses a false alienated consciousness because the subject fails to recognize its own essence in the objects it creates (whether these are conceptual or material objects). One major reason why the subject fails to truly comprehend essential reality is because the objects produced by the subject acquire an "alien" and "reified" form as a result of the subject's self-objectification. While the objective creations of the subject appear initially as "alien" realities, they are in truth symbolic and "reified" forms of subjective essences.

This Hegelian model appears in Feuerbach's critique of religion. According to Feuerbach, in the idea of God Christians unknowingly symbolize their own human "species-nature" and aspirations in an alien, supernatural and reified form. Like Hegel, Feuerbach interprets the ideas or ideologies of the alienated mind as the unrecognized symbols and conceptual reification of thought. However, unlike Hegel, it is not Absolute Mind which does the "reifying"; rather, for Feuerbach the human mind reifies its own essence. In any case, the following quote from Feuerbach's *The Essence of Christianity* gives evidence of the influence of the Hegelian model on Feuerbach's approach to the false, alienated consciousness. "Man has given objectivity to himself but has not recognized the object as his own nature."[2]

The Hegelian model appears in Marx's writings in a Feuerbachian mode. According to Marx, human producers unknowingly symbolize and reify their own productive powers in the commodities and forms of capital produced by their labor. While commodities and capital seem to circulate in their own world independent of human labor, for Marx they are in fact the alien and reified "appearances" of human labor in capitalist society.

In the following passage from the writings of Marx we see evidence of the background influence of Hegel's model on Marx: "...the object which labor produces—labor's product—confronts it as something alien, as a power independent of the producer..."[3]

Hegel's idealist metaphysics, then, laid the foundations for a novel conception of the false, alienated consciousness. In appropriating the model, Feuerbach developed important criticism of it while at the same time developing a materialist version of the Hegelian model. It was this Feuerbachian critique and materialist transformation of the Hegelian model which was later taken up by Marx (and Engels) in their own critique of the false, alienated consciousness.

However, while Feuerbach provided Marx with important insights about the alienated mind, Marx did not completely dismiss the relevance of the Hegelian model. As we will see, Marx was to utilize some of the principles of the Hegelian model to modify Feuerbach theory of the alienated mind. Hence, while Feuerbach's recasting of the Hegelian model was to have a considerable impact on Marx, the Hegelian model was to remain for Marx an important theoretical instrument.

In the following section, we will begin with an examination of how Feuerbach utilized the Hegelian model to develop a new kind of materialist critique of religion. In comparing Feuerbach's rather Hegelian approach to religion with that of the French Enlightenment's critique of religion, we will see how Feuerbach's critique served to lay new ground for understanding ideological false consciousness. In the last section of this chapter we will see how Feuerbach's critique of Hegelian philosophy, as well as Feuerbach's critique of religion, provided Marx with a model for understanding ideological false consciousness.

SEC. 5–2
FEUERBACH'S CRITIQUE OF RELIGION AND THE FRENCH ENLIGHTENMENT

According to the French Enlightenment critique, the religious mind was an alienated consciousness—a consciousness not in touch with reality, but lost in a world of illusions. But were religious "illusions" all pure fanatasies and imaginary nonsense?

The *philosophes* thought so. Holbach remarked about religious "chimeras,"

> ...whoever will deign to consult common sense upon religious opinion, and bestow in this inquiry the attention that is commonly given to objects...will easily perceive, that these opinions have no foundations; that all religion is an edifice in the air; that theology is only the ignorance of natural causes... that it is a long tissue of chimeras and contradiction.[4]

While concurring in the judgment that religion is like a dream-state of the human mind,[5] Feuerbach argued that religious dreams or illusions were not completely meaningless and imaginary nonsense. In a departure from the French Enlightenment tradition, he contended that religious illusions were often *symbolic* expressions of essential human desires and traits, Hence, far from being meaningless, religious dreams for Feuerbach were of the greatest significance, if interpreted correctly. As Feuerbach was to remark in preface to his *The Essence of Christianity*,

> Religion is the dream of the human mind. But even in dreams we do not find ourselves in emptiness or in heaven, but on earth in the realm of reality; we only see things in the entrancing splendour of imagination and caprice, instead of seeing them in the simple daylight of reality and necessity. Hence I do nothing more to religion—and to speculative philosophy and theology as well—than to open its eyes... i.e., I change the object as it is in the imagination into the object as it is in reality.[6]

In a move reflecting the Hegelian background of his theory of religion,[7] Feuerbach argued that the religious imagination was "the dreaming" consciousness of human self-alienation. In religion, according to Feuerbach:

> man separates himself from himself, but only to return always to the same point from which he sets out. Man negatives himself, but only to posit himself again, and that in a glorified form...[8]

> Religion is the disuniting of man from himself; he sets God before him as the antithesis of himself. God is not what man is—man is not what God is.[9]

Following Hegel's model of the alienated mind, Feuerbach contended that in religion human beings objectify or reify their own species-essence and natural-moral tendencies in the form of an alien, supernatural being who morally commands them.

> Religion is a dream, in which our own conceptions and emotions appear to us as separate existences, beings out of ourselves.[10]

> Man—this is the mystery of religion—projects his being into objectivity, and then again makes himself an object to this projected image of himself thus converted into a subject.[11]

Of course, human beings do not consciously realize that in worshipping God they are really adoring their own nature, nor are they aware that in the idea of God humans beings have made a "fetish" of their own human attributes.[12] From the standpoint of the religious imagination, God is a real, autonomous being. This fact indicates for Feuerbach that the religious consciousness is a false consciousness—because human beings do not recognize their own species-essence and aspirations in the symbolic imagery and ideas of religion.

> But when religion—consciousness of God—is designated as the self-consciousness of man, this is not to be understood as affirming that the religious man is directly aware of this identity; for on the contrary, ignorance of it is fundamental to the peculiar nature of religion...Man first of all sees his nature as if out of himself, before he finds it in himself...[13]

In a similar vein, in his work *The Preliminary Theses on the Reform of Philosophy* Feuerbach described the false consciousness of the Christian consciousness:

> ...the essence of the Christian religion is, in truth, the human essence. Yet in the consciousness of Christians it is something else, a non-human essence.[14]

Feuerbach argued that the "dreams" (or ideologies) of the Christian consciousness could be demystified simply by changing "the object as it is in the imagination into the object as it is reality." In practice what this Feuerbachian method of ideological interpretation often entailed was converting or "inverting" the subject and predicates of religious propositions in order to comprehend the humanistic meanings embodied in religious expressions. Since in Feuerbach's view all attributes of the Divine Being were really human attributes transfigured, one simply had to convert what the religious imagination had "upside-down" or inverted.

> ...we need only...invert the religious relations—regard that as an end which religion supposes to be a means—exalt that into the primary which in religion is subordinate,...—at once we have destroyed the illusion, and the unclouded light of truth streams in upon us.[15]

> The method of the reformatory critique of speculative philosophy in general does not differ from the critique already applied in the philosophy of religion. We only need always make the predicate into the subject and thus, as the subject, into the object. Hence we only invert speculative philosophy and then have the unmasked, pure, bare truth.[16]

Feuerbach argued that all of the personal characteristics which the religious consciousness attributes to God as a divine, supernatural Being are in truth abstract characteristics of the human species.

> All predicates which make God as God real...predicates like power, wisdom, goodness, love, even...personality... these predicates are first supposed in and with human beings.[17]

> [in religion] man converts the qualities of his own nature into the qualities of another being...[therefore] all predicates, all attributes of the Divine Being are fundamentally human...[18]

In a similar way, Feuerbach argued that all of the positive moral virtues which human beings value most about themselves are unconsciously projected onto God as divine perfections. God, therefore, symbolizes humanity's own unfulfilled ideal of moral perfection and at the same time compensates humanity for its moral shortcomings, acccording to Feuerbach.

> Of all the attributes which the understanding assigns to God, that which in religion, and especially in the Christian religion, has the pre-eminence, is moral perfection. But God as a morally perfect being is nothing else than the realised idea, the fulfilled laws of morality, the moral nature of man posited as the absolute being...[19]

Hence, in Feuerbach's theory, one of the characteristic features of the religious false consciousness is its inverted or "upside-down" way of understanding the aspirations and nature of human beings. In addition, Feuerbach also argued that religious ideologies were responsible for distorting and falsifying people's understanding of their real aspirations and moral duties. For example, the real reason why people are morally obligated to each other, according to Feuerbach, is because of their common humanity. Religion, however, has twisted this around to make moral obligation a matter of obedience to a superior authority. In this way, an authoritarian understanding of morality comes to prevail over a humanistic interpretation of morality.

Like the *philosophes*, then, Feuerbach criticized the religious consciousness as a false consciousness. However, in accounting for the origins of religious false consciousness, Feuerbach's account diverged from the explanations of the *philosophes*. For the *philosophes*, the sources of religious false consciousness were an unconstrained imagination, ignorance of Nature, and the deceitful manipulation of the social consciousness of human agents by members of the power elite. For Feuerbach, however, religious false consciousness was a manifestation of the alienation of the individual from his/her species-life and an expression of unfulfilled human needs.

On another point, though, Feuerbach did concur with the *philosophes* in the judgment of religion as an illusion harmful to humankind. (He remarked that because religion offers only a pseudogratification of human needs and because everything is inverted in the religious imagination, religious illusions were "injurious" to humankind.)[20] In particular, Feuerbach was critical of the way the natural moral ends of human action were distorted and inverted by the religious imagination.

According to Feuerbach, the real duties of human beings concern the common good and mutual respect, but religion requires human beings to treat their moral duties towards their fellow humanity as a means to divine grace and heavenly rewards. In this way, "all the best powers of humanity...are lavished on [an imaginary] being."[21]

> ...in religion man sacrifices some duty towards man—such as that of respecting the life of his fellow, of being grateful to him—to a religious obligation—sacrifices his relation to man to his relation to God.[22]

Hence, religion is morally harmful to humanity, according to Feuerbach, because humanity is treated as a means and God as the end in the Christian way of life. In opposing this "inverted" and mystified understanding of moral duty, Feuerbach encouraged the development of a collective self-awareness of one's natural obligations to fellow human beings. As Feuerbach defined this "species-consciousness":

> He therefore who lives in the consciousness of the species as a reality, regards his existence for others, his relation to society, his utility to the public, as that existence which is one with the existence of his own essence—as his immortal existence. He lives with his own soul, with his own heart, for humanity.[23]

Thus, while Feuerbach went beyond the *philosophes* in his theory of religion as the estranged consciousness of humankind, at the same time he preserved one of the basic themes of the materialist tradition on ideology: the belief that ideological illusions were antithetical to the real interests of humankind.

In conclusion, while the *philosophes* were satisfied with demonstrating the imaginary nature of religious beliefs (and their political utility to members of the ruling class), Feuerbach went a step further and demonstrated how the imaginary conceptions of religion expressed or "reflected" real human aspirations and characteristics in symbolic ways. Because religion was a symbolic expression of human alienation, Feuerbach argued, "the secret of theology is anthropology." It was this additional step taken by Feuerbach which was to constitute a major development in the materialist approach to ideology. Essentially, Feuerbach demonstrated that there was an meaningful component and material basis to the ideological consciousness and that ideologies were not completely nonsensical and irrational forms of thought. As Hans Barth said of the advance of Feuerbach's theory of religion over that of the French *philosophes*,

> To have explained the objectivity of God as a phantom was something; but to explain the objectivity of this phantom was something else, and equally necessary.[24]

Jorge Larrain summarized the advance of Feuerbach's theory of religion over that of the French *philosophes* from a different angle:

> Feuerbach's critique of religion goes much deeper than the theory of the priestly deceit. While the latter struggled against religious prejudices as if they were externally imposed upon the people, the former finds a much more profound connection between religion and the human essence...religion has a real basis; it is not an arbitrary invention of wicked priests who try to deceive the people, nor is it a totally irrational belief. This is a most important landmark in the critique of religion...and allows religion itself to be explained in terms other than lies, deceit or fantastic imagination.[25]

As I've suggested, Feuerbach's advance was made possible by his utilization of Hegel's model, which showed him a new way to understanding ideology.

SEC. 5–3
FEUERBACH'S CRITIQUE OF HEGEL AND ITS INFLUENCE ON MARX

While Hegel's model provided Feuerbach with insight into the phenomenon of the alienated mind, Feuerbach was critical of the idealist metaphysical character of Hegel's model and his overall philosophical system. Consequently, Feuerbach applied the critique of alienated mind to the theories of Hegel himself and demonstrated how Hegel's theories were indicative of alienated thinking.

Feuerbach's critique of Hegel's philosophy was essentially similar to his critique of the religious understanding: he criticized Hegel for his inverted and reified understanding of things. In this section we will begin with an examination of Feuerbach's critique of Hegel's philosophy and then show how this critique influenced the writings of Marx (and Engels).

According to Hegel,[26] Spirit or Absolute Mind is ontologically and causally prior to all things, and the objective world of nature and human history comes into being as a result of Spirit's self-alienation or self-objectification. Although the objective world is essentially spiritual in nature, Spirit initially fails to recognize objectivity as its own essential selfhood. In fact, the external world of objectivity appears to Spirit as an alien and antagonistic entity. However, since objectivity is essentially thought appearing in an alien form, and since Spirit is immanent in the thoughts of human beings, Spirit overcomes its self-alienation and acquires self-consciousness by means of the development of human self-consciousness and the recognition by human consciousness that objectivity is essentially spiritual in nature.

In criticizing Hegel, Feuerbach argues that Hegel's conception of Spirit or the Absolute Mind is simply a reification of abstract human thought understood in a religious (i.e., mystified and alienated) and idealist way.

> '[T]o abstract' means to suppose the essence of nature outside of nature, the essence of the human being outside the human being, the essence of thinking outside the act of thinking...Speculative philosophy has theoretically fixed this separation of the human being's essential qualities from the human being and thereby deified purely abstract qualities as self-sufficient essences.[27]

> the essence of Hegel's *Logic* is transcendent thinking, the thinking of human beings supposed outside of human beings.[28]

Since all of Hegel's philosophical theories presuppose this reified and mystical conception of human thought, Feuerbach argues that Hegel's speculative philosophy is itself an expression of an alienated human consciousness.

> In that its entire system rests upon these acts of abstraction, Hegelian philosophy has estranged the human being from its very self...[29]

Finally, Feuerbach argues that Hegel's idealist understanding of the relation between being and thought is backwards or inverted. According to Feuerbach, being does not come from thought, but thought from being. For Feuerbach, ultimate being or reality is material in nature and human thought acquires its ideas from the external material world by means of sense activity.

> The true relation of thinking and being is simply this: Being is the subject and thinking a predicate but a predicate such as contains the essence of its subject. Thinking come from being but being does not come from thinking.[30]

> I unconditionally repudiate absolute, immaterial, self-sufficing speculation—that speculation which draws its material from within...I found my ideas on materials which can be appropriated only through the activity of the senses. I do not generate the object from the thought, but the thought from the object; and I hold that alone to be an object which has an existence beyond one's brain.[31]

Hence, Feuerbach argues that, like religious thinking, idealist philosophical thought in general and the Hegelian system in particular are inverted and reified ways of understanding. And since they are reified and inverted ways of thinking (that is, alienated forms of consciousness), Feuerbach argued that one could apply to a critique of the "speculative philosophical imagination" the same "reformatory" or critical method utilized in the interpretation and criticism of the kind of errors and misconceptions characteristic of the religious imagination.

> The method of the reformatory critique of speculative philosophy in general does not differ from the critique already applied in the philosophy of religion. We only need always make the predicate into the subject and thus, as the subject, into the object. Hence we only invert speculative philosophy and then have the unmasked, pure, bare truth.[32]

One has to conclude on the basis of the texts of the young Marx that Feuerbach's philosophy exercised a profound influence on his thinking. Basically, Feuerbach's critical writings persuaded the young Marx to interpret nonreligious forms of human alienation and their corresponding ideological forms of consciousness on the basis of an analogy with religious alienation and the religious false consciousness. According to this analogy, the ideological consciousness is like the religious consciousness in that both are a mystified and inverted form of understanding and that both, therefore, perceive or comprehend reality in a mystified and upside-down manner. And since the ideological consciousness is like the religious consciousness, one can extend to the critique of the ideological consciousness in politics, law, morality, etc. the same method utilized for criticizing the religious alienated consciousness.

Feuerbach in his critique of the Hegelian philosophical imagination already had demonstrated how his critique of religion could be applied to other forms of thought. Following the example of Feuerbach, the young Marx ventured out to apply his version of the Feuerbachian method to a critique of ideological forms of social consciousness in the areas of law, politics, economics, etc. Feuerbach's critique of religion was used as a model for the analysis and critique of ideologies, and the young Marx endeavored to criticize the "inverted," "reified," "fetishized"—in short, "religious"—conceptions and modes of thought found in areas of law, politics, economics, and everyday practical social consciousness.

> For Germany, the criticism of religion has been largely completed; and the criticism of religion is the premise of all criticism...[Therefore] the immediate task of philosophy... is to unmask human self-alienation in its secular form, now that it has been unmasked in its sacred form. Thus criticism of heaven is transformed into the...criticism of law...and... the criticism of politics.[33]

For example, the influence of Feuerbach on the young Marx is evident in the latter's *On the Jewish Question*. In this text, the young Marx criticized the quasi-religious political conceptions of the state held by social agents in early modern capitalist society. According to Marx, in practice as well as in the political imagination of citizens the state has a status and function similar in nature to the status and role of God in traditional Christianity.

> The political state, in relation to civil society, is just as spiritual as is heaven in relation to earth. It stands in the same opposition to civil society, and overcomes it in the same manner as religion overcomes the narrowness of the profane world.[34]

In the area of economics, the influence of Feuerbach on the young Marx's theory of alienated labor is evident in the fact that Marx formulated his theory on the basis of an analogy with human self-alienation in religion. For example, in his *Economic and Philosophical Manuscripts* of 1844, the young Marx wrote:

> Just as in religion the spontaneous activity of the human imagination...operates independently of the individual—that is, operates on him as an alien, divine or diabolical activity—so [too] is the worker's activity not his spontaneous activity. It belongs to another; it is the loss of his self.[35]

In the area of philosophy, the influence of Feuerbach's critique of Hegel is evident in the young Marx's critique of the various philosophical theories of Hegel concerning the meaning of history, the nature of the state, etc. For example, in criticizing Hegel's speculative interpretation of history in his *Critique of Hegel's "Philosophy of Right"* (1843), the young Marx criticizes Hegel in familiar Feuerbachian terms:

> The inversion of the subjective into the objective and the objective into the subjective (which results from the fact that Hegel wants to write the life history of abstract substance, of the Idea, and that he wants to allow the essence of humanity to act for itself as an imaginary individual instead of acting in its real human existence) necessarily has the consequence that human activity must appear as the activity and result of something else...[36]

Finally, in the early stages of Marx's intellectual collaboration with Engels, the influence of Feuerbach is evident in their metaphorical description of the ideological perspective as an "upside-down" or "inverted" perspective on reality. Hence, in their often-quoted passage from *The German Ideology* (1845), Marx and Engels argue that ideological conceptions of reality are like the inverted images which result from the reflection of light through a "camera obscura."

> If in all ideology men and their circumstances appear upside-down as in a camera obscura, this phenomenon arises just as much from their historical life-process as the

inversion of objects on the retina does from their physical life-process.[37]

There is a considerable amount of textual evidence, then, which reveals the profundity of Feuerbach's influence on the thinking of the young Marx. Now, while this may be true of the young Marx, what about the writings of the mature "scientific" Marx? Did the mature "scientific" Marx continue to utilize Feuerbachian principles and conceptions in his writings, particularly his writings on ideology? Commentators have disagreed in their answer to this question. In the opinion of one group of commentators, the mature Marx did continue to utilize Feuerbachian and Hegelian conceptions and principles in his later "scientific" writings; they claim that in his later writings, Marx developed further many of the seminal ideas found in his earliest writings. For example, in his *Reason and Revolution: Hegel and the Rise of Social Theory*, Herbert Marcuse argued that:

> Marx's early writings are the first explicit statement of the process of reification through which capitalist society makes all personal relations between men take the form of objective relations between things. Marx expounds this process in his *Capital* as 'the fetishism of commodities'.[38]

In a similar vein, George Lichtheim opined that

> what Marx in *Capital* described as 'the fetishism of commodities' is only another aspect of what in the Paris Manuscripts of 1844 he had termed 'human self-alienation'.[39]

And finally, in a commentary by Jorge Larrain, Larrain argues that

> from the very early critique of religion to the unmasking of mystified economic appearances...there is a remarkable consistency in Marx's understanding of ideology. The idea of a double inversion in consciousness and reality is retained throughout, although in the end it is made more complex by distinguishing a double aspect of reality in the capitalist mode of production. Ideology, therefore, maintains throughout its critical and negative connotation, but is used only for those distortions which are connected with the concealment of a contradictory and inverted reality.[40]

However, in more recent years, some commentators have rejected the significance of the writings of the young Marx on ideology for understanding his "mature, scientific" conception of ideology. In some cases, commentators on Marx's conception of ideology have been influenced by the interpretation of Louis Althusser. Althusser argued that there exists an "epistemological break" between the early and later writings of Marx and that the mature "scientific" Marx rejected Hegelian and Feuerbachian philosophical conceptions like alienation in favor of such scientific conceptions as "class," "productive-forces," "productive relations," etc. In his essay "Lenin Before Hegel," Louis Althusser formulated the "epistemological break" interpretation of Marx's writings:

> The untenable thesis upheld by Marx in the 1844 Manuscripts was that History is the History of the process of alienation of a Subject, the Generic Essence of Man alienated in 'alienated labor'.
> But it was precisely this thesis that exploded. The result of this explosion was the evaporation of the notions of subject, human essence, and alienation, which disappears, completely atomized, and the liberation of a process without a subject, which is the basis of all the analyses in *Capital*.[41]

In general, the effect of Althusser's thesis on commentators has been to diminish the philosophical value of Marx's earlier writings on ideology while encouraging the interpretation of Marx's conception of ideology solely on the basis of his later writings and in abstraction from his Feuerbachian and philosophical past. For example, the influence of Althusser is evident in an article by John Mepham entitled "The Theory of Ideology in *Capital*." In his essay, Mepham contends that the "camera obscura" model of *The German Ideology* is "vague" and inadequate. In criticizing the passage containing the "camera obscura" analogy, Mepham asserts that the analogy

> ...is not a clear statement. Marx is here struggling to discover an adequate language and the result is a series of metaphors which are symptoms of his failure...[e.g.] camera obscura, reflexes, echoes, phantoms, sublimates...Also the passage is open to many different interpretations...[42]

I myself do not think that the "camera obscura" passage is "vague" and "open to different interpretations." In fact, as I have discussed above, the "camera obscura" analogy is understandable relative to the Feuerbachian influence on Marx and Engels. What the "camera obscura" analogy alludes to is the "inverted" nature of ideological "reflexes," and, by implication, the Feuerbachian influence on the thinking of Marx and Engels. I also do not believe that the use of metaphors and analogies in theories is necessarily symptomatic of conceptual inadequacy; in fact, metaphors and analogies are sometimes appropriate conceptual tools for conveying meaning, for simplifying descriptions of complex phenomena, and for facilitating insight into a complex phenomenon.

Most importantly, on the basis of the text itself I believe that Mepham's contention is simply wrong. If one examines closely Marx's discussions on the nature of the relationship between appearances and reality in *Capital*, one will observe that for Marx appearances represent reality in an inverted fashion. For example, in his discussion of the confusions caused by the wage form of labor, Marx makes evident his understanding of the inverted relationship between appearances and reality.

> In the expression of 'value of labor', the concept of value is not only completely extinguished, but inverted...It is an expression as imaginary as the value of the earth. These imaginary expressions arise, nevertheless, from the relations of production themselves. They are categories for the forms of appearance of essential relations. That in their appearance things are often presented in an inverted way is something fairly familiar in every science, apart from political economy.[43]

Now, if common sense only apprehends the appearances of reality, and if these appearances present reality in an inverted way, then common sense will view things in an upside-down manner as if it were a "camera obscura." This is what Marx argued in his various statements in *Capital* regarding the relationship between the commonsense appearance of things and the true reality of things in capitalist society. For instance, he says,

> The final pattern of economic relations as seen on the surface, in their real existence and consequently in the conceptions by which the bearers and agents of these relations

seek to understand them, is very much different from, and indeed quite the reverse of, their inner but concealed essential pattern and the conceptions corresponding to it.[44]

Hence, contrary to the opinion of Mepham, what Marx in fact did was to apply the "camera obscura" model of *The German Ideology* in a more systematic way to his analyses in Capital concerning the ideological nature of common sense.[45] In short, for Marx in *Capital*, the common sense of social agents in capitalism was a false, inverted consciousness, as the following passage from *Capital* makes clear:

> [A]ll the notions of justice held by both the worker and the capitalist, all the mystifications of the capitalist mode of production, all capitalism's illusions about freedom, all the apologetic tricks of vulgar economics, have as their basis the form of appearance discussed above, which makes the actual relation invisible, and indeed presents to the eye the precise opposite of that relation.[46]

But did Marx in *Capital* draw a connection between the inverted, mystified social consciousness of agents in capitalism and *alienated labor*? In Feuerbach's theory, the inverted and mystified, religious consciousness was linked with human self-alienation. This also was the case in the writings of the young Marx; for the young Marx, the inverted, mystified consciousness in politics, economics, philosophy, etc. was always linked with "secular" (i.e., social) forms of human self-alienation. Was this connection true for the mature Marx as well?

Contrary to the opinion of Althusser, I believe that the mature Marx continued to use "Feuerbachian and Hegelian-like" conceptions and principles in *Capital* for analyzing the ideological effects of alienated labor in capitalist society. According to my reading of Marx's analyses in *Capital*, for Marx the forms of appearances which represent the reality of capitalism in an inverted, fetishized, and "religious" way were symptomatic of the essentially *alienated* nature of social productive forces and human labor in capitalism.

The continued influence of the young Marx's philosophical heritage on his mature scientific analyses in *Capital* seems evident in the following passage from *Capital* in which Marx utilizes the notion of alienation to account for the socioeconomic illusions characteristic of capitalist society (illusions which he subsequently compares with the illusions of religion).

> It has been shown...how not merely at the level of ideas, but also in reality, the social characteristics of his labor confronts the worker as something not merely alien, but hostile and antagonistic, when it appears before him objectified and personified in capital...Thus at the level of material production, of the life-process in the realm of the social...we find the same situation that we find in religion at the ideological level, namely the inversion of the subject into object and vice versa...What we are confronted by here is the alienation of man from his own labor...[47]

> ...the bewitched, distorted and upside-down world haunted by Monsieur le Capital and Madame la Terre...this religion of everyday life...[48]

Moreover, I see no evidence for the claim of any absolute "epistemological break" between the writings of the young Marx and the mature Marx. If anything, it seems that in order to understand the full significance of Marx's 'theory of ideology in *Capital*' one must have an understanding of the young Marx's appropriation and modification of the Feuerbachian approach to ideology. Therefore, as a prelude to examining Marx's theory of ideology in *Capital* and the Feuerbachian influence on Marx's analyses there, let us begin with an examination of the young Marx's writings on alienation in the political state and in the economic sphere of society. In the course of this examination, we will see how the young Marx extended Feuerbach model of religion to an analysis of nonreligious forms of ideology, how Marx modified Feuerbach's model, and how his earlier writings prepared the theoretical grounds for his analyses in *Capital* concerning the quasi-religious appearances and conceptions prevailing in capitalist society.

6

Alienation and False Consciousness in the Writings of the Young Marx

SEC. 6–1
THE YOUNG MARX'S ANALYSIS OF THE STATE

One of the more interesting examples of the young Marx's application of Feuerbach's method of critique to nonreligious phenomena can be found in his *On the Jewish Question* (1843). While written for the specific purpose of criticizing the views of Bruno Bauer, Marx's general comments about the liberal republican state and the political consciousness of social agents in regards to the state are pertinent for illustrating his understanding of the political imagination of social agents in modern capitalist society on the basis of an analogy with the religious imagination of traditional Christianity.

According to the young Marx's Feuerbachian analysis of liberal democracy, just as God in the religious imagination of Christianity embodies all of the perfected moral virtues unobtainable by members of the human species in their earthly existence, so in the political imagination of most members of capitalist society, the liberal republican state represents all of the ideal aspirations of civil society (i.e., community and social unity, equality and equal rights, concern for the common good and public interest, mutual reciprocity and respect, guardianship of the social ethos, etc.) however unrealizable they may be. In short, in the opinion of the young Marx, the political consciousness of social agents in liberal democracy is religious because they look upon the liberal republican state as representative of their higher, universal "species-life" or social community in opposition to their "profane" selfish and competitive life in civil society.

> The members of the political state are religious because of the dualism between individual life and species-life, between the life of civil society and political life. They are religious in the sense that man treats political life, which is remote from his own individual existence, as if it were his true life; and in the sense that religion is here the spirit of civil society, and expresses the separation and withdrawal of man from man...[Hence] the political state, in relation to civil society, is just as spiritual as is heaven in relation to earth. It stands in the same opposition to civil society, and overcomes it in the same manner as religion overcomes the narrowness of the profane world; i.e., it has always to acknowledge it again, reestablish it, and allow itself to be dominated by it.[1]

Of course, the most outstanding example of a quasi-religious conception of the liberal republican state (and therefore an example of the quasi-religious political consciousness criticized by the young Marx) can be found in Hegel's theory of the state. According to Hegel, the state in capitalist society represents both the *idea* and the *reality* of civil society's higher, universal ethical life. Hegel astutely observed that as members of civil society, social agents could not know and experience any real social and ethical unity because civil society is the realm of egotism and private interest.[2] However, Hegel argued that as citizens of the state, social agents in capitalism could know and experience the reality of their higher, universal, spiritual social life because the state embodies the actualized rational and ethical substance of history and the universal Mind. Hegel therefore asserted that as the embodiment and realization of the universal, rational, ethical substance of history and the universal Mind, "the state is the divine Idea as it exists on earth." The contention that the state in capitalist society functions as the real cohesive spiritual force is acknowledged as such, according to Hegel, by the fact that in the political consciousness of social agents they themselves recognize in the idea of the state their own universal and higher social existence.

> The Idea is the interior; the State is the externally existing, genuinely moral life. It is the union of the universal and essential with the subjective will, and as such it is Morality. The individual who lives in this unity has a moral life...All the value man has, all spiritual reality, he has only through the State. For his spiritual reality is the knowing presence to him of his own essence, of rationality, of its objective, immediate actuality present in and for him. Only thus is he truly a consciousness, only thus does he partake in morality, in the legal and moral life of the state...The state [therefore] is the divine Idea as it exists on earth.[3]

For the young Marx, the liberal republican state might be the idea and "appearance" of social unity and human association (e.g., "species-being"), but the existing political state of capitalist society was neither the actuality nor realization of this ideal. Basically, the young Marx argued that the liberal republican state is only the idea and not the actual reality of human association because the liberal republican state does not really eliminate the social alienation which exists in civil society. It is therefore unsuccessful in unifying social agents in a higher kind of community. In elaborating on his view, Marx made three important points.

In the first place, since the liberal republican state takes a laissez-faire attitude in respect to the institutions of civil society (thereby leaving untouched the particularizing and divisive effects of civil society), social alienation and disunity continue to exist in the body politic.

> The state abolishes, after its fashion, the distinctions established by birth, social rank, education, occupation, when it decrees that birth, social rank, education, occupation are non-political distinctions; when it proclaims...that every member of society is an equal partner in popular sovereignty...But the state, none the less, allows private property, education, occupation, to act after their own fashion, namely as private property, education, occupation and to manifest their particular nature.[4]

In the second place, the young Marx argued that liberal democracy further complicates the alienated lives of social agents in capitalism by forcing them to lead two antithetical social lives. As citizens of the state individuals are expected to be public-minded and to value the common good above their own personal interests. However, the institutions of civil society still require individuals as members of civil society to lead selfish, private lives and to be competitive with each other. The two conflicting sets of principles make people in capitalist society lead "double lives," just as in the Christian religion the individual also has to live two separate lives—the higher life of spirit and the lower, profane life of the flesh.

> The perfected political state is, by its nature, the species-life of man as opposed to his material life. All the presuppositions of this egoistic life continue to exist in civil society outside the political sphere, as qualities of civil society. Where the political state has attained to its full development, man leads, not only in thought...but in reality, in life, a double existence—celestial and terrestrial. He lives in the political community, where he regards himself as a communal being, and in civil society where he acts simply as a private individual, treats other men as means...[5]

Finally, in opposition to the political imagination of all hopeful liberal democrats, the young Marx argued that the liberal republican state was essentially a bourgeois state and therefore not legally constituted for the purpose of elevating the atomistic individuals of civil society into a higher form of social association. According to the young Marx, since the liberal republican state was the product of the bourgeois-led political revolutions against feudal absolutism, the liberal republican state bears the mark of its bourgeois and historical origins. As a bourgeois state, the liberal republican state is essentially constituted for the sake of defending the property rights of individuals and for preserving and regulating the privately owned institutions of civil society. Since a defense of the principles of civil society and private property are embraced as the final ends of the liberal republican state, Marx concludes that the liberal republican state cannot really succeed in transforming "egoistic man" into a sociable "species-being." Hence, due to its very nature, the liberal republican state cannot succeed in fully emancipating humankind from the alienating conditions of civil society.

Now, in justifying his assertion that the liberal republican state is essentially a bourgeois state, the young Marx refers to the political declarations and constitutions of the new French republic created in the aftermath of the revolution of 1789. In these documents, Marx notes that French constitutionalists distinguished between "the rights of man and the rights of citizen," and that in the final analysis, it was the "rights of man" which were most important to the French constitutionists.

According to the French constitutionalists, the "rights of man" are "natural rights"; they include the right to "equality," "liberty," "security" and "property." Furthermore, the French constitutionalists argued that "the end of every political association is the preservation of the natural and imprescriptible rights of man."[6] In doing so, the French constitutionalists were giving expression to one of the familiar themes of bourgeois social contract theory, perhaps best expressed by John Locke, who argued,

> The supreme power cannot take from any man part of his property without his own consent. For the preservation of property being the end of government, and that for which men enter into society.[7]

Or, alternatively, as the young Marx was to interpret the social meaning of these "rights of man":

> ...the so-called rights of man...are simply the rights of a member of civil society...None of the supposed rights of man, therefore, go beyond the egoistic man...that is, an individual separated from the community, withdrawn into himself, wholly preoccupied with his private interest and acting in accordance with his private caprice...[8]

Since the liberal republican state is founded upon and aims at a defense of the "rights of man," Marx concluded, the liberal republican state is essentially a bourgeois state.

> [T]he political liberators reduce citizenship, the political community, to a mere means for preserving these so-called rights of man; and consequently, that the citizen is declared to be the servant of egoistic "man."...and that it is man as a bourgeois and not man as a citizen who is considered the true and authentic man...[and] the foundation and presupposition of the political state.[9]

This notion that the state should aim at protecting individual rights as they exist in civil society was an idea fairly common in classical liberal bourgeois thought (and one that continues to prevail today in contemporary political thought). It was an idea held by our own American constitutional leaders who, in addition, argued that the proper role of the state in society was to function as an arbiter mediating and regulating the competition and conflicts of private interest groups. For example, in one of the letters compiled and published as *The Federalist Papers*, James Madison remarked:

> Among the numerous advantages promised by a well-constructed Union, none deserves to be more accurately developed than its tendency to break and control the violence of faction...[T]he most common and durable source of factions, has been the various and unequal distribution of property. Those who hold, and those who are without property, have ever formed distinct interests in society...A landed interest, a manufacturing interest, a mercantile interest, a monied interest, with many lesser interests, grow up of necessity in civilized nations, and divide them into different classes, actuated by different sentiments and views. The regulation of these various and interfering interests forms the principal task of modern Legislation, and involves the spirit of party and faction in the necessary and ordinary operations of Government.[10]

Hence, the young Marx's assertion that the liberal republican state was essentially a bourgeois state was an assertion well justified by the documents and remarks of the republican constitutionalists in the period of the democratic revolutions of the eighteenth century. And since the liberal republican state was essentially a bourgeois state designed to preserve the institutions and property conditions of civil society, the young Marx concluded, liberal democracy could not really emancipate human beings from the "egotism" and alienation of civil society.

In summary, just as Feuerbach had argued that in the idea of God Christians unknowingly symbolize their own human species-nature and aspirations in an alien and supernatural form, so in his theory of liberal democracy the young Marx argued that in the idea of the state social agents symbolize their aspirations for a species-community and true human association in a secular, political form. However, just as the "heavenly kingdom of God" exists in a universe apart from this earthly "vale of tears," so too is the idealized life of social unity in the state remote from the egoism and disunity in civil society, according to the young Marx. The state might be the idea and symbol of social community—Marx argued that in the idea of "equal sovereignty and partnership" in the state social agents recognize each other in an indirect way as "species-beings"—but it was not by any means the actual reality of social "species-life." If social agents in their political imagination were to confuse the symbol for the reality, then like Christians they would possess false consciousness.

> The political state, in relation to civil society, is just as spiritual as is heaven in relation to earth. It stands in the same opposition to civil society, and overcomes it in the same manner as religion overcomes the narrowness of the profane world; i.e., it has always to acknowledge it again, re-establish it, and allow itself to be dominated by it...[Thus] in the state...where [the 'profane individual of civil society'] is regarded as a species-being, man is the imaginary member of an imaginary sovereignty, divested of his real, individual life, and infused with an unreal universality.[11]

Having seen how the young Marx relied on Feuerbachian principles in his criticism of the alienated, political false consciousness, we now can turn to a discussion of the differences in their accounts concerning the origin and nature of the alienated mind. Perhaps the major difference between Marx and Feuerbach exists in the fact that Marx "moved beyond Feuerbach...through his attempt to account for mystified consciousness as a social phenomenon."[12]

Basically, for Feuerbach the alienated mind was primarily an anthropological and psychological phenomenon. As an anthropological phenomenon, religious consciousness, according to Feuerbach, was an expression of humanity's self-alienation or the alienation of humanity from its own human nature. But alienated mind also was a psychological phenomenon, according to Feuerbach, because in religion human beings rationalize their moral inadequacies and seek psychological compensations for their moral deficiencies and unfulfilled psychological needs. The following quote from *The Essence of Christianity* gives an example of Feuerbach's psychological analysis of the religious mind.

> It is pleasanter to be passive than to act, to be redeemed and made free by another than to free oneself; pleasanter to make one's salvation dependent on a person than on the force of one's own spontaneity...The Redeemer...The God-Man, in opposition to the moral spontaneity of the natural or rationalistic man, satisfies immediately the inward moral wants and wishes, since he dispenses man on his own side from any intermediate activity...[13]

While Feuerbach was satisfied with giving a psychological interpretation of the fact that religious illusions serve collective human needs, the young Marx argued that there must be something wrong with the social life of humanity if it has a collective need for shared illusion. According to Marx's social explanation of the political false consciousness, social agents in capitalism are disposed to embrace a shared illusion of community in the state because of the absence of any real community and social solidarity in their practical lives as agents in civil society. This shared illusion of solidarity helps to compensate social agents for the lack of any real solidarity in civil society due to the class divisions and social alienation prevailing in civil society. From the perspective of the young Marx, therefore, the collective need for quasi-religious illusions was symptomatic of the social alienation of humanity.

> The wretchedness of religion is at once an expression of and a protest against real wretchedness...The abolition of religion as the illusory happiness of the people is a demand for their true happiness. The call to abandon illusions about their condition is the call to abandon a condition which requires illusions. Thus, the critique of religion is the critique in embryo of the vale of tears of which religion is the halo.[14]

A second way in which the young Marx's account of the alienated mind represented a social theory (as opposed to Feuerbach's psychological and anthropological theory) is evident in their different understanding of the symbolic "reifications" and "abstractions" of the alienated mind. For Feuerbach, "God" was a symbolic, *mental* abstraction or reification. For the young Marx, however, the state constituted a real, *objective* alienation or reification of human social powers vis-à-vis civil society.[15]

What Marx meant by his characterization of state power as a reification of human social powers is that although the modern state was created by social groups to look after the general interests of civil society as a governing body and institutional force, the state nonetheless stands opposed to its creators as an "alien" power and authority which controls and at times antagonizes its creators. For example, in being granted the authority and means of power to serve the general interests of civil society, state instituions like the police and legislature can exercise considerable power over its creators, i.e., individual property owners. Furthermore, the general interests of property owners served by the state can at times come into conflict with the particular interests of individual property owners. For example, the state may attempt to legislate laws and policies for protecting and furthering the common interests of individual property owners, and these state policies and laws may at times favor the particular interests of certain property owners over others. The state may think that tax breaks for big business will further the general interests of civil society, and the ensuing polices may hurt small businesses and homeowners who don't receive such tax breaks.

While this characterization of the state as objectified or reified human social powers and interests seems unusual, it makes sense. The modern state was a creation of human social struggles and hence human acts of will; the state has authority and power over civil society; and finally, in pursuit of the general interests of civil society, state policies and laws can contradict the particular interests of individuals.

Since the modern state can be understood as an alienated and reified, objective social entity, the ideological abstractions and mental "reifications" of the alienated mind can be understood as in part the reflections and expressions of an objective alienation and reification in society.[16] Thus, in opposition to Feuerbach, Marx could justifiably argue that there are social and objective origins for the alienated mind. In fact, Marx did say as much in his fourth thesis on Feuerbach:

> Feuerbach starts out from the fact of religious self-alienation, of the duplication of the world into a religious world and a secular one. His work consists in resolving the religious world into its secular basis. But that the secular basis detaches itself from itself and establishes itself as an inde-

pendent realm in the clouds can only be explained by the cleavages and self-contradictions within the secular basis.[17]

This understanding of alienation and reification as existing objectively in the external world indicates the influence of Hegel's theory of alienation on the young Marx, as we will see in the following section. In making use of Hegel's theory, Marx was able to demonstrate the relationship between quasi-religious forms of ideological consciousness and objective forms of human alienation in society. Hegel's theory also enabled Marx to go beyond Feuerbach account of the alienated false consciousness, as we will see more clearly in the pages ahead.

In summary, in this section we examined Marx's application of Feuerbach's theory of religion to an analysis of the political state in capitalism and Marx's analysis of the quasi-religious "political imagination" of social agents in respect to the state. In doing so, we examined Marx's critique of the Hegelian conception of the state and Marx's explanation of how the contradiction between civil society and liberal democracy fosters a political false consciousness. Finally, we examined the differences between the young Marx and Feuerbach's theory of alienation...

SEC. 6–2

*FALSE CONSCIOUSNESS AND ALIENATED LABOR
IN THE WRITINGS OF THE YOUNG MARX*

At the end of the preceding section we discovered that one of the major differences between Marx and his mentor Feuerbach was that for Marx alienation was a social phenomenon and the alienated false consciousness was a reflection and correlate of this social phenomenon. Since the young Marx believed there to be this kind of correlation between the alienated ideological understanding and social alienation, he reconceived the task of ideological criticism. He believed it should show how the ideologically symbolic and reified conceptions of the alienated consciousness were manifestations and reflections of the alienation and reifications in the objective, social world.

Now, perhaps the clearest illustration of this critical project in the writings of the young Marx can be found in his *Economic and*

Philosophical Manuscripts of 1844 concerning the economic self-alienation and false consciousness of human labor in capitalist society. In addition, Marx's account of money in his essay "On James Mill" (1844) is of importance in understanding the young Marx's conception of human alienation in the economic sphere of society.

According to Marx, human labor by nature is an objectifying activity which generates an objective world of human products: "It is only to be expected [of] a living, natural being equipped and endowed with objective (i.e., material) essential powers...that his self-alienation should lead to the establishing of a real, objective world..."[18] For Marx, the products of the activity of human labor embody the essence of human labor in an external, material form: "[T]he product of labor is labor which has been embodied in an object, which has become material: it is the objectification of labor..."[19] However, by virtue of becoming independent of their creators as a result of their production or "objectification," the products of human labor acquire an alien objectivity or appearance, and they now confront their producers as independent, opposing powers. Hence, for Marx, the self-objectification of human labor leads both to the alienation of human producers from their own products and to false consciousness, because human producers fail to recognize their own creative powers in the objects produced by their labor.

> [T]he object which labor produces—labor's product—confronts it as something alien, as a power independent of the producer...The alienation of the worker in his product means not only that his labor becomes an object, an external existence, but that it exists outside him, independently, as something alien to him, and that it becomes a power on its own confronting him. It means that the life which he has conferred on the object confronts him as something hostile and alien.[20]

Domination of the producers by their own products takes the form of money, according to Marx. In his essay "On James Mill" (1844), Marx argued that human alienation obtains its fullest form once money becomes the universal medium for the exchange of commodities. In *Capital*, the mature Marx would argue that money in essence is a symbol for equating the relationship between the productive activities of human labor with the exchange relations between the products of human labor. Marx anticipated this idea in his essay "On James Mill"; in this earlier writing on the nature of money, the young Marx argued that money in essence is a symbol for representing the social mediations between human labors and their products.

> The essence of money is...that the mediating activity or movement, the human, social act whereby man's products complete each other, is alienated and becomes the property of a material thing outside man, money.[21]

According to the argument in the above essay, once society began to use money as a symbol for representing the economic value of commodities, including the value of human labor itself, money itself acquired an incredible power over people because all other social values (e.g., social status and political power) were represented in the form of money. Society learned to evaluate the social status and personal worth of individuals in terms of the amount of wealth or money an individual owned.[22] Furthermore, society began to calculate the economic importance of different kinds of human labor in terms of their monetary value in the marketplace. Hence, with the institutionalization of a monetary system of exchange in society, people learned to evaluate their social relationship to others in terms of their monetary value.

This connection between money and modern alienation that the young Marx draws is evident in the following passage in his essay "On James Mill":

> ...the complete domination of the alienated thing over man is fully manifested in money...what was domination of person over person [in the master-slave societies of Antiquity and in the lord-serf societies of the Medieval Ages] is now the general domination of the thing over the person, of the product over the producer.[23]

In a further elaboration of these themes, Marx in his *German Ideology* (1845) states that the alienation and domination of human producers by their own products is a "historical fact," a fact which appears in the form of the "world market."[24] In the system of the world market, commodities appear to live a life of their own independent of the actions of their producers. The prices of commodities appear to result from the exchange rates between different types of commodities independent of the social labor involved in their production. Furthermore, the domination of human producers by their own products is a reality which takes the form of the laws of supply and demand which govern the exchange of commodities in the world market.

From the above discussions we see that by alienation, Marx signified a practical social process whereby human labor in producing products objectifies or "reifies" its own essential powers in its products, and because these products come to exist independently of their producers in the "world market," the products of human labor acquire an alien appearance and power over their producers which both mystifies and dominates them. Marx's conception of alienation was intended to describe a practical-social form of the reification, mystification and domination of human labor by its own products. As Marx remarked in his 1844 manuscripts: "the medium through which estrangement takes place is itself practical."[25]

Now, in the passages quoted from the writings of the young Marx we can see both the influence of Feuerbach's theory of religion on Marx's theory of the economic alienation of labor and the difference between the two theories. For example, just as for Feuerbach the falsity of the religious consciousness is due to the fact that religious believers fail to recognize their own human essence in the image of God, so for Marx human producers possess false consciousness because they fail to recognize their own human productive powers in the products of their labor.

However, one of the principal differences between Marx and Feuerbach is that for the latter human self-alienation is largely an intellectual phenomenon, whereas for Marx human self-alienation is an objective and social phenonomena. For Feuerbach human self-alienation is typified by the fact that human beings are dominated and mystified by their own *ideas* (e.g., the idea of "God"). The mystifying reifications confronting humanity in religion are thus the intellectual products of its own fantastic imagination, according to Feuerbach.

In contrast, for the young Marx human self-alienation is typified by the fact that human beings are dominated and mystified by real social objects. Human self-alienation and its correlate, the alienated false consciousness, are objective and social for the young Marx because in society human producers are really separated from their products and because human producers have no real control over the market disposition of their products. They also lack any real control over the social conditions of their labor. Hence, in distinction from Feuerbach, the young Marx asserted that human self-alienation was both a practical and social matter.[26] For Marx the mystifying reifications confronting human producers in capitalism were real objects and objects embodying their essential productive powers albeit in an alien, unrecognizable form as commodites.

In emphasizing the correlation between objective alienation in reality and an alienated false consciousness in thought, Marx's theory incorporated one of the major aspects of Hegel's theory on alienation. It was Hegel's notion that the self-alienation of Spirit or Mind creates a real, objective world which mystifies and opposes the Mind as an alien, antagonistic reality. This notion is evident in the following passage from Hegel's *Phenomenology of Spirit*:

> Although this world has come into being through individuality, it is for self-consciousness immediately an alienated world which has the form of a fixed and solid reality over against it...The Spirit whose self is an absolutely discrete unit has its content confronting it as an equally hard unyielding reality, and here the world has the character of being something external, the negative of self-consciousness. This world is, however, a spiritual entity...its existence is the work of self-consciousness, but it is also an alien reality already present and given, a reality which has a being of its own and in which it does not recognize itself...[27]

The rational possibilities implicit in Hegel's idealist and quasi-religious notion of the objective world as a reification of Spirit were not lost upon the young Marx.[28] What Hegel had discussed as the self-alienation and reification of Spirit by means of Spirit's self-objectification in the world as Substance was interpreted by the young Marx to mean the "alienation of the human essence through labor." In acknowledging the contribution of Hegel's theory to his own theory of alienation, the young Marx in his 1844 manuscripts praised Hegel's *Phenomenology of Spirit*.

> [T]he outstanding achievement of Hegel's *Phenomenology*...is...that Hegel conceives the self-creation of man as a

process, conceives objectification as loss of the object, as alienation and as transcendence of this alienation...he thus grasps the essence of labor and comprehends objective man...as the outcome of man's own labor...Labor is man's coming-to-be for himself within alienation, or as alienated man.[29]

Of course, what made possible Marx's appreciation of the "rational kernal" implicit within Hegel's mystified conception of alienation was Feuerbach's critique of Hegel's philosophy. Marx's reliance on Feuerbach in interpreting and criticizing Hegel's conception of alienation is evident in several places in the *Economic and Philosophical Manuscripts* of 1844. For example, following Feuerbach's interpretation of Hegel, Marx argued that Hegel's conception of Spirit was simply an abstract, reified expression of human self-consciousness: "[For Hegel] it is not real Man...who as such is made the subject, but only the abstraction of man—self-consciousness..."[30] Most importantly, it was Feuerbach's principle of inversion which made possible Marx's materialist interpretation of Hegel's idealist doctrine of alienation: "[For Hegel] real man and real nature become mere predicates—symbols of this esoteric, unreal mind of this unreal nature. Subject and predicate are therefore related to each other in absolute reversal..."[31]

Not surprisingly, prior to his analysis of Hegel's conception of alienation, Marx praised Feuerbach's critique of Hegel for proving

> that [Hegel's] philosophy is nothing else but religion rendered into thought and expounded by thought, hence equally to be condemned as another form and manner of existence of the estrangement of the essence of man.[32]

On the one hand, then, Feuerbach's critique assisted Marx in the transformation of Hegel's quasi-religious doctrine concerning Spirit's self-alienation in the world into a materialist and humanist theory concerning the self-alienation of human labor in the economic world. On the other hand, Hegel's writings aided Marx in understanding alienation and reification as an objective and social phenomenon. Together the theories of Feuerbach and Hegel helped Marx to better understand the objective and ideological dimension of human self-alienation.

In summary, in this section we examined the young Marx's theory of alienation of human labor, the differences between Marx and Feuerbach on the nature and basis of the alienated consciousness and reification, and finally, the influence of Hegel on the views of the young Marx. We discovered that for Marx the practical and social conditions of alienated labor produce a false consciousness whereby human producers fail to recognize their own productive powers and human essence in their products because their products acquire an alien appearance as the result of becoming commodites circulated in the world marketplace.

7

Alienation, the Fetishism of Commodities, and Ideology in Capital

In the previous chapter we examined the young Marx's distinctive theory of alienated labor and its correlate, the alienated false consciousness. According to the young Marx, the products and activity of human producers under certain social circumstances acquire a mystifying form which dominates their producers. In more complete terms, alienation, according to the young Marx, entailes: (a) a process of reification (in work human producers endow their products with their essential productive powers, and social circumstances separate human producers from their products); (b) mystification (the producers no longer recognize themselves in their products because their products acquire an alien appearance); and (c) domination (the products oppose their producers in the form of the market system and money).

In this section, we will demonstrate how this conception of alienation reappears in *Capital* in Marx's analyses of the mystifying and fetish-like appearances generated by the capitalist mode of production. According to Marx, the appearances generated by the capitalist mode of production constitute the basis for various ideological conceptions social agents have concerning the nature of capitalist society.

> All the notions of justice held by both the worker and the capitalist, all the mystifications of the capitalist mode of production, all capitalism's illusions about freedom, all the

apologetic tricks of vulgar economics, have as their basis the form of appearance discussed above, which makes the actual relation invisible, and indeed presents to the eye the precise opposite of that relation.[1]

Marx maintained that these phenomenal forms of reality constitute the basic categories of the commonsense conceptions held by all social agents in capitalism.

...the forms of appearance are reproduced directly and spontaneously, as current and usual modes of thought.[2]

What Marx's analysis establishes is that the commonsense understanding of social agents in capitalism constitutes an alienated false consciousness of the Hegelian-Feuerbachian kind. Hence, in addition to demonstrating the importance of the young Marx's conception of alienation to the mature Marx's theory of ideology in *Capital*, we will at the same time be demonstrating the continuing influence of the Feuerbachian-Hegelian heritage on the writings of the mature Marx. We will also show the continuity between Marx's earlier and later writings concerning his conception of ideology.

The order in which we will pursue the above objectives is as follows. We will begin with Marx's description of how social reality appears to people in the capitalist mode of production. We will then examine how the "socially valid" forms of common sense reappear in the categories and formulas of classical bourgeois political economists. Next, we will examine why Marx believed that the categories of common sense and classical political economy were mystifying and irrational forms of thought. According to Marx, because of the commodity form of the social division of labor (e.g., social relations of production) and the commodity form of the products of human labor in capitalism, social reality necessarily will appear in an inverted and false way to the social agents of capitalism. That is to say, the commodity forms of appearance are responsible for the social false consciousness of agents in capitalism as well as the "reified" and "fetishistic" appearances of society. However, in criticizing bourgeois political economy and commonsense modes of thought, Marx argued that it is necessary to account for the social and historical conditions which made possible the commodity form of the social division of labor and the commodity form of the products of human labor. In tracing Marx's account of the historical and social origins of the commodity form of social relations and the products of human labor-power, we will see the importance of Marx's conception of alienation. Specifically, I will demonstrate Marx's argument to the effect that it was the alienation of human labor from its products in capitalism which was ultimately responsible for the inverted, reified and fetishistic appearance of capitalism. Marx drew an analogy between the fetishism of commodities and the reified and inverted conceptions of religion, and we will discuss how this analogy demonstrates the continued influence of Feuerbach in Marx's analyses in *Capital*.

SEC. 7-1
MARX'S DESCRIPTION OF THE COMMONSENSE APPEARANCES OF CAPITALIST SOCIETY

According to Marx, the social relations of production and the products of human labor-power appear to common sense in forms very different from their real nature. Marx discusses in several places in *Capital* the common and theoretical conceptions held by social agents and bourgeois economists, respectively, concerning the nature of the capitalist relations of production. We will focus largely on Marx's analysis of the "trinity formula" from vol. 3, chap. 48 of *Capital* to see how this illustrates his description of the theoretical and commonsense understanding of capitalist social relations of production. In vol. 1, pt. 1 of *Capital*, Marx discusses to a greater extent the common and theoretical conceptions held by social agents and bourgeois economists, respectively, concerning the nature of economic value and the laws governing the products of human labor in the marketplace. Marx's description and analysis of the theoretical and commonsense conceptions of economic value and the capitalist relations of production are similar because both are instances of what he would describe as the fetishism attached to the commodity form of the social relations of productions and the products of human labor in the capitalist mode of production.

Marx used the expression "the fetishism of commodities" to refer to the "estranged" and "reified" appearances of the social relations of production and the products of human labor arising from the capitalist mode of production. According to Marx, the "trinity formula" used by some classical political economists is in essence a formulation of the "reified, " commonsense appearances of the social relations of production while the theories of economic value popular with many bourgeois political economists are reflections of the "fetish-like" appearances arising from the products of human labor under conditions of the capitalist system of commodity production. By fetishism of commodities, therefore, Marx signified a complex process whereby the social relations of production between people appear as a relationship between things or factors of production (e.g., as "reified") in which the powers of human labor appear as powers belonging to their products ("the personification of things").[3]

For the sake of convenience, we will examine separately each of these logically distinct aspects of Marx's "fetishism of commodities." We will begin by examining Marx's analysis and critique of the reified appearances of the social relations of production in capitalism as contained in his chapter on the "trinity formula" in vol. 3 of *Capital*.

HOW THE SOCIAL RELATIONS OF PRODUCTION BETWEEN PEOPLE APPEAR AS A RELATIONSHIP BETWEEN "THINGS" OR NATURAL FACTORS OF PRODUCTION

Marx argued that in capitalism, the social relations of production appear to common sense as a relationship between separate and autonomous economic "things" or "commodities" (i.e., as an external relationship between capital, wage-labor, and privately owned land). Marx also argued that the different components of economic value (i.e., profits, wages, and rent) appear to be generated from three different sources (namely, capital, wage-labor, and land). A clear expression of these claims appears in chap. 48 (on the "trinity formula") in vol. 3 of *Capital*.

> Capital, landed property and labor appear to those agents of production as three separate and independent sources, and it appears from these three arises three different components of the annually produced value...In the formula capital-interest, earth-ground rent, labor-wages, capital, earth and labor power appear respectively as sources or interest...ground-rent and wages as their products or fruit—one

ALIENATION, THE FETISHISM OF COMMODITIES, AND IDEOLOGY 131

the basis, the other the result; one the cause, the other the effect...[4]

Marx argued in vol. 1 of *Capital* that workers in capitalist society view their own labor-power as a commodity to be sold in the marketplace to the highest bidder (i.e., to an employer who would offer the highest wage). In turn, employers treat employees as if they are commodities to be purchased at the lowest cost, and they are utilized in the production process in much the same way one would treat one's personal possessions.

> The capitalist epoch is...characterized by the fact that labor power, in the eyes of the worker himself, takes on the form of a commodity...[5]

> ...the owners of the conditions of production treat living labor-power as a thing...[6]

In addition, instead of seeing themselves as being controlled and ruled by a social class of human owners (i.e., capitalists), workers view the power controlling their lives as emanating from impersonal and nature-like forces such as technology and the "natural" laws of the marketplace. This is so, according to Marx, because what workers directly encounter in their daily lives are not personal capitalists per se, but rather an established economic system of production and society's accumulated technical means of production. Hence, social appearances convey the impression that machines and market forces are the real, ultimate determinants of human-social destiny, not people.

> all material wealth confronts the workers as the property of the commodity possessors...as autonomous powers, personified in their owners...Hence the rule of the capitalist over the worker is the rule of things over man, of dead labor over the living, of the product over the producer...[7]

> to them, their own social action takes the form of the action of objects which rule the producers instead of being ruled by them.[8]

Of course, in the eyes of the capitalists, the social means of production are commodities, because they are their own private possessions. And as private property, they can be treated like any other commodity—used or sold, merged or abandoned, or treated in any other manner as their owners see fit.

Marx argued that in addition to viewing the social relations of production as independent things, social agents view the historical and socially specific form of capitalist social relations of production as "natural" and "normal" relations of production. Through experience, education and habit, both workers and capitalists come to view their mutual social productive relations as economic relations conformable to the principles of human nature and the so-called "natural laws" governing the economy, i.e., as an eternally valid form for the economic relations of production.

> The advance of capitalist production develops a working class which by education, tradition and habit looks upon the requirements of that mode of production as self-evident natural laws.[9]

> [To the bourgeois economist] production...is to be presented as governed by eternal natural laws which are independent of history, and at the same time bourgeois relations are clandestinely passed off as irrefutable natural laws of society *in abstracto*.[10]

In summary, then, on one side of the social relations of production, wage-labor appears as the natural form of human labor to social agents in the capitalist mode of production: "...it is not that wage-labor appears as a socially specific form of labor, but rather that all labor appears as wage-labor by nature (presenting itself like this to those trapped within the capitalist relations of production)."[11] On the other side of the relations of production, the private ownership of the means of production by capitalists appears as the natural form for the organization and control of the social means of production. Combining the two sides, we get the capitalist social relations of production, a social relationship between people which appears as a natural relationship between "things" or factors of production. Or as Marx was to phrase this idea:

> In capital, as in money, certain specific social relations of production between people appear as relations of things to people, or else certain social relations appear as the natural properties of things in society.[12]

HOW THE PRODUCTS AND THE ECONOMIC VALUE OF THE PRODUCTS OF HUMAN LABOR APPEAR TO COMMON SENSE

Marx argued that just as the social relations of production appear as natural relations between things to the common sense of social agents in capitalism, so the "social characteristics of men's own labor [appear] as objective characteristics of the products of labor themselves."[13] In other words, according to Marx, in the marketplace, economic value appears to be determined by the exchange relationships between different commodities—and ultimately, by the value inherent in the products independent of the social labor time necessary for producing commodities. For example, the idea that commodities determine their own economic value as a result of their exchange relationships with each other is enshrined in the popular notion concerning the infamous "laws of supply and demand" which govern the marketplace. Marx argued that the gold standard popular with monetarists for measuring the economic value of commodities is representative of the notion that the products of human labor (i.e., the gold mined and retrieved by human labor) are themselves a source of economic value. Marx cites the remarks of a monetarist of his time in illustration of this common conception of economic value:

> Value (i.e. exchange-value) is a property of things, riches (i.e. use-values) of man...A man or a country is rich...A pearl or a diamond is valuable as a pearl or a diamond.[14]

Marx discusses the nature of economic value, money and the market prices of commodities in the first part of vol. 1 of *Capital*. According to Marx, with the establishment of customary rates of exchange between commodities and with the conventional use of money as the universal measure for equating the economic value of commodities, the products of human labor appear to be the source of their own economic value independent of the social labor time necessary for their production.

> What initially concerns producers in practice when they make an exchange is how much of some other product can they get for their own; in what proportions can the product be exchanged? As soon as these proportions have attained a certain customary stability, they appear to result

from the nature of the products, so that, for instance, one ton of iron and two ounces of gold appear to be equal in value, in the same way as a pound of gold and a pound of iron are equal in weight, despite their different physical and chemical properties.[15]

Marx argued that with the establishment of customary rates of exchange between commodities in the marketplace, the *mysterious* appearance is conveyed that somehow commodities form their own "social" relationships with each other and lead a life of their own independent of the social relations between human producers. Hence, what the commodity form of the products of human labor does to mystify people is to represent their own social productive relationships with each other as a social relationship between their products. What in essence is an effect of the relationship between the social labors of the producers is represented in an inverted way by the commodity form as an effect of the determination of economic value by the products themselves. Hence, the commodity form of the products of human labor is the immediate cause for the mystifying appearances of the economic value of commodities.[16]

Finally, Marx argued that with the circulation of money in the marketplace the appearance is conveyed that somehow money or investment capital has a power of generating wealth independent of human labor and social production. For example, personal savings invested in the banking system appear to bear interest independent of any connection to the system of production. Marx was to refer to this seemingly self-valorizing property of money or investment capital as the "capital fetish" or as the "personification of things":

> If capital originally appeared on the surface of circulation as the capital fetish, value-creating value, so it now presents itself again in the figure of interest-bearing capital in its most estranged and peculiar form.[17]

In summary, the products of human labor as circulated in the marketplace (i.e., consumer items and capital) appear to have their own personal powers and social qualities similar to the qualities and powers of their human producers. This "personification of things" represents one aspect of what Marx referred to as the "fetishism of commodities." In the previous subsection we examined the other aspect of this phenomenon, i.e., the "reification of the relations of production."

SEC. 7–2
THE EMPIRICAL-SOCIAL VALIDITY OF THE CATEGORIES OF COMMON SENSE AND "VULGAR" BOURGEOIS ECONOMICS

Now, Marx argued that the categories of common sense are socially valid and objective forms of thought because they reflect the empirical appearances of capitalist society, such as the wage-relations between capital and labor, the market, private property, profit-oriented system of production, etc.

> [these commonsense] forms of thought...are socially valid, and therefore objective, for the relations of production belonging to this historically determined mode of social production.[18]

In a similar vein, in vol. 3 of *Capital*, Marx argued that the commonsense conceptions held by social agents are empirically valid because they reflect their experience with the institutional structures of capitalism.

> It is...quite natural...that the actual agents of production themselves feel completely at home in these estranged and irrational forms...for these are precisely the configurations of appearance in which they move, and with which they are daily involved.[19]

Significantly, in Marx's opinion, many of the classical bourgeois political economists simply generalized from these commonsense categories to arrive at their theoretical principles. In discussing bourgeois economic theory, Marx distinguishes between certain "vulgar" bourgeois political economists and the great classical bourgeois economists like Adam Smith and David Ricardo.[20] One of the differences between the two types of bourgeois economists, according to Marx, is that the former were naive empiricists and failed to distinguish between the appearances of things and the real nature of things. He speaks of "the bourgeois economist...whose limited mentality is unable to separate the form of appearance from the thing which appears within that form."[21] In fact, Marx opined that for these vulgar economists, appearances were reality: "...in their shallowness [vulgar economists] make it a principle to worship appearances only."[22] These vulgar bourgeois economists simply adopted the categories of common sense and gave them a systematic interpretation in their economic theories.

> Vulgar economics actually does nothing more than interpret, systematize and turn into apologetics the notions of agents trapped within bourgeois relations of production.[23]

According to Marx, the evidence for substantiating the claim that bourgeois economics simply gives a theoretical interpretation to the categories of common sense is obtainable merely by examining any popular economic textbook. What we will find, according to Marx, is the rationalization and justification of the "trinity formula."

> The folly of identifying a specific social relationship of production with the thing-like qualities of certain articles simply because it presents itself in terms of certain articles is what strikes us most forcibly whenever we open any textbook on economics and see on the first page how the elements of the process of production, reduced to their basic form, turn out to be land, capital and labor.[24]

In a footnote to the above citation, Marx refers to John Stuart Mill's *Principles of Political Economy* as an example of what he means. Opening Mill's *Principles* to bk. 1, ch. 11 we find this enumeration of the "universal" elements of the productive process: "the requisities of production being labor, capital and land..."

Predictably, Mill argued that the various economic rewards "naturally deserved" for their contributions to the productive process are wages for laborers, profit for capitalists, and rent for landowners:

> As wages of the laborer are the remuneration of labor, so the profits of the capitalist are properly, according to Mr. Senior's well-chosen expression, the remuneration of abstinence. They are what he gains by forbearing to consume his capital for his own uses, and allowing it to be consumed by productive laborers for their uses...Landed propri-

etors...have a claim to a share in the distribution of the produce [because] rent [is the "natural"] effect of this monopoly...[25]

More than a century after Mill, the popularity of the "trinity formula" with economists has not waned. For example, in a contemporary college textbook for an introductory economics course we find again the "trinity formula":

[T]he scarcity of goods and services, in turn, is attributed to the scarcity of the land, labor, and capital used to produce outputs...These resources are, after all, the means (instruments) of production, the inputs whose services cooperate in the production process...to yield both the commodities that people consume, as well as produced means of production (machines, locomotives, and so on).[26]

SEC. 7–3
MARX'S CRITIQUE OF THE CATEGORIES OF COMMON SENSE AND BOURGEOIS ECONOMICS

Now, in spite of the empirical validity of the "trinity formula" and the other categories of common sense, Marx argued that these theoretical and conventional forms of thought were mystifying, irrational, and "estranged" forms of thought inadequate for apprehending the real essence of capitalism. According to Marx, capital is not a "thing" any more than human labor is wage labor by nature. Marx rejected the commonsense notion that capital, labor and monopolized land are somehow natural factors of production, each the creator of a distinct type of economic value (such as capital-profits, labor-wages, and monopolized land-rent), and each somehow unrelated to the others except when joined externally through market exchange. Marx argued that each of these factors are internally related to each other in several ways; however, it is the commodity form of the social relations of production which conceals the interconnections between these various elements of the productive process and represents the real nature of capitalist society in a mystified and estranged way.

In criticizing the methodology of the "vulgar" bourgeois economists as well as the epistemological inadequacies of the notions of common sense, Marx argued that both of these modes of thought fail to comprehend the inner connection between the various factors of production, and hence the real essence of capitalism.

> ...the mode of thought of the philistine and the vulgar economist derives...from the fact that only the immediate form of appearance of relations is reflected in their brain, but not their inner connection. Incidentally, if the latter were true, what need for science at all?[27]

As we can see from the above citation, Marx believed that it is the task of science to grasp the essential inner connections between the objects presented to common sense. One of the reasons why real essences must be distinguished from appearances, according to Marx, is that the essential interconnections between objects are not given in empirical experience. Moreover, appearances often drastically diverge from the reality of things, even presenting reality in false and inverted ways, according to Marx. Because commonsense appearance of things is quite different from the real nature of things, it is the role of science to explain the former by the latter.

> ...the analysis of the actual intrinsic relations of capitalist production is a very complicated matter and very extensive: if it is the work of science to resolve the visible, merely external movement into the true intrinsic movement, it is self-evident that conceptions which arise about the laws of production in the minds of agents of capitalist production and circulation will diverge drastically from these real laws and will merely be the conscious expression of the visible movements.[28]

Now, because the essential interconnections between objects are not given in empirical experience, Marx argued, science must make use of theory or conceptual "abstractions" to reveal the real essence of things hidden behind appearances.

> ...in the analysis of economic forms neither microscopes nor chemical reagents are of assistance. The power of abstraction must replace both.[29]

According to Marx, the correct scientific method is one which analyzes empirical data and then uses universal theoretical principles to systematize and explain the relationships and laws governing the seemingly discrete entites of concrete, empirical experience. In Marx's opinion, David Ricardo's method was scientific because by means of his labor theory of value, Ricardo attempted to demonstrate abstractly the interconnections between the various empirical forms of value (e.g., profit, rent, wages).

> Ricardo establishes the truth of his formula by deriving it from all economic relations, and by explaining in this way all phenomena, even those like ground rent, accumulation of capital and the relation of wages to profit, which at first sight seem to contradict it; it is precisely that which makes his doctrine a scientific system.[30]

> It is the great merit of classical economists to have dissolved this...autonomization and ossification of the different social elements of wealth vis-à-vis one another...by reducing interest to a part of profit and rent to the surplus value above the profit, so that they both coincide in surplus-value; by presenting the circulation process as simply a metamorphosis of forms, and finally in the immediate process of production reducing the value and surplus-value of commodities to labor. Yet even its best representative remained more or less trapped in the world of illusion...[31]

In contrast to the method of Ricardo, the vulgar bourgeois economists, according to Marx, proceeded inductively from experience, thereby generalizing into principles the categories of common sense. Marx's distinction between the inductive method characteristic of vulgar bourgeois economics and the proper deductive method of science is evident in Marx's *Introduction to a Critique of Political Economy* (1857):

> The first procedure attenuates meaningful images to abstract definitions, the second leads from abstract definitions by way of reasoning to the reproduction of the concrete situation...The latter is obviously the correct scientific method.[32]

From the pattern of these quotes we see that for Marx the distinction between real essences and empirical appearances provided a basis for demarcating scientific from ideological conceptions of social reality.

Now, for Marx, the labor theory of value was important because it provided a basis for dissolving the reified appearances of capitalism as well as demonstrating the inner connections between the various social elements of the labor process. By the labor theory of value we understand a theory of economic value which argues that human labor is the sole value creating substance, while Nature is a source of use-values which have to be appropriated by human labor in order to be transformed into economic exchange-values. If labor is the sole value-creating substance, then capital in essence represents objectified labor. Profit, rent, and the other components of economic value are the various forms for the surplus-value of labor.

However, the labor theory of value was not completely adequate for a scientific understanding of the capitalist social relations of production and an explanation of the mystifying appearances of capitalism. Still needed, according to Marx, were historical and class analyses of the origins and nature of the commodity form of the capitalist social relations of production and products of human labor. But for various reasons, all of the bourgeois economists failed to investigate the historical origins of capitalism, and, in fact, presumed that that character of the capitalist social relations of production was given and "natural."

Marx criticized Mill and other bourgeois economists for failing to distinguish between those features of the productive process (i.e., labor, means of production, raw materials) which were universally valid and therefore characteristic of all social modes of production (such as primitive communism, classical slave economies, feudal serf economies, etc.), and those features of the productive process which were historical and socially relative, and thereby characteristic only of the capitalist mode of production (e.g., wage labor, private ownership of the means of production, the "trinity formula" and the commodity form of the social relations of production). In the section entitled "Results of the Immediate Process of Production" appended to the first volume of *Capital*, Marx describes how economists mistakenly confused the historical and socially relative elements of the capitalist mode of production with those elements of the productive process which were universally valid for all social modes of production:

> By confusing the appropriation of the labor process by capital with the labor process itself, the economists trans-

form the material element of the labor process into capital...we shall see above that this illusion is one that springs from the nature of capitalist production itself. But it is evident even now that this is a very convenient method by which to demonstrate the eternal validity of the capitalist mode of production and to regard capital as an immutable natural element in human production as such...the universal features of the labor process are independent of every specific social development. The materials and means of labor, a proportion of which consists of the products of previous work, play their part in every labor process in every age and in all circumstances. If, therefore, I label them 'capital'...then I have proved the existence of capital is an eternal law of nature of human production.[33]

As Marx was to argue elsewhere in the first volume of *Capital*, the social division of labor and commodity market economy characteristic of capitalism were not typical of all other socioeconomic modes of production.

One thing is clear...Nature does not produce on the one side owners of money or commodities, and on the other men possessing nothing but their own labor-power. This relation has no natural basis, nor is its social basis one that is common to all historical periods...Capital, therefore, announces from its first appearance a new epoch in the process of production.[34]

For example, not all economic systems in history have been commodity-producing systems of production. Many economic systems in history—ancient agrarian economic systems, medieval feudalism, North American Indian tribal economic systems, and others—were not oriented towards a market system of production. Hence, the capitalist mode of production is not a universal and naturally determined form of human production. In addition, societies in history such as ancient slave economies and feudal serf economies have had a social division of labor different from the wage-labor division characteristic of capitalism. Hence, the commodity form of the capitalist social relations of production is not of a natural and universal kind.

Marx believed that this lack of historical awareness concerning the historical and socially relative character of the capitalist social relations of production and the commodity form of this relationship was something characteristic of all bourgeois political economists.

> Economists explain how production takes place in the above-mentioned relations...but what they do not explain is how these relations themselves are produced, that is, the historical movement which gives them birth.[35]

In fact, Marx argued that it was the class interests of the bourgeois political economists which predisposed them to ignore the historical origins of the commodity form of capitalist social relations of production and to preconceive these relationships as the natural and legitimate form for the social relations of production.

> [T]he vulgar economist thinks he has made a great discovery when he insists, in opposition to the revelation of the inner connectedness, that things look different in experience...But there is also another side to the question. Once insight into the connectedness has been gained, all theoretical belief in the permanent necessity of existing conditions collapses before the practical collapse. So here there is an absolute interest of the ruling class in eternalizing the thoughtless confusion. And why else are these sycophantic gossipers paid...[36]

> This [trinity] formula...corresponds to the self-interest of the dominant class, since it preaches the natural necessity and perpetual justification of their sources of income and erects this into a dogma.[37]

Marx argued that by adopting the categories of common sense as a foundation for their own theories, these vulgar economists simply gave a rational legitimacy to the "reified" appearances of capitalist social relations of production as well as a justification and apology for the social inequalities and misery which result from these social relationships.

Now, if the capitalist division of labor between two different commodity owners[38]—a social division between wage-laborers and private owners of the means of production—was not a "natural" and universal form for the social relations of production, then the big question for Marx was how this division came about in history and how its historical development contributed to the subsequent reified and fetishistic appearances of capitalism. At this point, the younger Marx's theory of alienation became very important to the mature Marx's analyses and explanations in *Capital*.

According to the *Economic and Philosophical Manuscripts* of the young Marx, human labor and the products of human labor can appear in a mystifying and dominating form only if workers have lost control over the conditions of their labor and consequently, over the products of their labor.

> Till now we have been considering...the alienation of the worker only in one of its aspects, i.e., the worker's relationship to the product of his labor. But the estrangement is manifested not only in the result but in the act of production, within the producing activity, itself. How could the worker come to face the product of his activity as a stranger, were it not that in the very act of production he was estranging himself from himself?[39]

Now, if workers have lost control over the "means of life" and the "products" of their labor, this can only mean, according to the young Marx, that the activity of production and the products of labor belong to someone other than the worker, namely the capitalist. This private ownership of the means of production by someone other than workers and the control over the product of labor by someone other than the producers are necessary conditions for the alienation of human labor. The origins of alienation in private property are commented on in the following passage from the *Economic and Philosophical Manuscripts* of 1844:

> ...if the product of his labor...is for him an alien, hostile, powerful object independent of him, then his position towards it is such that someone else is master of this object...If his own activity is to him related as an unfree activity, then he is related to it as an activity performed in the service, under the domination, the coercion, and the yoke of another man.[40]

Some twenty years after these youthful writings, Marx in *Capital* essentially reproduced his earlier theory of alienated labor to describe and interpret a historical process leading to the development of a social division of labor between two different commodity owners: wage-laborers and capitalists. According to Marx in *Capital*, the historical origins of the social division of labor in capitalism arose through a process of primitive accumulation whereby the producers were forcibly separated or "alienated" from the means of production and transformed into wage-laborers, while the means of production through a succession of "hostile takeovers" were eventually appropriated by a small number of capitalists as their own private possession.

> The capital-relation presupposes a complete separation between the workers and the ownership of the conditions for the realization of their labor. As soon as capitalist production stands on its own feet, it not only maintains this separation, but reproduces it on a constantly extending scale. The process, therefore, which creates the capital-relation can be nothing other than the process which divorces the worker from the ownership of the conditions of his own labor; it is a process which operates two transformations, whereby the social means of subsistence and production are turned into capital, and the immediate producers are turned into wage-labourers. So-called primitive accumulation is nothing else than the historical process of divorcing the producer from the means of production.[41]

In essence, as Marx describes it, primitive accumulation was a historical process whereby in becoming wage-laborers human producers lost control over the means of production and consequently lost control over the products of their labor as well. This control passed over to somone other than the workers, namely the capitalists. Hence, primitive accumulation was for the mature Marx the origin of what the young Marx had referred to as the alienation of human labor arising from private property. For him this "original alienation" underlay the development of the commodity form of capitalist social relations of production and was the foundation for the subsequent reified and fetishistic appearances of the social reality of capitalism.

Now, how does the alienation of human labor in capitalism provide the foundation for the reified and fetishistic appearances of capitalist social reality? According to Marx, as a result of the original alienation of human labor arising from the primitive accumulation of capital, capitalists were able to gain control of the means of production, the organization and conduct of work, and the products of human labor. By organizing and controlling the work activities of wage-laborers as well as the products of their work, the capitalists were able to exploit the wage-laborers. In turn, the exploitation of wage-labor provided the means by which capitalists could appropriate the unpaid surplus-value produced by workers. According to Marx's labor theory of value, this surplus-value appropriated from the productivity of workers provides the basis for all other forms of value such as the profits owned and controlled by capitalists.

If, for example, capitalists decide to reinvest their profits in the production process by purchasing new means of production, their profits thereby would be transformed into objective forms of capital such as machines and physical plants. However, because capital has its source in the surplus-value produced by human labor, Marx argued, in essence capital is objectified labor.

Although capital is essentially objectified labor because it is owned and controlled by someone other than the workers, capital *appears* to the workers as an autonomous, self-generated entity. And because the workers do not themselves control the various consumer products they produce, the economic value of their products *appears* to be determined solely by independent market forces (such as the laws of supply and demand). In short, as a result of the alienation and exploitation of human labor by capitalists and the commodity form of their products, workers cannot *perceive* that the wealth manifest in the commodity world of bourgeois society is their own creation.

In vol. 1 of *Capital*, Marx describes the reifying and dominating aspects of the alienation of human labor resulting from the control of the social production process and products of human labor by capitalists:

> Since, before he enters the process, his own labor has already been alienated from him, appropriated by the capitalist, and incorporated with capital, it now, in the course of this process, constantly objectifies itself so that it becomes a product alien to him. Since the process of production is also the process of the consumption of labor-power by the capitalist, the worker's product is not only constantly converted into commodities, but also into capi-

tal, i.e. into value that sucks up the worker's value-creating power, means of subsistence that actually purchase human beings, and means of production that employ the people who are doing the producing. Therefore the worker himself constantly produces objective wealth, in the form of capital, an alien power that dominates and exploits him.[42]

According to Marx, because of the alienation and exploitation of human labor in capitalism, all of the value-creating powers of human labor *appear* as the self-valorizing powers of capital. Capital, in other words, is a reified form for the essential value-creating power of human labor. Marx describes this reified nature and seemingly self-valorizing powers of capital as the fetishism which attaches to the products of human labor as a result of the alienation of human labor in capitalism.

> The objective conditions essential to the realization of labor are alienated from the worker and become manifested as fetishes endowed with a will and soul of their own. Commodities, in short, appear as the purchasers of persons.[43]

> It is not only the workers' products which are transformed into independent powers, the products as masters and buyers of their producers, but also the social powers and interconnecting forms of this labor also confronts them as properties of their products.[44]

> The mystification inherent in the capital-relation is that the value-sustaining power of labor appears as the self-supporting power of capital; the value-creating power of labor as the self-valorizing power of capital.[45]

In a similar vein, Marx again refers to the mystifying and false appearances which characterize the products of human labor as a result of the alienation of human labor in capitalism:

> It is the natural property of living labor to keep old value in existence while it creates new. Hence...labor maintains and perpetuates an always increasing capital-value in an ever-renewed form. This natural power of labor appears as a power incorporated into capital for the latter's own self-

preservation, just as the productive forces of social labor appear as inherent characteristics of capital, and just as the constant appropriation of surplus labor by the capitalists appear as the constant self-valorization of capital. All the powers of labor project themselves as powers of capital...[46]

These passages demonstrate that Marx uses the term "alienation" in *Capital* and that this concept was important for him in explaining the origins of the commodity form of capitalist social relations of production and thereby the ultimate origins of the reified and fetishistic appearances of social reality in capitalism. The conception of alienation he propounds includes all the component features of this phenomenon as first described by him in his *Economic and Philosophical Manuscripts* of 1844. Hence, what we have found here in Marx's mature work, *Capital*, is the conception of the alienation of labor with all the various components—the reifying, mystifying and dominating aspects of alienation—which were first outlined by the young Marx.

In summary, in following Marx's critique of the categories of common sense and "vulgar" bourgeois economists we discovered the importance of the essence/appearance distinction to Marx, and how this distinction provides a basis for distinguishing between scientific and ideological conceptions. We contrasted the importance of Marx's historical perspective with the ahistorical perspective of bourgeois economists. In doing so, we discovered the importance of the concept of alienation to Marx's analysis of the ultimate origins of the reified and fetishistic appearances of capitalist social reality

SEC. 7–4
ANALOGY OF THE FETISHISM OF COMMODITIES
TO RELIGIOUS REFLECTIONS

In previous sections, I have documented and discussed how for Marx the commodity form of the products of human labor and the social relations of production give rise to the inverted, reified and fetishistic appearances of capitalist society. However, while the commodity form is the proximate cause of a pervasive social false consciousness in capitalism, the ultimate cause of the mystifying appearances of capitalism is the historical and social alienation of human producers from the means of production and their products. It was this historical and social alienation which made possible the social division between two different commodity owners and the workers' loss of control over their products, according to Marx.

In fact, in his concluding remarks concerning the ultimate origins of the fetishism of commodities, Marx alludes to the idea of alienation. According to Marx, the various formulas and categories characteristic of the bourgeois economists and the common sense of social agents all bear the symptoms of the alienation of labor in capitalism.

> [T]hese formulas...bear the unmistakable stamp of belonging to a social formation in which the process of production has mastery over man, instead of the opposite...[47]

In other words, because the producers do not have control over their own products, workers will not be able to recognize that society is their own creation. Instead, society will appear to them as an alien objectivity governed by powers and laws beyond their control.

For example, even though capital and the profits of capital are forms of objectified labor and the surplus value produced by workers, because workers do not control the products of their labor, capital and profits came to appear as self-generated forms of value. Furthermore, because the commodities they produce are not controlled by their own conscious social plans but are allowed to be exchanged freely in the marketplace, their own products can come to control them by means of the external market forces and laws governing the exchange relationships between commodities. Finally, since workers cannot participate in the decision-making process of corporations because of the capitalist division into labor and management, workers have no control over *how* things will be produced or *what* things will be produced. Hence, the "trinity formula" and "laws of supply and demand" popular with bourgeois economists reflect the alienation of human producers from their work and products, and the domination of the producers by their own products in capitalism. Marx said of this inverted, alienated situation reflected in the trinity formula and other categories of common sense,

> Their own movement within society has for them the form of a movement made by things, and these things, far from being under their control, in fact, control them.[48]

In a move which shows the influence of Feuerbach, Marx compares the inverted and fetishistic appearances arising from the commodity form of capitalist society with the mystifying ideas of religion. According to Marx, just as in religion "the products of the human brain appear as autonomous figures endowed with a life of their own, which enter into relations with each other and with the human race," so the products of human labor appear to be endowed with self-valorizing powers of their own. In both cases, the creations of human beings appear to them as alien entities with powers opposed to their own.[49]

To continue the analogy further, just as in religion people view themselves as "subject to higher beings," so in the marketplace workers view themselves as subject to the "inevitable" laws of profit and "supply and demand." Hence, just as religion expresses the fact that people are not yet masters of their situation, so the trinity formula and other formulas of bourgeois political economy express the fact that the workers do not have control of their situation. Thus, just as religion for Feuerbach expressed the alienation of human consciousness, the formulas of bourgeois political economy expressed for Marx the alienation of human labor.

In several other passages in *Capital* Marx also compared the mystifying and inverted character of the forms of appearance of capitalism with the mystifying and inverted nature of religious ideas. For example, in vol. 1, Marx argued that the basis for the inverted ideological appearances of capitalism is a real inversion between the producers and their products in capitalism: the inversion of subject and object.

> Hence the rule of the capitalist over the worker is the rule of things over man,...of the product over the producer... Thus at the level of material production...we find the same situation that we find in religion at the ideological level, namely the inversion of the subject into object and vice versa...What we are confronted by here is the alienation of man from his own labor...[50]

Hence, the ultimate basis for the upside-down view of reality characteristic of the common sense of social agents in capitalism and "vulgar" bourgeois economists is the real inversion between the producers and their products, an inversion which arises, according to Marx, from the alienation of the producers from their products.

Interestingly, in 1844 Marx also drew an analogy between the alienation of workers from their products and the alienated consciousness of religion. According to the young Marx,

> Just as in religion the spontaneous activity of the human imagination...operates independently of the individual—that is, operates on him as an alien, divine or diabolical activity—so is the worker's activity not his spontaneous activity. It belongs to another; it is the loss of his self.[51]

In addition, in his essay "On James Mill" (1844), the young Marx compared the power of money in the economic world with the religious conception concerning the power of God.

> It is clear that this mediator [use of money as the medium for exchange] has now become a real God, for the mediator is the real power over and what it mediates to me.[52]

Hence, from his youthful to his mature writings, Marx found it appropriate to compare social and economic ideologies with religious ideologies. Furthermore, the principle of inversion Marx learnt from Feuerbach proved to be as useful in his mature writings on social and economic ideologies as it did in his earlier writings on political ideologies. Even in his mature writings, Marx continued to find use for the "camera obscura" metaphor for describing the ideological conceptions arising from reality. As we have documented, according to Marx's analysis in *Capital*, the appearances of reality are themselves inverted.

Now, Marx argued in *Capital* that the liberation of human consciousness from the quasi-religious, ideological conception of society can occur only if the producers regain control over their products and regulate the production and distribution of their products according to a collective social plan.

> [T]he religious reflections of the real world can...vanish only when the practical relations of everyday life between man and man, and man and nature, generally present themselves to him in a transparent and rational form. The veil is not removed from the countenance of the social life-process... until it becomes production by freely associated men, and stands under their conscious and planned control.[53]

ALIENATION, THE FETISHISM OF COMMODITIES, AND IDEOLOGY

In a related vein, Marx argued in the *Grundrisse* (1857) that progress in the overcoming of the alienated false consciousness can come about only when workers recognize that capital and the commodities in the marketplace are their own products.

> [W]hen the worker recognizes the products as being his own and condemns the separation of the conditions of his realization as an intolerable imposition, it will be an enormous progress in consciousness...[54]

Hence, alienated false consciousness can be overcome by restoring to the producers control over their products, i.e., by reversing what is inverted in capitalism. In overcoming the alienation of the producers from their products the roots of social false consciousness can be eradicated.

Not surprisingly, Engels in his later writings expressed views similar to Marx's concerning the origins and overcoming of social false consciousness. For example, in his *Origins of the Family, Private Property and the State* (1884), Engels accounts for the origins of alienated false consciousness by saying it comes from the alienation of human producers from their products, an alienation resulting from the emergence of primitive market relationships and a social division of labor in precapitalist Western society. Engels argued that in ancient "communistic" societies, this alienated false consciousness did not exist, because in these "communistic communities" the producers had control over their products, there existed a nonhierarchical division of labor, and because the producers treated their products as use-values and not as commodities. And because the products of labor "could not grow beyond the control of the producer," Engels argued, no alien beings could arise having "any strange, phantom powers against them, as is the case regularly and inevitably under civilization."[55]

Like Marx, Engels argued that alienated false consciousness can be overcome only when "anarchy in social production gives place to a social regulation of production upon a definite plan."[56] Engels proposed this solution in his pamphlet "Socialism: Utopian and Scientific" (1880). According to this pamphlet, a true understanding of the nature and laws governing society can be effected only by means of the socialization of the means of production and the regulation of production according to a social plan. As with Marx, for Engels the social revolution promises to effect a revolution in human consciousness as well.

> [T]he laws of his own social action, hitherto standing face to face with man as laws of Nature foreign to, and dominating him, will then be used with full understanding, and so mastered by him. Man's own social organization, hitherto confronting him as a necessity imposed by Nature and history, now becomes the result of his own free action. The extraneous objective forces that have hitherto governed history pass under the control of man himself.[57]

Thus, the textual evidence from the writings of both Marx and Engels support the interpretation that in their opinion, the form of false consciousness we have discussed in this chapter has its origins in the alienation of human producers from their products.

In summary, we have discussed in this section why it is that appearances necessarily represent the reality of capitalism in an inverted manner. According to Marx, because of the alienation of human producers from their products in capitalism, appearances necessarily will represent the reality of capitalism in inverted, fetishistic manner. In comparing these inverted, "fetishistic" appearances of capitalism to the inverted conceptions of religion, we discovered the influence of Feuerbach on Marx's analyses in *Capital*. Like religious ideologies, the social and economic ideologies of capitalism necessarily convey an inverted picture of the world. For Marx as for Feuerbach, the principle of inversion is important for analyzing the ideological conceptions arising from alienation. Finally, we discussed how Engels shares similar views with Marx concerning the origins and overcoming of social false consciousness.

SEC. 7–5
CONCLUSION: ALIENATION AND THE ESSENCE/APPEARANCE DISTINCTION IN CAPITAL

Throughout this chapter we have demonstrated the importance to Marx of the distinction between the essence and appearances of capitalism. We've noted how Marx utilized this distinction in *Capital* for demarcating scientific from ideological conceptions. The importance of this distinction for understanding Marx's theory of ideology in *Capital* has been noted by a number of commentators. For example, John Mepham in his essay "Theory Ideology in *Capital*" states:

It is a distinction that contains a substantial epistemological theory about the relation between thought and reality and about the origins of illusions about reality. This theory is that the origins of ideological illusions are in the phenomenal forms of reality itself.[58]

Norman Geras, in his essay on "Marx and the Critique of Political Economy," notes how Marx's essence/appearance distinction constitutes a basic methodological requirement for all sciences.

In such passages Marx presents the conceptual distinction between appearance and reality as a form of scientificity as such, by notifying us that the method he is applying in political economy is simply a general requirement for arriving at valid knowledge, one which he has taken over from the other sciences where it has long been established.[59]

Finally, Derek Sayer in his book *Marx's Method: Ideology, Science and Critique in "Capital"* notes how Marx's account of the disparity between empirical appearances and the real relations of capitalism provides a basis for understanding the experiential origins of false, ideological beliefs.

Marx's view of consciousness allows but one type of explanation of ideology. If ideological accounts of the world are false, then their falsity must be explained in terms of the nature of experience which is capable of sustaining such illusions...Such divergence of forms and relations provides the basis for Marx's conception of ideology and at the same time defines the project of his science.[60]

As much as I agree with these commentators that Marx's essence/appearance distinction provides the basis for demarcating scientific from ideological conceptions, I believe we also need to know why it was important to Marx to insist upon this distinction. As Norman Geras remarked in his essay on Marx and political economy, we need to know why Marx believed it was necessary to extend to the social sciences an "abstract procedural rule" characteristic of the natural science.

Taken on its own, the answer does not yet specify why it is appropriate to extend the methods of astronomy to the subject matter of political economy.[61]

As I have shown, Marx called upon political economists to distinguish between the essence and appearance of capitalism because the appearances of capitalism necessarily represent the reality of capitalism in an inverted and false way. According to Marx, the commodity forms of the immediate appearance of capitalist society conceal the real nature of capitalism as well as representing the reality of this society in several distorted ways. For example, in discussing Marx's theory of the fetishism of commodities, we examined how the commodity form of the social relations of production represent human relations in a reified way as thing-like relationships between commodities or factors of production. We then discussed how the commodity form of the products of human labor represent the self-valorizing powers of human labor in a fetishistic way as self-valorizing powers belonging to the products of human labor. In discussing the dominant ideological conceptions arising from the wage-relationship between wage-labor and capital, we considered how this commodity form represents exploitative social-economic relationships as fair and just relationships, and socioeconomic relations of domination and dependence as relationships of freedom and equality. In short, in Marx's opinion, the commodity forms of the social relations of production and of the products of human labor in capitalism are immediately responsible for the misconceptions and false perceptions social agents have concerning the real nature of capitalism, i.e., their social false consciousness.

However, as I argued, for Marx the commodity forms of the appearance of capitalism are not sufficient for understanding the origins of the mystifying appearances of capitalism. According to Marx, one needs to account for the origins of the commodity forms of appearance, and hence the real social and historical conditions which made it possible for the products of human labor and the socioeconomic relationships between people to appear in mystifying ways. In other words, one needs to investigate the social and historical causes which transformed human labor into a commodity, and the products of human labor into commodites. Finally, one needs to explain how it is possible for the products and commodities of human labor to dominate their producers.

We discovered that for Marx, the key to explicating the ultimate origins of the reifying, fetishistic, and inverted appearances is the concept of alienation. Consequently, we demonstrated the importance of the young Marx's conception of alienation to the mature

Marx's analyses in *Capital*. In doing so, we avoided the error of omission made by many commentators who fail to see how the concept of alienation was important to the mature Marx for explaining the ultimate reified, fetishistic, and inverted appearances of capitalism as well as for justifying his methodological requirement that the essence and appearances of capitalism be distinguished.[62]

8

Conclusion

When I began this book, I assumed the burden of proving the claim that Marx had a concept of false consciousness and that contemporary attempts to attribute to Marx a nonepistemological, functionalist concept of ideology as the practical rationality of a class were in error. From the perspective of these functionalist interpreters, the notion of false consciousness is, in the words of Joe McCarney,

> ...an aberration, an instance of that curious uncertainty of touch [Engels] could sometimes display, even on matters supposedly central to doctrines held jointly with Marx...[1]

As opposed to this "aberrant" notion, what Marx is purported to have meant by ideology, according to McCarney's version of the functionalist interpretation, is the following:

> ...the role of ideas in the class struggle constitutes the substance of Marx's conception of ideology. To say this is to imply a systematic indifference on his part to other sorts of consideration; an indifference that extends to the cognitive status of the forms of consciousness that fall within the ideological realm. For Marx, it may be said, ideology is not an epistemological category.[2]

In accordance with this functionalist approach to social ideologies, the main problem with "social Darwinist" ideologies or "supply-side economics" ideologies is not that they are false ideas but that they are bourgeois conservative ideas. In the functionalist view bourgeois ideas are not always a problem, because in the overthrow of feudalism bourgeois ideologies served revolutionary and hence progressive interests. From the functionalist perspective what matters is not the truth or falsity of an ideology but how an ideology "functions" in the class struggle (i.e., is it progressive or reactionary? conservative or radical?) and what class interests an ideology serves (i.e., ruling classes or the oppressed).

Now, I do not deny the contention that the social-political significance of ideas was important to Marx and that the study of ideology for Marx was a study of ideas and modes of thought having social-practical significance for social agents in class-divided societies. But as this functionalist interpretation stands, it is deficient and textually inaccurate, because for Marx ideologies are *false* collective ideas and *false* collective modes of thinking which have significance for the outcome of class-divided societies. In other words, an ideological consciousness is a false consciousness for Marx, and the class struggle for Marx was a political struggle conducted with a false consciousness.

Thus, I have criticized how the functionalist reading of Marx omits the centrality of Marx's *critique* of the *false* ideological perceptions and interpretations of social agents. For example, I have shown how Marx criticized ruling classes in general and the bourgeoisie in particular for misrepresenting their particular group interests as the interest of the majority.[3] It was this type of collective fallacious thinking on the part of ruling classes in history which Marx criticized as the distinctive false consciousness of dominant social classes.[4] In addition, we have examined Marx's views concerning how even ruling classes can be deceived by the appearances of their societies, as well as self-deceived by their ideologies.

We examined Marx's (and Engels's) views on how the ideologies of the oppressed deluded and distorted their social understanding, and generally prevented these oppressed groups from having a clear and rational view of the historical and class dynamics of their situation and their real (as opposed to ideological) political aims.[5] Hence, if anything characterizes the ideological rationality of the oppressed proletariat, it is the misguided nature of their "practical" thinking, according to Marx.

In short, epistemological analyses of the "practical" and the "commonsense" social consciousness of social actors are quite important to Marx because in his view the practical social consciousness of social agents is a false consciousness. In addition, as I have shown, for Marx ideologies *qua* beliefs are shared, *false* beliefs social agents hold concerning: (a) their social institutions (e.g., about economic matters, about the nature and functions of the political state, etc.); (b) the utility of dominant social values (e.g., the social utility of the profit motive, selfishness, competition, etc); (c) the justice of their social relationships (e.g., market relationships as relations of "freedom, equality and justice"); (d) the validity and origins of the ideas in their heads (e.g., social and historically relative ideas as eternally valid, *a priori* ideas); (e) scientific methodologies and philosophies (e.g., "vulgar bourgeois economic" and idealist philosophies); and (f) the common self-understandings of social agents (e.g., an "atomistic individualist" self-identity or a nationalist self-identity—both of which exclude a class consciousness of social realities).

Accordingly, it is my opinion that the functionalist reading of Marx is in error because it assumes that the cognitive content of ideologies were irrelevant to Marx and that falsehood was not an essential characteristic of ideological ideas for Marx.

As I have argued, the functionalist conception of ideology has various shortcomings. For example, while functionalists may reject the relevance of epistemological evaluations to ideological analysis, they themselves must presume some kind of rational, hence epistemological, criteria when distinguishing between "progressive" and "reactionary" ideologies. In addition, the functionalist interpretation has implications for Marx's critique of ideology which I find to be unacceptable. For the functionalist the problem with "bourgeois ideology" is not that it is false or unreasonable, but that it is "bourgeois" or that it serves the conservative interests of the bourgeoisie.[6] If this were the case, then when Marx criticized ideologies, he in essence would be engaged in a kind of fallacious *ad hominem* attack against his class opponents rather than be engaged in any rational critique of their ideas. Marx's criticisms would simply amount to saying: "Well, you only think that way because you are bourgeois (i.e., because of your social position) or because it serves your class interests to think that way."

But as we have seen, when Marx's criticized ideologies he did so on the ground that they were false or unreasonable. That is the case with Marx's critique of the trinity formula as ideology; with Marx's critique of the inverted and alienated methodology of idealist social sciences; and with Marx's critique of the nonscientific methodology of vulgar bourgeois economy. Hence, I believe that it is a serious distortion of Marx's views to suggest that for him epistemological considerations were irrelevant to his critique of ideologies.[7]

Finally, I have argued that the nonepistemological reading of Marx is incorrect in its assertion that Marx used a functional criterion to distinguish between science and ideology (e.g., science qua theoretical reason and knowledge function; ideology qua practical reason, noncognitive social function) rather than a true/false criterion.[8] As I have shown, Marx distinguished between science and ideology according to a true/false criterion and this is evident throughout his writings. For example, it appears in his critique of idealist perspectives in the social sciences and his advocacy of a materialist approach; in his distinction between societal appearances and social essences; and in his methodological dictum that social scientists should distinguish between the social conceptions in the minds of social agents with their actual social realities as known by means of scientific materialist analyses. In short, for Marx science is distinguished from ideology both by its methods and its relative truth.

In summary, I fail to see any validity in the claim that Marx was "indifferent to epistemological considerations" and that functionalist interpretations of ideology were his sole concern. If anything, epistemological considerations of ideology were extremely important to him because in his view false and illusory social views were practically disadvantageous for both oppressed groups and society as a whole. He believed that ideologies were practically disadvantageous to the oppressed because ideology prevented them from having a true insight into the social causes of their misery as well as a true understanding of their political aims. In this respect, I believe it is significant to note how Marx resisted the demands of his political colleagues to give a "higher, universal and ideal orientation" to the political platform of the communist working class party and insisted upon a class-conscious perspective in theory and practice.[9]

Marx's criticisms suggest that dominant social ideologies are practically disadvantageous for society as a whole because they prevent societies from having a rational and comprehensive understanding of their own quasi-natural "laws of development." In addition,

Marx's criticisms suggest that dominant social ideologies lead to a collective "narrow-mindedness" or "one-dimensional" thinking in that the prevailing social consciousness is unable to envision alternatives to the status quo's ways of doing things.[10]

As for the contention that the notion of false consciousness was an "aberration," I think it would be more accurate to say that the forms of false consciousness noted in the writings of Marx and Engels represent the culmination of a history-making theoretical reflection concerning: (1) misguided and alienated modes of social consciousness; (2) the common mind's social and historical unconsciousness; (3) social delusionary thinking; and (4) a falsified and distorted collective understanding and perception of reality.

The identification of forms of false consciousness within the writings of Marx and Engels "echoed" the diverse theoretical insights of Marx's (and Engels's) predecessors—i.e., Bacon, Holbach, Helvetius, Hegel, and Feuerbach. Though each of Marx's predecessors had something distinctive to say about the nature and origins of the ideological false consciousness, at the same time, each thinker built upon the views of his predecessor. As a result, an overall theoretical development towards new and more sophisticated conceptions of the ideological false consciousness materialized in the course of history. To briefly recapitulate the distinctive moments and advances in this historical-theoretical development, we must begin with Francis Bacon's theory of idols.

Francis Bacon laid the foundations for the modern theory of the ideological false consciousness by defining false consciousness in the most basic terms as a false understanding and distorted perception of reality. Bacon's complaint that ideological ideas were responsible for deflecting human thought away from empirical studies of natural realities laid the foundations for one version of the alienated false consciousness. Bacon was to remark concerning the distorted nature of human thought:

> ...let men please themselves as they will in admiring and...adoring the human mind, [but] this is certain: that as an uneven mirror distorts the rays of objects according to its own figure and section, so the mind, when it receives impressions of objects through the senses, cannot be trusted to report them truly, but in forming its notions mixes up its own nature with the nature of things...[11]

Bacon's views were to be taken up by his immediate successors, the *philosophes* of the French Enlightenment, and they in turn added a distinctive social dimension to Bacon's conceptions. According to the conspiratorial views of the *philosophes*, ruling elites deliberately took advantage of the ignorance and credulousness of their subjects to give a false direction to their thoughts thereby leading to a misguided social consciousness. These power elites, particularly priests, conspired to fill the common mind with purely imaginary and nonsensical metaphysical and religious ideas which prevented the common person from understanding his/her real interests and the common good. For Holbach and the French Enlightenment, the result was a misguided and manipulated social false consciousness.

> Men will always deceive themselves by abandoning experience to follow imaginary systems…All the errors and all the disputes of men, have their foundation in this, that they have renounced experience and the evidence of their senses, to give themselves up to the guidance of notions which they have believed infused or innate, although in reality they are no more than the effect of a distempered imagination; of prejudices in which they have been instructed from their infancy; with which habit has familiarized them; and which authority has obliged them to conserve.[12]

Following the *philosophes*, Hegel in his philosophy of history was to strike a new note regarding the nature of ideological deception. While the *philosophes* had criticized their political rulers for being self-conscious, ideological deceivers, Hegel suggested that all history-making agents including the power elite of history were themselves deceived by their ideologies and unaware of the real historical aims their ideologies served. As Hegel said, "Such individuals had no consciousness of the general Idea they were unfolding…"[13]

In short, for Hegel social agents were for the most part unconscious or oblivious to the systematic historical forces impelling their thoughts and actions. At the same time, Hegel suggested that social agents had illusions about their real motives; hence for Hegel, there was a kind of deluded quality to the common mind's historical unconsciousness.

Hegel's theory of alienation suggested a new way for conceiving the alienated false consciousness. For Bacon and the *philosophes*, human thought had become alienated from reality as a result of being dominated by imaginary ideas. Hegel, however, argued that all of the realities created by thought invariably acquire an "alien" appearance as a result of the reification or projection of thought. All thought involved false consciousness because consciousness cannot recognize itself in the objective products created by its projections. As Hegel remarked, concerning this sense of the alienated false consciousness:

> Although this world has come into being through individuality, it is for self-consciousness immediately an alienated world which has the form of a fixed and solid reality over against it...This world is, however, a spiritual entity...its existence is the work of self-consciousness, but it is also an alien reality already present and given, a reality which has a being of its own and in which it does not recognize itself.[14]

This Hegelian version of the alienated false consciousness suggested to Feuerbach a new way for conceiving the religious false consciousness. According to Feuerbach, in the ideas of religion human beings had unknowingly symbolized their own essential nature and aspirations in alien and inverted, supernatural forms. As Feuerbach was to remark concerning the religious false consciousness,

> Religion is a dream in which our conceptions and emotions appear to us as separate existences, beings out of ourselves.[15]

The theoretical advance Feuerbach achieved in understanding religion in this rather Hegelian way was to show how collective ideological illusions could be expressions of meaningful and essential aspirations though appearing in symbolic and distorted forms. In this way, Feuerbach's theory of ideology went beyond that of the *philosophes* who for the latter conceived of all ideological ideas as a bunch of meaningless nonsense.

However, while Feuerbach's theory went beyond the views of the *philosophes* in disclosing the objective content concealed within ideological forms (he claimed that "the secret of theology is anthropology"), Feuerbach's critique of religion lacked the political and social awareness characteristic of the French Enlightenment's critique of religion. For Marx, there was something about both theories he liked as well as elements in both which he disliked.

While Marx was appreciative of the social and political dimensions of the *philosophes'* critique of religion, he argued that there must be a more profound systematic basis for social false consciousness than ruling-class conspiracies and propaganda. Furthermore, for Marx the emotional attachment of oppressed groups to the religious and political ideologies of the ruling class could only be explained if religious and patriotic sentiments had some positive and genuine meaning for the oppressed.[16]

From Marx's standpoint Feuerbach's theory helped to explain why ruling-class illusions could be meaningful to the oppressed, but Feuerbach was blind to the fact that religious sentiments and human alienation were ultimately the product of societal and historical conditions.[17] In other words, for Marx, if the key to understanding the misguided collective imagination was human alienation, and if the secret of human alienation was society, then the ultimate origins of the collective false consciousness existed in the objective conditions of society.

In turning to an examination of objective social conditions for explaining ideological false consciousness, Marx's theory once again drew upon the theories of Hegel and the Baconian-French materialist tradition. Marx's theory incorporated Hegel's insights regarding how ignorance of systematic historical forces fosters false consciousness and how alienated false consciousness is rooted in the alien appearances of objective reality. It drew upon the Baconian-French materialist tradition in explaining how ideological ideas originate from and "reflect" or "echo" societal appearances.[18]

At the same time, the "mature" Marx didn't discard Feuerbachian principles in his analysis of the "alien" appearances of capitalist society. For as Marx was to remark in *Capital*, there was a certain quasi-religious quality to the "alien" and "inverted" appearances of capitalist society, and the concomitant false common sense of social agents in capitalism. Marx summarized this in *Capital*:

> It has been shown...how not merely at the level of ideas, but also in reality, [that] the social characteristics of his labor confront the worker as something not merely alien, but hostile and antagonistic...Thus at the level of material production...we find the same situation that we find in religion at the ideological level, namely, the inversion of

the subject into object and vice versa...What we are confronted by here is the alienation of man from his own labor.[19]

By incorporating the diverse insights from the Baconian-French Enlightenment tradition and the Hegelian-Feuerbachian tradition, Marx was able to explain why the ideologies of the ruling classes could dominate the social consciousness as "natural and self-evident" forms of thought. Marx remarked concerning the systematic origins and illusory nature of dominant ideological conceptions,

> It is also quite natural...that the actual agents of production themselves feel completely at home in these estranged and irrational forms...for these are precisely the configurations of appearance in which they move, and with which they are daily involved...All the notions of justice held by both the worker and the capitalist, all the mystifications of the capitalist mode of production, all capitalism's illusions about freedom...have as their basis the forms of appearance... which makes the actual relation invisible, and indeed presents to the eye the precise opposite of that relation.[20]

As we have seen, it was these collective illusions which intellectuals "idealized" in their theories[21] and which social classes used in their political struggles with each other.

In summary, the forms of false consciousness found in the writings of Marx and Engels represent the influences of a diverse heritage. Some might argue that because of the diverse meanings of false consciousness, Marx's notion of the ideological false consciousness is incoherent. In reply to this criticism, I have tried to show how the various senses of false consciousness denote different kinds of ideological errors and modes of collective false thinking criticized by Marx. Hence, instead of criticizing the notion as incoherent, we should talk about the rich complexity conveyed by Marx's notion of false consciousness.

For Marx, these diverse forms of false consciousness all shared a "common denominator":[22] a social consciousness which takes certain false things to be true about matters having significance to the outcome of class-divided societies. For Marx these forms of false collective thinking are determined by various kinds of social factors (such as the social division of labor, social position and class interests, empirical forms of societal appearances, education, etc.). Finally, Marx thought it was in the interest of both the oppressed proletariat and society in general to reject its social illusions because in the final analysis false ideas do not really emancipate or serve the common good.

Notes

CHAPTER ONE. INTRODUCTION

1. Engels, Letter to Mehring, 14 July 1898, reprinted in *The Marx-Engels Reader*, ed. Robert C. Tucker (New York: W. W. Norton, 1972), p. 648–49.

2. Cf. the analysis of Engels's definition by Richard Norman in his *The Moral Philosophers: An Introduction to Ethics* (Oxford: Clarendon Press, 1983), p. 182: ideology is a "product of motives which remain unrecognized by the thinker himself."

3. Martin Seliger, *The Marxist Conception of Ideology: A Critical Essay* (New York: Cambridge University Press, 1977), p. 30.

4. David Braybrooke, S.V. "Ideology," *The Encyclopedia of Philosophy*.

5. Cf. Joe McCarney, *The Real World of Ideology* (Atlantic Highlands, N.J.: Humanities Press, 1980), p. 80:

> [T]he thesis of this essay is that the role of ideas in the class struggle constitutes the substance of Marx's conception of ideology. To say this is to imply a systematic indifference on his part to other sorts of consideration; an indifference that extends to the cognitive status of the forms of consciousness that fall within the ideological realm. For Marx, it may be said, ideology is not an epistemological category.

6. Ibid., pp. 93–94.

7. Ibid., p. 95.

8. Ibid., p. 97.

9. Cf. Paul Hirst, *On Law and Ideology* (Atlantic Highlands, N.J.: Humanities Press, 1979); John B. Thompson, *Studies in the Theory of Ideology* (Berkeley: University of California Press, 1984); Chantel Mouffe, "Hegemony and Ideology in Gramsci," in *Culture, Ideology, and Social Process: A Reader*, ed. Tony Bennett et al. (London: Open University Press, 1981).

10. David McLellan, *Ideology* (Minneapolis: University of Minnesota Press, 1986), p. 18.

11. Ibid.

12. Cf. Jorge Larrain, *The Concept of Ideology* (Athens: University of Georgia Press, 1979) and *Marxism and Ideology* (London: Macmillan Press, 1983).

13. Louis Althusser, *For Marx* (London: NLB Verso Press, 1965), p. 231.

14. Istvan Meszaros, *Philosophy, Ideology, and Social Science* (New York: St. Martin's Press, 1986), p. xii.

15. Ibid., pp. xiii, xv–xvi.

16. Alex Callinicos, *Marxism and Philosophy* (Oxford: Oxford University Press, 1983), p. 135.

17. For the skeptical view, cf. the remarks of P. Berger and H. Kellner as quoted by Roger Trigg in his *Understanding Social Science: A Philosophical Introduction to the Social Sciences* (New York: Basil Blackwell, 1985), p. 37:

> 'False consciousness' as a concept implies 'correct consciousness', which in turn implies a direct access to reality which the sociologists cannot supply.

18. George Lichtheim, "The Concept of Ideology," *History and Theory* 4 (1965), p. 172.

19. Erich Fromm, *Beyond the Chains of Illusion: My Encounters with Marx and Freud* (New York: Touchstone Books, 1985), p. 102.

20. Arnold Hauser, "Propaganda, Ideology and Art" in *Aspects of Historical Consciousness*, ed. Istvan Meszeros (Boston: Routledge, Kegan & Paul, 1977), p. 137.

21. John McMurty, *The Structure of Marx's World-View* (Princeton: Princeton University Press, 1978), p. 125.

22. Concerning the social nature of false consciousness, cf. the remarks of John Plamenatz in his *Ideology* (London: Macmillan, 1970), p. 23:

> By false consciousness, Marx appears to have meant a set of mistaken beliefs about matters important to them shared by a whole group of persons or even a whole community. False consciousness is pervasive and has extensive social consequences. It consists of a number of closely related illusions common to all or nearly all persons whose situations or roles in the society are the same.

In a similar vein, see the comments of J. G. Merquior in his *The Veil and the Mask: Essays on Culture and Ideology* (London: Routledge & Kegan Paul, 1979), p. 34:

> Ideology theory today [must try] to recover the sense of group false consciousness determined by social structure and social process.

23. Cf. remarks of Raymond Williams in his *Culture and Society: 1780/1950* (New York: Harper and Row, 1958), pp. 266–67: "[Marx's remarks sometimes suggests that for him] the superstructure is mere rationalization."

24. Jorge Larrain, *Marxism and Ideology*, p. 103.

25. David McLellan, *Ideology*, p. 18.

26. Cf. Larrain's encyclopedia article "Ideology" in *Dictionary of Marxist Thought*, ed. Tom Bottomore (Cambridge: Harvard University Press, 1983), p. 220:

> From the very early critique of religion to the unmasking of mystified economic appearances...there is a remarkable consistency in Marx's understanding of ideology. The idea of a double inversion, in consciousness and reality, is retained throughout...In this sense the often-quoted definition of ideology as false consciousness is not adequate in so far as it does not specify the kind of distortion which is criticized, thus

opening the way for a confusion of ideology with all sorts of errors.

27. Allen Wood, *Karl Marx* (London: Routledge & Kegan Paul, 1981), p. 10.

28. Walter Carlsnaes, *The Concept of Ideology and Political Analysis: A Critical Examination of Its Usage by Marx, Lenin and Mannheim* (Westport, Conn.: Greenwood Press, 1981), pp. 46–47.

29. Cf. George Thomson's Marxist-inspired critique of the metaphysical thought of the early Greek philosophers in his *The First Philosophers: Studies in Ancient Greek Society* (London: Lawrence & Wishart, 1955), pp. 340–42:

> ...with this division between intellectual and manual labor, theory was continually being drawn apart from practice and so losing touch with reality...[Consequently, philosophers fell into the illusion] that his new categories of thought were endowed with an immanent validity of the social and historical conditions which had created them. This is the 'socially necessary false consciousness' which...has prevented philosophers from recognizing the limitations which are inherent in their 'autonomy of reason' in virtue of its origin as the ideological reflux of commodity production.

30. Carolyn Porter, "Reification and American Literature," in *Ideology and Classic American Literature*, eds. S. Bercovitch and M. Jehlen (Cambridge: Cambridge University Press, 1986), p. 189.

31. Brian Fay, *Critical Social Science: Liberation and its Limits* (Ithaca: Cornell University Press, 1987), p. 53.

32. In Ron Eyerman's book *False Consciousness and Ideology in Marxist Theory* (New Haven: Yale University Press, 1983), p. 18, Eyerman links Georg Lukacs's work on false consciousness with Marx's analyses of commodity fetishism:

> Lukacs developed the concept of reification out of Marx's notion of fetishism of commodities. False consciousness was rooted in the daily life of capitalist society where exchange relations came to dominate every

form of human expression. There social reality appears to be objective, thing-like...

33. Alex Callinicos, *Making History: Agency, Structure and Changes in Social Theory* (Oxford: Basil Blackwell, 1987), p. 139.

34. Ibid.

35. Richard Schmitt, *Introduction to Marx and Engels: A Critical Reconstruction* (Boulder, Colo.: Westview Press, 1987) p. 56.

36. Nicholas Abercrombie, *Class, Structure and Knowledge: Problems in the Sociology of Knowledge* (New York: New York University Press, 1980), p. 18.

37. David Rubinstein, *Marx and Wittgenstein: Social Praxis and Social Explanation* (Boston: Routledge & Kegan Paul, 1981), p. 55.

CHAPTER TWO. BACON'S THEORY OF IDOLS AND MARX ON IDEOLOGICAL FALLACIES

1. Bernard Williams, *Descartes: The Project of Pure Inquiry* (Sussex, England: Harvester, 1978), p. 26.

2. For a comprehensive historical overview of Bacon's milieu, see chapter 8 of Sterling Lamprecht's *Our Philosophical Traditions: A Brief History of Philosophy in Western Civilization* (New York: Appleton-Century-Crofts, 1955).

3. Descartes, *Meditations*, reprinted in *The Rationalists* (Garden City, N.Y.: Anchor Books, 1974), p. 112.

4. Bacon, *The New Organon*. Selections are reprinted in *The Philosophy of the 16th and 17th Centuries*, ed. Richard Popkin (New York: Free Press, 1966), pp. 83–84 (hereafter referred to as "Bacon selections, Popkin").

5. Bacon, *The New Organon* (New York: Macmillan, 1985), Library of Liberal Arts, aphorism 38, p. 47 (hereafter referred to as "Bacon").

6. Bacon selections, Popkin, p. 92, aphorism 41.

7. Bacon, aphorism 49, p. 52.

8. Bacon selections, Popkin, p. 95.

9. Bacon, aphorism 51.

10. Cf. "the adventitious come into the mind from without... the innate are inherent in the very nature of the intellect" (Bacon selections, Popkin, p. 87).

11. Marx, *Capital*, vol. 1, trans. Ben Fowkes (New York: Vintage Books, 1977), p. 714 and p. 679 (hereafter referred to as "CAP").

12. Marx and Engels, *The German Ideology* (New York: International Publishers, 1978), p. 52 (hereafter referred to as "GI").

13. Marx, GI, pp. 65–66.

14. Cf. Roger Gottlieb, "A Marxian Concept of Ideology," *Philosophical Forum* (Boston) 6, no. 74–75; David Miller in his article "Ideology and the Problem of False Consciousness," *Political Studies* 20(1972) lists this fallacy as one of four fallacies often discussed by Marxist writers.

15. Marx, *The Poverty of Philosophy* (New York: International Publishers, 1982), p. 189.

16. Marx, *Introduction to a Critique of Political Economy*. This selection is printed in GI, p. 127.

17. Marx, CAP, p. 273.

18. Cf. Marx, CAP, p. 165.

19. Marx, CAP, p. 766, note 4.

20. Cf. Karl Mannheim, *Ideology and Utopia: An Introduction to the Sociology of Knowledge* (New York: Harcourt Brace Jovanovich, 1936), p. 61:

> it is only when we...seek to discover the sources of their untruthfulness in a social factor, that we are properly making an ideological interpretation.

See also Alex Callinicos, *Making History: Agency, Structure and Change in Social Theory* (Oxford: Basil Blackwell, 1987), p. 139:

> Explaining why an individual holds ideological beliefs is a matter of analyzing social processes, not of diagnosing intellectual error or individual pathology. Ideology is social consciousness.

21. Marx, *Theories of Surplus Value: Part Two* (Moscow: Progress Publishers, 1966), p. 119.

22. Marx, CAP, p. 98:

> In so far as such a critique represents a class, it can only represent the class whose historical task is the overthrow of the capitalist mode of production and the final abolition of all classes—the proletariat.

23. Ibid., p. 103:

> In its rational form it is a scandal and an abomination to the bourgeoisie and its doctrinaire spokesmen, because it includes in its positive understanding of what exists a simultaneous recognition of its negation, its inevitable destruction; because it regards every historically developed form as being in a fluid state, in motion, and therefore grasps its transcient aspect...in its very essence [the dialectical method is] critical and revolutionary.

24. Cf. Marx's letter to Klings, 4 October 1864, reprinted in *Letters on Capital*, trans. Andrew Drummond (London: New Park Publications, 1983), p. 93:

> ...I hope to finish [*Capital*] in a couple of months and to deal a theoretical blow to the bourgeoisie from which they will never recover...Farewell and rely on it that the working class will always find a loyal champion in me.

25. Marx, *Theories of Surplus Value*, p. 120.

26. Cf. Marx, *The Poverty of Philosophy*, p. 125:

> Just as the economists are the scientific representatives of the bourgeois class, so the Socialists and the Communists are the theoreticians of the proletarian class.

27. Marx, *Theories of Surplus Value*, pp. 119–20.

28. Cf. Marx, CAP, p. 96:

> In so far as political economy is bourgeois, i.e., in so far as it views the capitalist order as the absolute and ultimate form of social production, instead of as a historically transient stage of development, it can only remain a science while the class struggle remains latent

> or manifests itself only in isolated and sporadic phenomena.

29. Cf. Engels's letter to Schmidt, 8 October 1888, reprinted in *Letters on "Capital"*, p. 240:

> I am not at all astounded that you have finally arrived at the Marxist viewpoint in the course of your studies, for I believe that anyone who approaches the matter objectively and fundamentally will do the same.

CHAPTER THREE. IDEOLOGY AND THE FRENCH ENLIGHTENMENT

1. Cf. Hans Barth, *Truth and Ideology*, trans. Frederic Lilge (Berkeley: University of California Press, 1976), p. 28.

2. Holbach, *The System of Nature*, trans. H. D. Robinson (New York: Burt Franklin, 1970), p. 263.

3. My statement here is something of a paraphrase of a passage from Nietzsche's *Ecce Homo*, aphorism 10, which reads:

> What mankind has so far considered seriously have not even been realities but mere imaginings—more strictly speaking, lies prompted by the bad instincts of sick natures that were harmful in the most profound sense—all these concepts, 'God', 'soul', 'virtue', 'sin', 'beyond', 'truth', 'eternal life'...All the problems of politics, of social organization, and of education have been falsified through and through because one mistook the most harmful men for great men—because one learned to despise 'little' things, which means the basic concerns of life.

As Nietzsche's remarks make evident, the influence of the *philosophes* on modern theories of ideology is considerable.

4. Holbach, *The System of Nature*, p. 284.

5. Ibid., pp. 11, 84.

6. Cf. ibid., p. 300. As Holbach envisioned it, the goal of ideological critique was to

> destroy chimeras prejudical to the human species, in order to reconduct man back to nature, to experience, and to reason.

7. Condillac, *Essay on the Origin of Knowledge*. Selections reprinted in *18th-Century Philosophy*, ed. Lewis White Beck (New York: Free Press, 1966), pp. 169–70.

8. Cf. Holbach, *The System of Nature*, p. 79:

> If, as Aristotle asserted...'nothing enters the mind, but through the medium of his senses'; it follows as a consequence, that every thing that issues from it, must find some sensible object to which it can attach its ideas, whether immediately, as a man, a tree, a bird, etc., or in the last analysis or decomposition, such as pleasure, happiness, vice, virtue, etc. Whenever, therefore, a word or its ideas, does not connect itself with some sensible object, to which it can be related, this word, or this idea, is unmeaning, void of sense.

9. Ibid., p. 163.

10. In his *Studies in the Theory of Ideology* (Berkeley: University of California Press, 1984), p. 5, John Thompson summarizes the difference between materialist-realist and nonrealist approaches to ideology as follows:

> we must also resist the view that ideology is pure illusion, our inverted or distorted image of what is 'real'...Once we recognize that ideology operates through language and that language is a medium of social action, we must also acknowledge that ideology is partially constitutive of what in our societies is 'real'. Ideology is not a pale image of the social world but is part of that world, a creative and constitutive element of our social lives.

11. Condillac summarized his basically Lockean epistemological position in his statement: "all our knowledge comes from the senses...both particular and general." Cf. his *Treatise on System*, selections of which are reprinted in *The Enlightenment: A Comprehensive Anthology*, ed. Peter Gay (New York: Simon and Schuster, 1973), p. 522.

12. Holbach, *The System of Nature*, p. 80. The arguments and materialist outlook of Holbach and Condillac concerning the empirical

origins of so-called rational *a priori* truths were not unlike Marx's own arguments in his *Notes on Wagner* concerning the practical-empirical origins of the fundamental logical categories of thought. According to Marx, reflections of the basic properties of external objects were "impressed upon" the mind as a result of humankind's practical interaction with nature. In turn, through rational abstraction and syntheses, these raw perceptions were worked up into class concepts and eventually acquired a prima facie *a priori* status with the development of logic. Thus, like Condillac, in his *Notes on Wagner*, Marx emphasized the material basis of so-called metaphysical, *a priori* ideas.

13. Helvetius also argued "that sensibility alone produces all our ideas...[and hence] every thing is reducible to feeling [i.e., sense experience]." Cf. his *Essay on Mind* (New York: Burt Franklin, 1970), p. 7.

14. Holbach, *The System of Nature*, p. 93.

15. Cf. George Boas, S.V. "Destutt de Tracy," *Encyclopedia of Philosophy*, p. 357.

16. Cited by Emmet Kennedy in *A Philosophe in the Age of Revolution: Destutt De Tracy and the Origins of Ideology* (Philadelphia: American Philosophical Association, 1978), p. 45.

17. Cf. Marx and Engels, *The Holy Family*. Selections reprinted in *Reader in Marxist Philosophy*, ed. Howard Selsam and Harry Martel (New York: International Publishers, 1980) pp. 53–55.

> The French Enlightenment of the 18th century, in particular French materialism, was not only a struggle against the existing political institutions and the existing religion and theology; it was just as much an open struggle against the metaphysics of the 17th century...[The French Enlightenment] anti-theological, anti-metaphysical, and materialistic practice demanded corresponding anti-theological, anti-metaphysical and materialistic theories.

18. Nicholas Abercrombie in his *Class, Structure, and Knowledge: Problems in the Sociology of Knowledge* (New York: New York University Press, 1980) has noted that there exist two variations in Marx's writings on the principle concerning the social determination of thought. According to Abercrombie (p. 25):

> The doctrine 'social being determines consciousness' tends to suggest that there are powerful reasons, chiefly class-interest, for supposing that each class will have its own distinctive system of beliefs...[whereas] the 'base determines superstructure' doctrine, on the other hand, tends to argue that class-specific systems of belief become incorporated within a dominant ideology.

19. Cf. Engels's remark in *Anti-Düring*, trans. Emile Burns (New York: International publishers, 1976), p. 118.

> The idea of equality...is itself a historical product, the creation of which required definite historical conditions which in turn themselves presuppose a long previous historical development. It is therefore anything but an eternal truth. And if today it is taken for granted by the general public...if, as Marx says, it "already possesses the fixity of a popular prejudice," this is not the consequence of its axiomatic truth, but the result of the general diffusion and the continued appropriation of the ideas of the eighteenth century.

See also Marx's remarks in *Capital*, vol. 1, p. 152, concerning the idea of equality as a "fixed popular opinion."

> The secret of the expression of value, namely the equality and equivalence of all kinds of labor...could not be deciphered until the concept of human equality had already acquired the permanence of a fixed popular opinion. This however becomes possible only in a society where the commodity-form is the universal form of the product of labor, hence the dominant social relation is the relation between men as possessors of commodities.

20. Perhaps the views of Charles Darwin in *The Origin of Species* illustrate the way that social conditions may influence purportedly "objective" and "unbiased" observations of nature. Both Marx and Engels were fascinated by and appreciative of Darwin's work. However, in a series of letters, they commented on the underlying social influences on Darwin's theory. In a letter to Engels dated 18

June 1862 (reprinted in *Letters on "Capital,"* trans. Andrew Drummond [London: New Park Publications, 1983], p. 74), Marx writes,

> It is notable that Darwin recognizes among the beasts and plants his own English society with its division of labor, competition, opening of new markets...and Malthusian 'struggle for existence'.

In a letter to Lavrov dated 12 November 1875 (*Letters on "Capital,"* p. 180), Engels says,

> The whole Darwinist doctrine of the struggle for existence is simply Hobbes's doctrine...and the bourgeois doctrine of competition, together with the Malthusian population theory, transferred from society into natural life. Once this trick has been performed...then these same theories can be transferred back from organic nature to history, and one could then claim that their validity as eternal laws of human society has been established.

Finally, John McMurty, on page 126 of his *The Structure of Marx's World-View* (Princeton: Princeton University Press, 1978), quotes the following revealing passage from Darwin's work:

> We sometimes see the contest [between varieties of plant species] soon decided: for instance, if several varieties of wheat be sown together, and the mixed seed resown, some of the varieties will beat the others, and so yield more seed, and will consequently in a few years supplant the other varieties.

21. Cf. Marx's remarks in his *The Poverty of Philosophy* (New York: International Publishers, 1982), pp. 105, 186–89, concerning how historically contingent categories of political economy (e.g., the idea of "competition") are transformed by economists into "pre-existing, eternal ideas."

22. Friedrich Engels, *Ludwig Feuerbach and the End of Classical German Philosophy* (Moscow: Progress Publishers, 1969), pp. 19–20:

> The great basic question of all philosophy...is that concerning the relation of thinking and being...which

> is primary, spirit or nature…The answers which the philosophers gave to this question split them into two great camps…

23. Cf. Sean Sayers, *Reality and Reason: Dialectic and the Theory of Knowledge* (New York: Basil Blackwell, 1985) and Samuel E. Stumpf, *Philosophical Problems: Selected Readings*, 3d ed. (New York: McGraw, Hill, 1989) who argue that Marx has a materialist reflection theory of ideas like Engels. For a contrasting view, see Joseph Femia's *Gramsci's Political Thought: Hegemony, Consciousness, and the Revolutionary Process* (Oxford: Clarendon Press, 1981).

24. Did Marx have a materialist reflection theory of ideas? The following remarks from his postface to *Capital*, vol. 1, suggest he did:

> My dialectical method is, in its foundation, not only different from the Hegelian, but exactly opposite to it. For Hegel, the process of thinking, which he even transforms into an independent subject, under the name of 'the Idea', is the creator of the real world, and the real world is only the external appearance of the idea. With me the reverse is true: the ideal is nothing but the material world reflected in the mind of man, and translated into forms of thought.

25. Cf. Engels's letter to Joseph Bloch, 21 September 1890, and letter to Conrad Schmidt, 27 October 1890.

26. Cf. Marx's remark in *Capital*, vol. 1, trans. Ben Fowkes (New York: Vintage Books, 1977), p. 899:

> The advance of capitalist production develops a working class which by education, tradition and habit looks upon the requirements of that mode of production [i.e., capitalism] as self-evident natural laws.

27. Cf. Marx's remark in *The Eighteenth Brumaire of Louis Bonaparte*, quoted in *The Marx-Engels Reader*, ed. Robert C. Tucker (New York: W. W. Norton, 1972), p. 462:

> …one must not form the narrow-minded notion that the petty bourgeoisie, on principle, wishes to enforce an egoistic class interest. Rather, it believes that the special conditions of its emancipation are the general

conditions under which modern society can alone be saved...

28. Marx, *Poverty of Philosophy*, p. 186.

29. Engels, letter to Conrad Schmidt, 27 October 1890, reprinted in *The Marx-Engels Reader*, pp. 645–46.

30. Ibid., p. 645:

> In a modern state, law must not only correspond to the general economic conditions and be its expression, but must also be an internally coherent expression which does not, owing to inner contradictions, reduce itself to nought. And in order to achieve this, the faithful reflection of economic conditions suffers increasingly.

31. Cf. Engels, *Ludwig Feuerbach*, p. 49.

32. Marx, *Poverty of Philosophy*, p. 189.

33. Marx, letter to Schweitzer, 24 January 1865, printed in the appendix to *The Poverty of Philosophy*, p. 197.

34. Engels, *Ludwig Feuerbach*, p. 50.

35. Marx and Engels, *The German Ideology.* Part One, ed. C. J. Arthur (New York: International Publishers, 1978), pp. 51–52:

> Division of labor only becomes truly such from the moment when a division of material and mental labor appears...From this moment onwards consciousness can really flatter itself that it is something other than consciousness of existing practice, that it really represents something without representing something real...

36. Ibid., pp. 47, 118.

37. Ibid., p. 48.

38. See *Capital*, vol. 1, postface to 2d ed., pp. 102–3 for Marx's remarks on the "rational kernal" within the mystified philosophy of Hegel.

39. Cf. Marx's "Critique of Hegelian Philosophy," in *The Economic and Philosophic Manuscripts of 1844*, trans. Martin Milligan (New York: International Publishers, 1982).

40. In *Rules and Meaning*, ed. Mary Douglas (Harmondsworth: Penguin Books, 1973), p. 20, Alfred Schutz's remarks concerning Max Weber's postulate of *"Verstehen"*:

> the postulate of subjective interpretation has to be understood in the sense that all scientific explanations of the social world can, and for certain purposes must, refer to the subjective meaning of the actions of human beings from which social reality originates.

See also see Roger Trigg, *Understanding Social Science: A Philosophical Introduction to the Social Sciences* (New York: Basil Blackwell, 1985), p. 2, for comments concerning what the hermeneutical tradition takes as the goal of social science. Trigg says,

> [According to the European hermeneutical tradition] the social world is constituted by the meanings and purposes of rational agents. The function of social science is then to interpret and render intelligible rather than to invoke causes.

Finally, see Charles Taylor's essay "Interpretation and the Sciences of Man," in *Understanding and Social Inquiry*, ed. Fred Dallmayr and Thomas McCarthy (Notre Dame: University of Notre Dame Press, 1977). Concerning the interpretative role of social scientists, Taylor writes:

> [Social scientists should aim at] a consideration of social reality as characterized by intersubjective and common meanings...the intersubjective meanings, which are constitutive of the social matrix in which individuals find themselves and act...

For the contrasting materialist view on social science, see Emile Durkheim's remarks praising the virtues of the Marxist approach to social science (quoted by David Rubinstein in his *Marx and Wittgenstein: Social Praxis and Social Explanation* [Boston: Routledge & Kegan Paul, 1981], p. 14):

> I consider extremely fruitful this idea that social life should be explained, not by the notions of those who participate in it, but by more profound causes which are unperceived by consciousness.

41. Marx, *Capital*, vol. 1, p. 290.

42. Cf. Marx's preface to *Critique of Political Economy* (1859):

    In the social production which men carry on they enter into definite relations that are indispensable and independent of their will…The sum total of these relations of production constitutes the economic structure of society…

43. Rubinstein, *Marx and Wittgenstein*, p. 14.

44. Cf. Marx and Engels, *The German Ideology*, p. 46:

    The social structure and the state are continually evolving out of the life-process of definite individuals, but of individuals not as they may *appear* in their own or other people's *imagination*, but as they *really* are, i.e., as they operate, produce materially, and hence as they work under definite material limits, presuppositions and conditions independent of their will.

In their *Small Town in Mass Society: Class, Power and Religion in a Rural Community*, a classic study of the disparity between social consciousness and social realities, Arthur Vidich and Joseph Bensman utilized a class analysis to expose the false consciousness of the members of a small rural township in the state of New York, circa 1950. In the preface to their work, Vidich and Bensman said of their method [p. xviii],

> The class and political analysis opened our perception to a number of sharp contradictions in the community's institutions and values. The public enactment of community life and public statements of community values seemed to bear little relationship to the community's operating institutions and the private lives of its members.

In discussing the consequences of the study by Vidich and Bensman for the *Verstehen* methodological approach, Maurice Stein says in his *The Eclipse of Community*, p. 290,

> This disparity between public imagery and social realities put the field workers in an odd position. The familiar and indispensable sociological injunction to

explore the meanings that social structures hold for the people whose behavior they pattern led them up a blind alley. Since the essential structural features of the community...are not recognized by the participants, these structures cannot possibily hold any meaning for them...[there] appears to be a kind of 'latent' social structure. The elements are not only unrecognized and unintended, but the mere suggestion that they exist arouses intense antagonism.

45. Marx says in *The Eighteenth Brumaire of Louis Bonaparte*:

> As, in private life, the distinction is made between what a man thinks of himself and says, and that which he really is and does, so, all the more, must the phrases and notions of parties in historic struggles be distinguished from their real organism and their real interests, their conceptions from their reality.

See also see Paul Ricoeur's grouping of Marx, Freud, and Nietzsche as the "three masters of suspicion," in *Freud and Philosophy: An Essay on Interpretation*, trans. David Savage (New Haven: Yale University Press, 1970), p. 32.

46. Alex Callinicos, *Marxism and Philosophy* (Oxford: Oxford University Press, 1983), p. 105.

47. Marx and Engels, *The German Ideology*, p. 67; see also p. 60:

> For instance, if an epoch imagines itself to be actuated by purely 'political' or 'religious' motives, although 'religion' and 'politics' are only forms of its true motives, the historian accepts this opinion. The 'idea', the 'conception' of the people in question about their real practice, is transformed into the sole determining, active force, which controls and determines their practice.

For an illustration of the historical materialist methodology applied to interpreting history, see Charles A. Beard's classic *An Economic Interpretation of The Constitution of the United States* (New York: Free Press, 1913). In particular, see Beard's opening chapter, in which he criticizes idealist historical accounts of U.S. constitutional history. For example, on pages 10 and 11, Beard writes:

> ...the juristic theory of the origin and nature of the Constitution is marked by the same lack of analysis of determining forces which characterized older historical writing in general...In the juristic view, the Constitution is not only the work of the whole people, but it also bears in it no traces of the party conflict from which it emerged...Nowhere in the commentaries is there any evidence of the fact that rules of our fundamental law are designed to protect any class in its rights, or secure the property of one group against the assaults of another...

Beard concludes that as a result of the idealist nature of the juridical viewpoint, the juridicial viewpoint results in a superficial and vague understanding of legal history. Cf. page 8:

> In the absence of a critical analysis of legal evolution [particularly, in the absence of any examination of the influence of economic factors on the evolution of law], all sorts of vague abstractions dominate most of the thinking done in the field of law...[e.g., it is believed that] law is made out of some abstract stuff known as 'justice'...[But what needs to be explained is:] What was the standard in the beginning and why does it advance?

48. Cf. Howard Zinn's formulation of the dominant ideology thesis in his *Declarations of Independence: Cross-Examining American Ideology* (New York: Harper Collins, 1990), pp. 3–4.

49. Holbach, *Common Sense*, selections of which are reprinted in *18th-Century Philosophy*, ed. Lewis White Beck (New York: Free Press, 1966), p. 182.

50. Holbach, *Common Sense*, as quoted in *Readings in Philosophy*, ed. John Herman Randall et al (New York: Barnes and Noble, 1946), p. 369; see also Holbach, *System of Nature*, trans. H. D. Robinson (New York: Burt Franklin, 1970), pp. 264, 275.

51. Holbach, *Common Sense*, selections reprinted in *18th-Century Philosophy*, p. 182; see also *System of Nature*, pp. 15, 256.

52. Cf. Holbach, *System of Nature*, p. 207:

> the notions of Divinity…have been [utilized] by legislators…[and] priests…who have prescribed systems of worship to the uninformed; who have availed themselves of their existing prejudices…to submit them to their yoke; who have obtained a dominion over their minds by seizing on their credulity—by making them participate in their errors—by working on their fears…

53. Ibid., p. 309; see also pp. 207, 270, and 273.

54. Cf. Holbach's remarks in ibid., p. 69, on social contract theory as an alternative to the theory of the divine right of kings.

55. Ibid., p. 126.

56. Ibid., p. 152.

57. Holbach, *Common Sense*, selections reprinted in *Readings in Philosophy*, p. 359.

58. Helvetius, *Treatise on Man*, vol. 2, trans. W. Hosper (New York: Burt Franklin, 1969), p. 356.

59. Helvetius, *Essay on the Mind* (New York: Burt Franklin, 1970), p. 173.

60. Ibid., p. 172.

61. Ibid., p. 177.

62. Cf. Gunter Remmling's remark in *Road to Suspicion: A Study of Modern Mentality and the Sociology of Knowledge* (New York: Appleton-Century-Crofts, 1967), pp. 155–56, on the influence of the French Enlightenment on Marx's theory of ideology:

> [Marx] incorporated Helvetius's psychology of interests into his theory of ideology: ideas are the expression of human interests; they are always modified by the class position of those who produce them…

63. Helvetius, *Treatise on Man*, vol. 1, p. 198.

64. Cf. G. William Domhoff, *The Powers That Be: Processes of Ruling Class Domination in America* (New York: Viking Books, 1979); see also Graham Murdock, "Mass Communication and the Construction of Meaning," in *Reconstructing Social Psychology*, ed. Nigel Armistead (Harmondsworth: Penguin Books, 1974).

65. Cf. Marx's remarks on the effects of the dominant democratic-republican ideology on the social-political consciousness of the proletariat in early nineteenth-century Europe. For example, in his essay "The King of Prussia and Social Reform" (August 1844) reprinted in *Karl Marx: Early Texts*, ed. David McLellan (New York: Barnes and Noble, 1972), p. 219, Marx says,

> the workers in Lyon thought they were only pursuing political ends and were only soldiers of the republic, whereas in reality they were soldiers of socialism. Their political understanding obscured for them the roots of social misery, falsified their insight into their true aims, and belied their social instinct.

See also Marx's explanations of the political defeat of the French proletariat in the 1848 revolution in his *The Eighteenth Brumaire of Louis Bonaparte*. Finally, in his and Engels's *Address of the Central Committee to the Communist League*, Marx warned the German proletariat to avoid being "seduced...by the hypocritical phrases of the democractic petty bourgeois" and get clear as to their real political interest in revolution, and not democratic reforms.

66. Cf. Marx and Engels, *The German Ideology:* Part One, ed. C. J. Arthur (New York: International Publishers, 1978), pp. 65–66:

> For each new class which puts itself in the place of one ruling before it, is compelled...to represent its interest as the common interest of all the members of society...

See also Marx's speech delivered on 8 February 1849 entitled "The Trial of The Rhenish District Committee of Democrats," reprinted in *The Revolution of 1848–49: Articles from the "Neue Rheinische Zeitung,"* trans. S. Ryanzanskaya (New York: International Publishers, 1972), p. 233. In this speech, Marx argued that the conservative opponents of a centralized German political legislature were "asserting [their] minority interests as if they were the predominant interests, when they [were] no longer dominant."

67. Marx and Engels, *The German Ideology*, p. 64; see also their *The Communist Manifesto* (Northbrook, Ill.: AHM Publishing, 1955), p. 30: "The ruling ideas of each age have ever been the ideas of its ruling class."

68. Marx and Engels, *The German Ideology*, p. 64.

69. Cf. Marx's remark in *Capital*, vol. 1, trans. Ben Fowkes (New York: Vintage Books, 1977), p. 682: "these forms of appearances are reproduced directly and spontaneously as current and usual modes of thought." See also *The German Ideology*, p. 47:

> We set out from real, active men, and on the basis of their real life-process we demonstrate the development of the ideological reflexes and echoes of this life-process. The phantoms formed in the human brain are also, necessarily, sublimates of their material life-process, which is empirically verifiable and bound to material premises.

70. Cf. Marx's editorial in the *New York Daily Tribune*, 24 October 1854, reprinted in *Reader in Marxist Philosophy*, ed. Howard Selsam and Harry Martel (New York: International Publishers, 1963), p. 240; see also G. A. Cohen's remark in *Karl Marx's Theory of History: A Defence* (Princeton: Princeton University Press, 1978), pp. 290–91, on Marxist theory and conspiracy theories of ideology:

> ...it is also necessary to point out that Marxists can be too sensitive to the charge that they perceive conspiracies. There is more collective design in history than inflexible rejection of 'conspiracy theories' would allow...Thus, while ideologies are not normally invented to fit the purposes they serve, a fairly deliberate and quite concerted effort to maintain and protect an existing ideology is not unusual.

71. Cf. John Mepham's remark in his essay "The Theory of Ideology in *Capital*," printed in *Issues in Marxist Philosophy*, Vol. 3: *Epistemology, Science, Ideology*, ed. John Mepham and David-Hillel Ruben (Atlantic Highlands, N.J.: Humanities Press, 1979), p. 143:

> To say that the bourgeoisie produce ideas is to ignore the conditions that make this possible, to ignore that which determines which ideas are thus produced, and to conceal the real...origins of ideology. It is not the bourgeois class that produces ideas but bourgeois society.

72. Cf. Marx, *Capital*, vol. 1, p. 680:

> All the notions of justice held by both the worker and the capitalist, all the mystifications of the capitalist mode of production, all capitalism's illusions about freedom, all the apologetic tricks of vulgar economics, have as their basis the form of appearance [of capitalist social relations].

73. Marx, *Capital*, vol. 3, trans. David Fernbach (New York: Vintage Books, 1981), p. 969; *Capital*, vol. 1, ibid., pp. 169, 682.

74. Cf. Marx, *Poverty of Philosophy* (New York: International Publishers, 1982), pp.120–21:

> Economists have a singular method of procedure. There are only two kinds of institutions for them, artificial and natural. The institutions of feudalism are artificial...those of the bourgeoisie are natural...When the economists say that present-day relations—the bourgeois relations of production—are natural...they imply [that these historically contingent relations] are eternal laws which must always govern society...

75. Cf. Engels, *Anti-Duhring*, trans. Emile Burns (New York: International Publishers, 1976), p. 118:

> The idea of equality...is itself a historical product, the creation of which required definite historical conditions which in turn themselves presuppose a long previous historical development. It is therefore anything but an eternal truth. And if today it is taken for granted by the general public...if, as Marx says, it 'already possesses the fixity of a popular prejudice', this is not the consequence of its axiomatic truth, but the result of the general diffusion and the continued appropriation of the ideas of the eighteenth century.

Cf. Marx's remark in *Capital*, vol. 1, p. 152, concerning the idea of equality as a fixed popular opinion.

76. Cf. Holbach, *System of Nature*, p. 11: "Men will always deceive themselves by abandoning experience to follow imaginary systems..."

77. My interpretation of a basic continuity between *The German Ideology* and *Capital* is not shared by many contemporary crit-

ics of Marx. To begin with, many contemporary critics argue that Marx's formulation of the dominant ideology thesis in *The German Ideology* remains essentially similar to the eighteenth-century "conspiratorial" view concerning the origins of ideology. Secondly, contemporary critics argue that Marx's theory of ideology in *Capital* is substantially different from his earlier views in *The German Ideology* concerning the origins of dominant ideological conceptions.

For example, in a recent book by Alex Callinicos (*Making History: Agency, Structure and Change in Social Theory* [Oxford, Basil Blackwell, 1987]), Callinicos argues that with the exception of a class theoretical approach, Marx's formulation of the dominant ideology thesis in *The German Ideology* remains essentially the same as the view of the *philosophes:*

> [Marx's] analysis is evidently a development of the Enlightenment critique of religion as a conspiracy of priests and rulers to keep the masses in the dark. It differs primarily in rooting the generation of mass illusions in broader class relations. But it is vulnerable to the kind of objection made to the *philosophes*, namely that it treats the subordinate classes as passive receptacles of ideas inculcated in them from above.

In a somewhat similar vein, Rachel Sharp in her recent book *Knowledge, Ideology and the Politics of Schooling: Towards A Marxist Analysis of Education* (Boston: Routledge & Kegan Paul, 1980), objects to the "naive conspiracy" theory of ideology which she believes to be implied by *The German Ideology* version of the dominant ideology thesis. Referring to Marx's remarks on the role of ideologists who make a living by "perfecting" and disseminating the "illusions" of the ruling class, Sharp argues that the theory of ideology in *The German Ideology*

> ...sometimes leads to a conceptualization of subordinate classes as passively manipulated victims of propaganda disseminated by a cynical and self-interested, but all-knowing ruling class; it thus reinforces a naive conspiracy theory of society, and tends to reduce the concept of ideology to nothing but lies.

I believe that the above criticisms are valid against the *philosophes'* version of the dominant ideology thesis, but not against Marx's theory of ideology in *The German Ideology*. By means of a selective reading of *The German Ideology*, these critics distort Marx's views concerning the origins and content of dominant ideological conceptions; they omit important passages which would invalidate their critique of Marx.

For example, the attempt by critics to attribute to *The German Ideology* a conspiratorial view regarding the origins of false consciousness is the result of their exclusive focus on Marx's remarks concerning the role played by professional "ideologists" who earn their living by rationalizing and popularizing the "illusions" of the ruling class. What these critics overlook are Marx's account of the structural basis of ruling-class ideologies and his realistic interpretation of the content of ruling-class ideologies. They ignore Marx's observation that

> the ruling ideas are nothing more than the ideal expression of the dominant material relationships, the dominant material relationships grasped as ideas; hence of the relationships which make the one class the ruling one, therefore, the ideas of its dominance.

This propensity on the part of contemporary critics to read *The German Ideology* in a narrow and distorted manner is also the source of another erroneous contemporary interpretation: the thesis that Marx's theory of ideology in *Capital* breaks with his earlier views in *The German Ideology* concerning the origins and content of dominant ideological conceptions. According to the critics, what distinguishes *Capital* from *The German Ideology* is that in the former, Marx emphasizes the structural origins of dominant ideological conceptions (e.g., market relationships, division of labor, etc.), whereas in the latter it is the economic, political and intellectual dominance of the ruling class as a class which accounts for the origins of false consciousness. For example, according to Alex Callinicos, Marx argued in *Capital* (but not in *The German Ideology*), that

> there is...a material basis for bourgeois ideology...Far from depending on some conspiracy by the ruling class the acceptance of ideological beliefs is spontaneously generated by capitalist relations of production themselves.

In a somewhat similar spirit, Richard Lichtman in his essay also contends that the theory of ideology in *Capital* is substantively different from Marx's views in *The German Ideology*. Lichtman says,

I think it is clear that throughout the entire analysis of fetishism in *Capital*, Marx treats the mystification of consciousness as intrinsic to the form of capitalist production. The position of *The German Ideology* is transformed. It is no longer merely the case that economic power confers power over intellectual production which is 'falsified' for the purpose of social control. The account is more profound. Ideology is generated out of the mode of production itself...The earlier view was that control over the media in the superstructure—press, schools, churches, etc.—gave the ruling class control over the formation of working class consciousness. Now, as I grasp and extend Marx's position, the mystification of consciousness is viewed as ingredient in and constitutive of economic exploitation.

Now, as I have tried to demonstrate, *The German Ideology* is not as one-sided or unsophisticated as these critics would have it to be. Like *Capital*, *The German Ideology* emphasizes the structural origins of ideological conceptions. For example, in his analysis of idealist and religious forms of false consciousness, Marx cites the structural division between mental and manual labor as a fundamental factor in the formation of these forms of false consciousness. In *The German Ideology*, Marx says of the structural origins of ideology,

> Division of labor only becomes truly such from the moment when a division of material and mental labor appears (the first form of ideologists, priests, is concurrent). From this moment onwards consciousness can really flatter itself that it is something other than consciousness of existing practice, that it really represents something without representing something real... (pp. 51–52)

In a similar vein, in discussing the structural origins of modern utilitarian ideologies, Marx argued in *The German Ideology* (p. 109) that the various "abstract" philosophical formulations of utilitarianism by French and English writers reflect the fact that in capitalism, all social relations "are subordinated in practice to the one abstract monetary-commercial relation."

Finally, what these critics overlook is the fact that in *Capital*

Marx applies to an analysis of a specific dominant ideology (namely, bourgeois ideology) the basic theoretical principle of *The German Ideology* that "the ruling ideas are nothing more than the ideal expression of the dominant material relationships..."

In a different though related type of contemporary critique of *The German Ideology*, John Mepham argues in his essay "The Theory of Ideology in *Capital*" that Marx's utilization in *Capital* of the categories of "essence" and "phenomenal forms of appearances" constitutes a major conceptual innovation not found in the "epiphenomenalist" doctrine of *The German Ideology*. Mepham remarks,

> It is this theoretical advance [i.e., Marx's use of the essence/appearance distinction in *Capital*] that... allows Marx to make a decisive move beyond the ambiguities of his earlier remarks on ideology." (p. 148)

But this claim is textually inaccurate. In all of Marx's texts where he mentions the historical materialist methodology, including *The German Ideology*, the categories of essence and appearance are implied in the distinction Marx draws between social consciousness and social reality (i.e., thought and reality). For example, the implicit connection between the essence/appearance distinction and the thought/reality distinction is evident in the following passage from *The German Ideology*:

> the social structure and the State are continually evolving out of the life-process of definite individuals, but of individuals, not as they may *appear* in their own or other people's *imagination*, but as they *really* are, i.e., as they operate, produce materially, and hence as they work under definite material limits, presuppositions and conditions independent of their will. (p. 46)

The reason why the essence/appearance distinction is implied in the thought/reality distinction Marx explicitly draws in *The German Ideology* has something to do with Marx's materialist reflection theory of ideology. The basic idea of Marx's materialist reflection theory is that the ideological conceptions of social agents have their origins in the appearances generated by the "material-life process" or society of social agents. In other words, what Mepham interprets as an "epiphenomenalist" theory is in fact Marx's materialist reflection theory. According to Marx's statement of his materialist reflection theory in *The German Ideology*:

> We set out from real, active men, and on the basis of their real life-process we demonstrate the development of the ideological reflexes and echoes of this life-process. The phantoms formed in the human brain are also, necessarily, sublimates of their material-life process... (p. 47)

Furthermore, Marx's use of the essence/appearance distinction in *Capital* also entails his materialist reflection theory. For example, in the following passage from *Capital* (vol. 1, p. 677, 682) the materialist reflection theory is quite evident in Marx's claim that the *basic* ideological conceptions of capitalist society *directly* emanate from the forms of appearances generated by the social relations characteristic of capitalism. I quote:

> These imaginary expressions arise...from the relations of production themselves. They are the categories for the forms of appearance of essential relations...[and] the forms of appearance are reproduced directly and spontaneously, as current and usual modes of thought...

Hence, if Mepham believes that *The German Ideology* is epiphenomenalist because of its materialist reflection theory of ideas, then I fail to see how Marx's *Capital* is any less epiphenomenal.

78. Marx, *Capital*, vol. 1, p. 280.

79. Ibid., p. 680.

80. Ibid., p. 899.

81. Ibid., p. 719.

82. Allen Buchanan, *Marx and Justice: The Radical Critique of Liberalism* (Totowa, N.J.: Rowman & Allanheld, 1982), p. 53.

83. Marx, *Capital*, vol. 1, p. 729.

84. Cf. Marx's remark in ibid., p. 173:

> The religious reflections of the real world can...vanish only when the practical relations of everyday life... become production by freely associated men...

Compare Holbach's remark in his *System of Nature*, p. 174, on the role of knowledge and education as the key to eliminating false consciousness:

> If the ignorance of nature gave birth to the Gods, the knowledge of nature is calculated to destroy them... Man, when instructed, ceases to be superstitious.

85. Cf. David-Hillel Ruben's remarks in his *Marxism and Materialism: A Study in Marxist Theory of Knowledge* (Atlantic Highlands, N.J.: Humanities Press, 1979), p. 113:

> ...it is not necessary that men take those appearances for reality, although it is natural that they should tend to do so...They can come to know that such appearances are not indicative of what their situation essentially is...

86. For example, in *Capital* Marx argued that vulgar bourgeois economists simply take for granted capitalist productive relations as "natural" socioeconomic relations and from that seek to summarize the principles of the marketplace in capitalism without seeking knowledge of the deeper social and political truths of capitalism. By popularizing and instructing others in these formulas, vulgar economists disseminate a distorted and superficial view of capitalism which, in addition, is socially advantageous to the bourgeois ruling class because such formulas and distorted knowledge serve to rationalize and justify their incomes and class position in the division of labor. Cf. Marx on the trinity formula in *Capital*, vol. 3; see also Marx's letter to Kugelmann, 11 July 1868.

In addition, Marx argued that members of the ruling and middle classes were often biased and partisan in their perceptions and intellectual judgments as a result either of the effect of their practical class interests on their understanding or as a result of the limits imposed upon their understanding by their class position in society.

In Marx's opinion the theories of Thomas Malthus were openly biased and partisan in favor of the interests of the ruling class of England—and, in particular, of the traditional landowning aristocracy of England. In accounting for the biased character of Malthus's work, Marx utilized a class-interest explanation of bias. Marx wrote:

> [T]he scientific conclusions of Malthus are 'considerate' towards the ruling classes in general and towards the reactionary elements of the ruling classes in particular; in other words, he falsifies science for these inter-

ests. But his conclusions are ruthless as far as they concern the subjugated class" (*Theories of Surplus Value*, vol. 2 [Moscow: Progress Publishers, 1986], p. 120).

As for middle-class social prejudices, the following passage from Marx's *The Eighteenth Brumaire of Louis Bonaparte* illustrates Marx's class-positional explanation of bias, i.e., the notion that one's social understanding can be biased as a result of the limits placed upon one's social understanding by one's objective class position in the social structure.

> ...one must not form the narrow-minded notion that the petty-bourgeoisie, on principle, wishes to enforce an egoistic class interest. Rather, it believes that the special conditions of its emancipation are the general conditions under which modern society can alone be saved and the class struggle avoided. Just as little must one imagine that the democractic representatives are all shopkeepers or enthusiastic champions of shopkeepers...What makes them representative of the petty bourgeoisie is the fact that in their minds they do not go beyond the limits which the latter do not go beyond in life, that they are consequently driven theoretically to the same tasks and solutions to which material interest and social position practically drive the latter.

For a further discussion of the interest explanation of ideology and the positional explanation of ideology, see Jon Elster's essay "Belief, Bias and Ideology," in his *Sour Grapes: Studies in the Subversion of Rationality* (Cambridge: Cambridge University Press, 1983).

CHAPTER FOUR. IDEOLOGY AND POLITICAL CLASS STRUGGLE: HEGEL'S PHILOSOPHY OF HISTORY AND THE POLITICAL FALSE CONSCIOUSNESS IN THE WRITINGS OF MARX AND ENGELS

1. Cf. Marx's remark from his *Theories on Surplus Value* (in *Karl Marx: Selected Writings in Sociology and Social Philosophy*, edited by T. B. Bottomore and Maximilien Rubel (London: McGraw-Hill, 1956), p. 82):

> ...there corresponds to the capitalist mode of production a type of intellectual production quite different

from that which corresponds to the medieval mode of production. Unless material production itself is understood in its specific historical form, it is impossible to grasp the characteristics of the intellectual production which corresponds to it or the reciprocal action between the two.

2. Cf. Aristotle's *Politics*, bk. 1, ch. 5 concerning the natural basis of the master-slave social relationship:

> But is there any one thus intended by nature to be a slave, and for whom such a condition is expedient and right, or rather is not all slavery a violation of nature?
>
> There is no difficulty in answering this question, on grounds both of reason and of fact. For that some should rule and others be ruled is a thing not only necessary, but expedient; from the hour of their birth, some are marked out for subjection, others for rule.

3. Cf. Marx's remarks in the first volume of *Capital*, trans. Ben Fowkes (New York: Vintage Books, 1977), p. 152:

> The secret of the expression of value, namely the equality and equivalence of all kinds of labor...could not be deciphered until the concept of human equality had already acquired the permanence of a fixed popular opinion. This however becomes possible only in a society where the commodity-form is the universal form of the product of labor, hence the dominant social relation is the relation between men as possessors of commodities.

4. Cf. the writings of John of Salisbury (c. 1150–80), secretary to Thomas Becket of Canterbury, for an illustrative example of medieval political thinking. According to Salisbury's "organic" model of political relations,

> A commonwealth...is a certain body which is endowed with life by the benefit of divine favor...Those things which establish and implant in us the practice of religion...fill the place of the soul in the body of the commonwealth. And therefore those who preside over in the practice of religion should be looked up to and ven-

> erated as the soul of the body...The place of the head in the body of the commonwealth is filled by the prince, who is subject only to God and to those who exercise His office and represent Him on earth [i.e., the Church]...The place of the heart is filled by the Senate...The duties of eyes, ears, and tongue are claimed by the judges and the governors of provinces. Officials and soldiers correspond to the hands...[And] the husbandmen [i.e., the serfs and artisans] correspond to the feet, which always cleave to the soil, and need the more especially the care and foresight of the head...

This selection is taken from Franklin Le Van Baumer's edited anthology entitled *Main Currents of Western Thought*, 4th ed. (New Haven: Yale University Press, 1978), pp. 72–73.

5. Engels, "Juridical Socialism," reprinted in *Dynamics of Social Change: A Reader in Marxist Social Science*, edited by David Goldway, Harry Martel, and David Selsam (New York: International Publishers, 1983), p. 60.

6. Cf. in ibid., p. 60, Engels's remark concerning the continued influence of feudal religious ideologies on the political consciousness of the emerging bourgeosie:

> ...the Catholic world outlook fashioned on the pattern of feudalism, was no longer adequate for this new class [i.e., the bourgeoisie] and its conditions of production and exchange. Nevertheless, this new class remained for a long time a capitive in the bonds of almighty theology. From the 13th to the 17th century all the reformations and the struggles carried out under religious slogans that were connected with them were, on the theoretical side, nothing but repeated attempts of the burghers and plebians in the towns and the peasants who had become rebellious by contact with both of the latter to adapt the old theological world outlook to the changed economic conditions and the conditions of life of the new class.

See also remarks of C. Michael Otten in his *Power, Values and Society: An Introduction to Sociology* (Glenview, Ill: Scott, Foresman and Co., 1981), p. 186:

the ideal of personal liberty may have started as a rich person's ideology, but in the name of liberty the poor and the middle class have opposed the rich.

7. Cf. in Engles, "Juridical Socialism," p. 61, the remark:

> As the bourgeoisie in its time had by force of tradition dragged the theological outlook with it for a while in its fight against the nobility, so, too, the proletariat at first took over the juristic outlook from its opponent and sought in it weapons against the bourgeoisie.

For example, in the nineteenth century the dominant political ideology was liberal democracy (and still is, for that matter). While liberal democratic ideas were important for developing the political consciousness of the proletariat, Marx and Engels criticized democratic ideology for impeding the formation of a revolutionary class consciousness. In their view democratic ideology was a "reformist," hence, nonrevolutionary ideology which deflected the political consciousness of the proletariat from their real interest, i.e., the "abolition of class society." Thus, in their *Address of the Central Committee to the Communist League* (1850), Marx and Engels admonished the political leaders of the German proletariat to get clear in their minds

> as to what their class interests are, by taking up their position as an independent party as soon as possible and by not allowing themselves to be seduced for a moment by the hypocritical phrases of the democratic petty bourgeosie...

This address is reprinted in *The Marx-Engels Reader*, ed. Robert C. Tucker (New York: W. W. Norton, 1972), p. 373.

8. Cf. the remarks of Andrew Collier in his "Scientific Socialism and the Question of Socialist Values," reprinted in *Marx and Morality*, edited by Kai Nielsen and Steven Patten, Supplementary Volume 7 of the Canadian Journal of Philosophy (Guelph, Ont.: Canadian Assn. for Publishing in Philosophy, 1981), pp. 143 and 144:

> ...'equality', without further specification, is a concept without content...concepts like freedom and equality only acquire content in the context of concrete class struggles...

9. Cf. Marx's editorial in the *New York Daily Tribune*, 24 October 1854, in which he comments on how sections of the ruling class allied with each other used religion as a counter to the demand for democracy by subordinate social groups:

> Nobility and clergy, lords temporal and lords spiritual, found themselves equally threatened by the popular movement, and it naturally came to pass that the upper classes of Europe threw aside their skepticism in public life and made an outward alliance with the State churches and their system.

Reprinted in *Reader in Marxist Philosophy*, ed. Howard Selsam and Harry Martel (New York: International Publishers, 1963), p. 240.

10. Marx, *Introduction to the Critique of Hegel's "Philosophy of Right,"* trans. Annette Jolin and Joseph O'Malley (Cambridge: Cambridge University Press, 1978), p. 131.

11. Cf. Engels, *Anti-Dühring*, trans. Emile Burns (New York: International Publishers, 1976), p. 117:

> in the same way the bourgeois demand for equality was accompanied by the proletariat demand for equality. From the moment when the bourgeois demand for the class privileges was put forward, alongside it appeared the proletariat demand for the abolition of the classes themselves.

12. Nicholas Emler, "Morality and Politics: The Ideological Dimension in the Theory of Moral Development," in *Morality in the Making*, ed. H. Weinreich-Haste and D. Locke (New York: John Wiley & Sons, 1983), p. 48.

13. Istvan Meszaros, *Philosophy, Ideology and Social Science* (New York: St. Martin's Press, 1986), p. xii.

14. Joe McCarney, *The Real World of Ideology* (Atlantic Highlands, N.J.: Humanities Press, 1982), p. 80.

15. Chantel Mouffe, "Hegemony and Ideology in Gramsci," in *Culture, Ideology, Social Process: A Reader*, ed. Tony Bennett et al (London: Open University Press, 1981), p. 226.

16. Alex Callinicos, *Marxism and Philosophy* (Oxford: Oxford University Press, 1983), p. 135.

17. McCarney, *The Red World of Ideology*, p. 8.

18. For those theorists who reject a rigid pejorative conception of ideology and favor pragmatic evaluations of political ideologies, one of the preferred pragmatic criteria for evaluating ideologies entails an evaluation of its "progressive" or "reactionary" character. On this pragmatic type of view, see the excellent essay by R. N. Berki in *Knowledge and Belief in Politics: The Problem of Ideology* ed. Berki, Robert Benewick and B. Parekh (London: Allen & Unwin, 1973). Philosophers in the former Soviet Union also tend to follow this pragmatic view (cf. the *Soviet Encylopedia*, S.V. "Ideology").

According to this pragmatic view, what determines the "correctness" or "incorrectness" of an ideology are the historical interests represented by the ideology. An ideology is "correct" if it represents an historically ascendent class and progressive historical interests, while an ideology is "incorrect" if it represents reactionary historical interests. Hence, on this pragmatic view, an ideology could be "correct" at one point in history and "incorrect" at another point in history. So, for example, bourgeois liberal-democratic ideology was "correct" or progressive when it served as a "revolutionary" ideology against the obsolete feudal system, but became "incorrect" or reactionary when it became the dominant ruling-class ideology opposed to socialism.

Now, two of the reasons why I reject the pragmatic view are the following. First of all, the pragmatic view *begs the question* regarding how one is to "correctly" distinguish between "progressive" and "reactionary" historical interests. Presumably, one would need some kind of rational criteria or "theory," in order to make such distinctions; and if so, what then determines the "truth" or "falsity" of the "theory"? So again, I don't think we can escape the use of epistemological criteria in evaluating ideologies. Secondly, as I have argued in the text of this chapter, even the once "historically progressive" ideologies of bourgeois liberalism contained many false views which served to limit and falsify the social-political consciousness of social agents. And this continues to be the case with current ideologies of bourgeois liberalism.

With regard to the various falsehoods inherent in bourgeois liberalism and social contract theory, see the writings of C. B. Macpherson.

19. Cf. remarks of P. Berger and H. Kellner, as quoted by Roger Trigg in his *Understanding Social Science: A Philosophical Introduction to the Social Sciences* (New York: Basil Blackwell, 1985), p. 37:

'False consciousness' as a concept implies 'correct consciousness', which in turn implies a direct access to reality which the sociologists cannot supply.

20. Cf. Graham Kinloch's *Ideology and Contemporary Sociological Theory* (Englewood Cliffs, N.J.: Prentice-Hall, 1981), p. 3:

> ...there is growing...awareness of the extent to which...all 'knowledge' is ideological, in that it represents the vested interests and viewpoints of particular social groups...

21. Cf. Martin Seliger's remarks concerning "the Mannheim paradox," in his *The Marxist Conception of Ideology: A Critical Essay* (New York: Cambridge University Press, 1977), pp. 21–22. Seliger contends that Marx's theory of false consciousness is just as ideological as the views Marx criticized as being 'ideological', because like them Marx's theory is socially determined. Seliger seems to assume that all socially determined thought is ideological. The paradox in Marx's theory, according to Seliger

> is to assume that the unexceptional conditioning of our ideas precludes their objectivity while at the same time claiming objectivity for this proposition and the social analysis resting on it.

In my opinion, Seliger's criticisms are based on faulty assumptions. Marx did not argue that the social determination of thought 'precludes' the objectivity of thought. Moreover, it is not the *general* social determination of thought that creates an ideological false consciousness; according to Marx (and what I have so far demonstrated), only the determination of consciousness by certain kinds of social factors can lead to ideological false consciousness.

22. Cf. Karl Mannheim, *Ideology and Utopia: An Introduction to the Sociology of Knowledge,* trans. Louis Wirth and Edward Shils (New York: Harcourt Brace Jovanovic, 1936), p. 40. In the following passage Mannheim argues that both "ideological" and "utopian" thinking are modes of thought distorted by the class interests of their respective groups:

> the concept 'ideology' reflects...that ruling groups in their thinking become so intensively interest-bound to a situation that they are simply no longer able to see

> certain facts which would undermine their sense of domination...The concept of utopian thinking reflects the opposite discovery...namely that certain oppressed groups are intellectually so interested in the destruction and transformation of a given condition of society that they unwittingly see only those elements in the situation which tend to negate it.

23. Ibid., pp. 120, 125.

24. What's being described here is referred to by some as the "standpoint" epistemology theory. Recent feminist philosophy has resurrected this theory from the writings of Hegel and Marx. See the writings of Nancy Hartsock and Sandra Harding in *Discovering Reality: Feminist Perspectives on Epistemology, Metaphysics, Methodology, and Philosophy of Science*, ed. S. Harding and M. Hintikka (Dordrecht, Holland: Reidel, 1983); see also Allison Jagger's *Feminist Politics and Human Nature* (Totowa, N.J.: Rowman and Allanheld, 1983) pp. 370–71 concerning the superior knowledge perspectives of the oppressed compared to those of the ruling classes.

25. Hegel, *Reason in History: A General Introduction to the Philosophy of History*, trans. Robert S. Hartman (Indianapolis, Ind.: Bobbs-Merrill, 1953), pp. 26, 31.

26. Ibid., p. 43.

27. Shlomo Avineri, *Hegel's Theory of the Modern State* (Cambridge: Cambridge University Press, 1972), p. 233.

28. Hegel, *Reason in History,* p. 94–95.

29. Engels, *Ludwig Feuerbach and The End Of Classical German Philosophy* (Moscow: Progress Publishers, 1969), p. 44.

30. Ibid.

31. Ibid.

32. Cf. the following selections from *The Holy Family* in *Karl Marx: Selected Writings in Sociology and Social Philosophy*, ed. T. B. Bottomore and M. Rubel (New York: McGraw-Hill, 1956), pp. 57–58, 63:

> Hegel's conception of history presupposes an abstract or absolute spirit which develops in such a way that humanity is nothing more [than] a mass which more or less consciously bears it along...History thus becomes...a

separate entity, a metaphysical subject…[However,] [i]t is not 'history' which uses men as a means of achieving—as if it were an individual person—its own ends. History is nothing but the activity of men in pursuit of their ends.

33. Engels, *Ludwig Feuerbach*, pp. 43–44.

34. Ibid., p. 45.

35. Engels, letter to Conrad Schmidt, 27 October 1890, reprinted in *The Marx-Engels Reader*, ed. Robert C. Tucker, p. 249.

36. Cf. Marx and Engels, *The German Ideology* (New York: International Publishers, 1978), p. 60:

> If an epoch imagines itself to be actuated by purely 'political' or 'religious' motives, although 'religion' and 'politics' are only the forms of its true motives…

37. Engels, *The German Revolutions: "The Peasant War in Germany," and "Germany: Revolution and Counter-Revolution,"* edited and introduced by Leonard Krieger (Chicago: University of Chicago Press, 1967), pp. 4, 33.

38. Ibid., p. 44.

39. cf. Engels, "Juristic Socialism," p. 60:

> …this theological welding was not only in ideas, it existed in reality…[The] Church, which, owning about a third of the land in every country, occupied a position of tremendous power in the feudal organization…Besides, the clergy was the only educated class. It was therefore natural that Church dogma was the starting point and basis of all thought…

40. Engels, *Ludwig Feuerbach*, p. 50.

41. Marx, *The Eighteenth Brumaire of Louis Bonaparte*, p. 458.

42. Ibid., p. 459.

43. Ibid.

44. Ibid.

45. Ibid.

46. Cf. Marx's remarks on the misrepresentation of particular sectional interests as general interest in his *The German Ideology*, p. 138:

> For each new class which puts itself in the place of one ruling before it, is compelled, merely in order to carry through its aim, to represent its interest as the common interest of all members of society...

47. Marx, *The Eighteenth Brumaire of Louis Bonaparte*, p. 462.

48. Cf. J. G. Merquior's comment on Marx's theory in *The Veil and the Mask: Essays on Culture and Ideology* (London: Routledge & Kegan Paul, 1979), pp.11-12:

> [according to Marx in his *The Eighteenth Brumaire*,] the false consciousness of the petty bourgeois...is not a function of any transparently conscious class interest—rather, it is a function of the limits imposed by their 'life-activities' upon their ways of conceiving social reality.

49. On the other hand, Marx did recognize and acknowledge that members of the ruling class could be (and had been, at times) deliberately deceitful in representing their partisan class interests as the common interest in the effort to manipulate others and to win consent to their political agendas. For example, in his analysis of the political ideologies used by conservative members of the German provincial diets during the revolution of 1848, Marx suggests that these representative of the landed ruling class of Germany may have been consciously deceitful in their appeal to political federalism as a reason to reject a centralized, republican democratic state. cf. Marx, "The Trial of Rhenish District Committee of Democrats," in Marx and Engels, *The Revolution of 1848-49: Articles from the "Neue rheinische Zeitung,"* trans. S. Ryazansaya (New York: International Publishers, 1972), p. 233:

> To maintain the old laws in face of the new needs of social development is essentially the same as hypocritically upholding the out-of-date particular interests of a minority in face of the up-to-date interests of the community. This maintenance of the legal basis aims at asserting minority interests as if they were the predominant interests, when they are no longer dominant...Relying on these phrases about the legal basis, which arise either from conscious deceit or unconscious self-deception, the United Provincial Diet was

convoked, and this Diet was made to frame organic laws for the National Assembly.

50. Marx, "The King of Prussia and Social Reform," in *Karl Marx: Early Texts*, ed. David McLellan (New York: Barnes and Noble, 1972), p. 219.

51. Marx, *The Eighteenth Brumaire of Louis Bonaparte*, p. 464; see also Marx's remark in his *Class Struggle in France, 1848–1850* (New York: International Publishers, 1964), pp. 53–54:

> [they] saw in the whole of France, at least in the majority of Frenchmen, *citoyens* with the same interests, the same understanding, etc. This was the cult of the people...of...imaginary people.

52. Marx, *Class Struggle in France, 1848–1850*, ibid., pp. 44, 142.

53. Marx, *The Civil War in France*, in *The Marx-Engels Reader*, p. 554.

54. Marx and Engels, "Programmes of the Radical-Democratic Party of the Left at Frankfort" (June 1848), in *The Revolution of 1848–49: Articles from the "Neue rheinische Zeitung,"* p. 34.

55. Marx, "The Trial of the Rhenish District Committee Democrats," p. 241.

56. Ibid., p. 242.

57. Ibid., p. 241.

58. Marx and Engels, "Programmes of the Radical-Democratic Party of the Left at Frankfort," p. 33.

CHAPTER FIVE. THE HEGELIAN AND FEUERBACHIAN APPROACH TO THE ALIENATED MIND

1. Hegel, *The Phenomenology of Spirit*, trans. A. V. Miller (Oxford: Clarendon Press, 1977), pp. 229, 294.

2. Feuerbach, *The Essence of Christianity*, trans. George Eliot (New York: Harper Torchbooks, 1957), p. 13. Except for the reference in note 11 *infra*, all references to *The Essence of Christianity* are to Eliot's translation.

3. Marx, *The Economic and Philosophical Manuscripts of 1844*, trans. Martin Milligan (New York: International Publishers, 1964), p. 108.

4. Holbach, *Common Sense*, selections reprinted in *The Enlightenment*, ed. Frank E. Manuel (Englewood Cliffs, N.J.: Prentice-Hall, 1965), p. 57.

5. Feuerbach, *The Essence of Christianity*, pp. 104, 204.

6. Ibid., preface, p. xxxix

7. Cf. Feuerbach's repeated critical remarks on Hegel's "speculative doctrine," in ibid., p. xxxiv, 226–30.

8. Ibid., pp. 181–82.

9. Ibid., p. 33.

10. Ibid., p. 204.

11. Feuerbach, *The Essence of Christianity*, selections reprinted in *19th-Century Philosophy*, ed. Patrick L. Gardiner (New York: Free Press, 1969), p. 244.

12. Cf. Feuerbach on religion and "fetishism," in *The Essence of Christianity*, p. 13.

13. Ibid.

14. Feuerbach, *Provisional Theses for the Reformation of Philosophy*, selections reprinted in *The Young Hegelians*, ed. Lawrence Stepelevich (Cambridge: Cambridge University Press, 1983), p. 159.

15. Feuerbach, *The Essence of Christianity*, p. 274.

16. Feuerbach, *Provisional Theses*, p. 157.

17. Ibid.

18. Feuerbach, *The Essence of Christianity*, pp. 222, 226.

19. Ibid., p. 46.

20. Cf. Feuerbach's remarks on the "injurious" nature of religious illusions in his *The Essence of Christianity*, p. 274.

21. Ibid., p. 272.

22. Ibid.

23. Ibid., p. 170.

24. Hans Barth, *Truth and Ideology*, trans. Frederic Lilge (Berkeley: University of California Press, 1976), p. 59.

25. Jorge Larrain, *The Concept of Ideology* (Athens: University of Georgia Press, 1979), p. 32.

26. My explication of Hegel's theory of alienation is based primarily on my reading of his *Phenomenology of Spirit*. Paragraph 37 of Hegel's preface to the *Phenomenology of Spirit* epitomizes his view on alienation:

> What seems to happen outside of [Spirit or Mind], to be an activity directed against it, is really its own doing, and Substance shows itself to be essentially Subject.

See also the chapter on "Culture and the Realm of Self-alienated Spirit."

27. Feuerbach, *Provisional Theses*, pp. 159, 170.

28. Ibid., p. 158.

29. Ibid., p. 159.

30. Ibid., p. 167.

31. Feuerbach, *The Essence of Christianity*, p. xxxiv.

32. Feuerbach, *Provisional Theses*, p. 157.

33. Marx's introduction to his *Critique of Hegel's "Philosophy of Right"*, reprinted in *The Marx-Engels Reader*, ed. Robert Tucker (New York: W. W. Norton Co., 1972), pp. 11, 12.

34. Marx, *On The Jewish Question*, in *The Marx-Engels Reader*, ed. Robert Tucker, p. 32.

35. Marx, *The Economic and Philosophical Manuscripts of 1844*, trans. Martin Milligan (New York: International Publishers, 1964), p. 111.

36. Marx, *Critique of Hegel's "Philosophy of Right"*, by Erica Sherover-Marcuse in her *Emancipation and Consciousness: Dogmatism and Dialectical Perspectives in the Early Marx* (New York: Basil Blackwell, 1986), p. 58.

37. Marx, *The German Ideology* ed. C. J. Arthur (New York: International Publishers, 1970), p. 47.

38. Herbert Marcuse, *Reason and Revolution: Hegel and the Rise of Social Theory* (Boston: Beacon Press, 1960), p. 279.

39. George Lichtheim, "Freud and Marx," in *Freud: The Man, His World, His Influence*, ed. Jonathan Miller (Boston: Little, Brown, 1972), p. 61.

40. Jorge Larrain, S.V. "Ideology," in *A Dictionary of Marxist Thought*, ed. Tom Bottomore (Cambridge: Harvard University Press, 1983), p. 220

41. Louis Althusser, "Lenin Before Hegel," in his *Lenin and Philosophy and Other Essays*, trans. Ben Brewster (New York: Monthly Review Press, 1971), p. 121.

42. John Mepham, "Theory of Ideology," in *Issues in Marxist Philosophy*, vol. 3, Epistemology, Science, Ideology, ed. John Mepham and David-Hillel Ruben (Atlantic Highlands, N.J.: Humanities Press, 1979), p. 144

43. Marx, *Capital*, vol. 1, trans. Ben Fowkes (New York: Vintage Books, 1977), p. 677.

44. Ibid. Cf. Jorge Larrain, "Ideology," p. 220.

45. In fact, any comprehensive look at the writings of Marx and Engels on ideology will reveal that from their point of view the "camera obscura" analogy (and by implication, Feuerbach's principle of the inverted nature of the mystified consciousness) was quite appropriate for depicting the ideological consciousness.

For example, one of the "commonsense" ideologies Marx criticizes in his writings was the ideology of individualism. According to Marx, social agents began to conceive of themselves as essentially "atomistic individuals" without any natural ties to society as a result of the waning of feudal social ties and the emergence of market relationships. Market relationships were especially important to the development of this individualistic self-understanding because market relationships forced social agents to contract with employers as private individuals.

As the following passage from his *Introduction to a Critique of Political Economy* makes evident, Marx argued that the individualist viewpoint characteristic of capitalist society is not only ahistorical but it inverts the proper causal and ontological relationship between individuals and their societies.

> The prophets of the eighteenth century, on whose shoulders Adam Smith and Ricardo were still standing...saw this individual not as an historical result, but as the starting-point of history; not as something evolving in the course of history, but posited by nature,

because for them this individual was in conformity with nature, in keeping with their idea of human nature.

Of course, in the opinion of bourgeois thinkers, individuals naturally exist prior to society, and society only comes into existence as a result of contracts between atomistic individuals. In Marx's opinion, however, "Man is...not only a social animal, but an animal that can individualize himself only within society" (*Grundrisse*).

Of course, the individualism characteristic of capitalist society pervades many different forms of thought, both practical and theoretical. In social sciences, methodological individualism is contrasted with holistic or institutional methods of analyses. In law and political theory, the individual subject with rights represents one of the dominant categories for analysis as well as a desirable social norm. In economic theory and moral theory, the individual utility-seeking agent serves as a model for analysis. And, of course, in philosophy, the individual cogito of epistemology serves as a model for human consciousness.

In any event, for Marx, the individualist viewpoint characteristic of the self-understanding of social agents in capitalist society was an inverted, mystified viewpoint.

Marx also found evidence of an inverted consciousness in legal thinking. In his discussion of the "juridical illusion" characteristic of legal philosophy, Marx argued that jurists operate under the illusion that legal rules are independent of any social determination and in fact are the primary and constitutive factors in the formation of civil societies. Furthermore, because jurists assume that legal rules are autonomous, this justifies their belief that the rationality of legal systems can be understood independently of social and material factors. However, from Marx's perspective, jurists have things backwards. He says in *Capital*, vol. 1, p. 766, n. 4:

> ...from the standpoint...of [the] juridical illusion, he does not regard the law as a product of the material relations of production, but rather the reverse: he sees the relations of production as products of the law. Linguet overthrew Montesquieu's illusory 'esprit des lois' with one word: L'esprit des lois, c'est la propriété.

Finally, Marx also employed Feuerbach's principle of inversion in criticizing Proudhon's idealism. The following citation from Marx's *Poverty of Philosophy* contains both Marx's criticism of

Proudhon's idealist "inverted" understanding concerning the origin and nature of ideas and Marx's own materialist perspective:

> Economic categories are only the theoretical expressions, the abstractions of the social relations of production. M. Proudhon, holding things upside down like a true philosopher, sees in actual relations nothing but the incarnation of these principles...

Thus, we see that Marx used extensively the camera obscura analogy and its implicit Feuerbachian principle of inversion for understanding and criticizing forms of ideological thought. In addition, Feuerbach's principle of inversion also had a considerable influence on Engels, who like Marx favored the "camera obscura" metaphor for depicting the ideological process. In a letter to Conrad Schmidt (October, 1890), Engels once again made use of the terminology he and Marx had used to describe ideology as far back as their work *The German Ideology* (1846). Engels said in the letter,

> Economic, political and other reflections are like those reflections in the human eye—they pass through a convex lens and appear inverted, on their heads...The money-market man will see the movement of industry and of the world market only in its inverted reflections of the money and stock markets, and so, for him, effect becomes cause.

Engels goes on to describe in his letter to Schmidt how these inverted appearances of reality contribute to the political false consciousness of social agents.

> Just as the movement of the industrial market is...reflected in the money market [as] naturally inverted,— so [in] the struggles of the opposing classes which existed beforehand is reflected in the struggle between government and opposition...no longer directly, but indirectly, not as a class struggle but as a struggle for political principles, and so inverted...

Engels in his letter to Schmidt also, like Marx, criticizes lawyers for their inverted consciousness.

> ...the reflection of economic relations as the principles of law is equally necessarily one which stands on its

> head: it proceeds without entering the consciousness of the person involved; the lawyer imagines he can operate with *a priori* phrases, while these are really only reflections of the economy...

Finally, in ending his discussion on the nature of the ideological consciousness, Engels informs Schmidt:

> And it seems to me to be natural that this inversion, which, as long as it is not recognized, constitutes the thing we call an ideological viewpoint.

All of these passages suggest that Marx and Engels were actually quite spellbound by the camera obscura analogy and its Feuerbachian principle of inversion.

46. Marx, *Capital*, vol. 1, p. 680.

47. Ibid., pp. 990, 1024.

48. Marx, *Capital*, vol. 3, trans. David Fernbach (New York: Vintage Books, 1981), p. 969.

CHAPTER SIX. ALIENATION AND FALSE CONSCIOUSNESS IN THE WRITINGS OF THE YOUNG MARX

1. Marx, *On the Jewish Question*, in *The Marx-Engels Reader*, ed. Robert C. Tucker (New York: W. W. Norton & Co., 1972), pp. 32, 37.

2. Cf. Hegel's *Philosophy of Right*, para. 187: "Individuals in their capacity as burghers in this state are private persons whose end is their own interest."

3. Hegel, *Reason in History*, trans. Robert S. Hartman (Indianapolis, Ind.: Bobbs-Merrill, 1953), pp. 50, 52–53.

4. Marx, *On the Jewish Question*, p. 31.

5. Ibid., pp. 31–32.

6. Ibid., p. 41.

7. John Locke, *Second Treatise on Government*, para. 138.

8. Marx, *On the Jewish Question*, pp. 40, 41.

9. Ibid., pp. 41, 43.

10. James Madison, "The Federalist No. 10."

11. Marx, *On the Jewish Question*, p. 32.

12. Erica Sherover-Marcuse, *Emancipation and Consciousness: Dogmatism and Dialectical Perspectives in the Early Marx* (New York: Basil Blackwell, 1986), p. 62.

13. Feuerbach, *The Essence of Christianity*, trans. George Eliot (New York: Harper Torchbooks, 1957), pp. 140–41.

14. Marx's introduction to *Critique of Hegel's "Philosophy of Right,"* trans. Annette Jolin and Joseph O'Malley (Cambridge: Cambridge University Press, 1978), p. 131.

15. Cf. Marx, *On the Jewish Question*, pp. 44–45 concerning the state as a "real abstract universal" and reification of human social powers:

> when he has recognized and organized his own powers...as social powers so that he no longer separates this social power from himself as political power.

16. Erica Sherover-Marcuse, *Emancipation and Consciousness*, p. 63, remarks on the difference between the young Marx and Feuerbach on abstraction:

> For Feuerbach abstraction is a mental process which is fundamentally misguided...For Marx, on the other hand, abstraction is characteristic not only of people's thinking but their lives as well.

17. Marx, "Theses on Feuerbach," #4.

18. Marx, *The Economic and Philosophical Manuscripts of 1844*, trans. Martin Milligan (New York: International Publishers, 1964), p. 178.

19. Ibid., p. 108.

20. Ibid.

21. Marx, "On James Mill," in *Karl Marx: Early Texts*, ed. David McLellan (New York: Barnes and Noble, 1972), p. 189.

22. Cf. Thomas Hobbes, *Leviathan*, selections reprinted in *Approaches to Ethics*, ed. W. T. Jones et. al (New York: McGraw-Hill, 1977), p. 178:

> The value or worth of a man is, as of all other things, his price—that is to say, so much as would be given for the use of his power...

23. Marx, "On James Mill," p. 198.
24. Marx and Engels, *The German Ideology*, p. 55.
25. Marx, *The Economic and Philosophical Manuscripts of 1844*, p. 116.
26. Cf. in ibid., p. 110, Marx's remark on the practical and social nature of alienation:

> Till now we have been considering...the alienation of the worker only in one of its aspects, i.e., the worker's relationship to the products of his labor. But the estrangement is manifested not only in the result but in the act of production, within the producing activity, itself. How could the worker come to face the product of his activity as a stranger, were it not that in the very act of production he was estranging himself from himself?

See also his comment in ibid., p. 111, on ownership:

> Lastly, the external character of labor for the worker appears in the fact that it is not his own, but someone else's, that it does not belong to him...but to another...

27. Hegel, *Phenomenology of Spirit*, pp. 229, 294.
28. Marx, *The Economic and Philosophical Manuscripts of 1844*, p. 176:

> ...inasmuch as [Hegel's *Phenomenology of Spirit*] grasps steadily man's estrangement, even though man appears only in the shape of Mind, there lies concealed in it all the elements of criticism, already prepared and elaborated in a manner often rising far above the Hegelian standpoint.

29. Ibid., p. 177.
30. Ibid., p. 180.
31. Ibid., p. 188.
32. Ibid., p. 172.

CHAPTER SEVEN. ALIENATION, THE FETISHISM OF COMMODITIES, AND IDEOLOGY IN CAPITAL

1. Marx, *Capital*, vol. 1, trans. Ben Fowkes (New York: Vintage Books, 1977), p. 680.
2. Ibid., p. 682.
3. Cf. *Capital*, vol. 3, trans. David Fernbach (New York: Vintage Books, 1981), p. 962, where Marx says,

> It is the great merit of classical economists to have dissolved this false appearance and deception, this autonomization and ossification of the different social elements of wealth vis-à-vis one another, this personification of things and reification of the relations of production...

N. B. Marx distinguished between "vulgar" economists and the "great classical economists" like Smith and Ricardo. According to Marx, the theories and formulas of the "vulgar" economists remained captivated by the false appearances of the capitalist economy.

4. Ibid., vol. 3, pp. 955, 961.
5. Ibid., vol. 1, p. 274.
6. Ibid., p. 989.
7. Ibid., pp. 990, 1003.
8. Ibid., p. 167, as cited by Georg Lukacs in his *History and Class Consciousness: Studies in Marxist Dialectics*, trans. Rodney Livingstone (Cambridge: MIT Press, 1971), p. 49.
9. Marx, *Capital*, vol. 1, p. 899.
10. Marx, *Introduction to a Critique of Political Economy*. Selections are reprinted in the New World paperback edition of *The German Ideology* (New York: International Publishers, 1978), p. 127.
11. Marx, *Capital*, vol. 3, p. 963.
12. Ibid., vol. 1, p. 1005.
13. Ibid., pp. 164–65.
14. Ibid., p. 177.
15. Ibid., p. 167.
16. Cf. p. 168:

> It is however precisely the finished form of the world of commodities—the money form—which conceals

the social character of private labor and the social relations between the individual workers, by making these relations appear as relations between material objects.

17. Ibid., vol. 3, p. 968.

18. Ibid., vol. 1, p. 169.

19. Ibid., vol. 3, p. 969.

20. Cf. ibid., vol. 1, p. 174, note 34.

21. Ibid., p. 714.

22. Ibid., p. 679.

23. Ibid., vol. 3, p. 956.

24. Ibid., vol. 1, p. 998.

25. John Stuart Mill, *Principles of Political Economy*, bk. 2, ch. 15; bk. 2, ch. 16.

26. William Baumol and Alan Binder, *Economics: Principles and Policy, Macroeconomics*, 4th ed. (Orlando, Fla.: Harcourt Brace Jovanovich, 1988), p. 37.

27. Marx, letter to Engels, 27 June 1867, in *Letters on "Capital,"* trans. Andrew Dummond (London: New Park Publications, 1983), p. 109.

28. Marx, *Capital*, cited by Derek Sayers in his *Marx's Method: Ideology, Science and Critique in "Capital"* (Atlantic Highlands, N.J.: Humanities Press, 1979), p. ix.

29. Marx, *Capital*, vol. 1, see the preface to first edition, p. 90.

30. Marx, *Poverty of Philosophy* (New York: International Publishers, 1982), p. 49.

31. Marx, *Capital*, vol. 3, p. 969.

32. Marx, *Introduction to a Critique of Political Economy*, p. 141.

33. Marx, *Capital*, vol. 1, pp. 998–99.

34. Ibid., p. 273.

35. Marx, *Poverty of Philosophy*, as cited by Mihaly Vajda in "Truth or Truths," *Cultural Hermeneutics* 3 (1975), p. 35.

36. Marx, letter to Kugelmann, 11 July 1868, in *Letters on "Capital,"* p. 149.

37. Marx, *Capital*, vol. 3, p. 969.
38. Ibid., vol. 1, p. 874. Marx says:
> on the one hand, the owners of money, means of production, means of subsistence, who are eager to valorize the sum of values they have appropriated by buying the labour-power of others; on the other hand, free workers, the sellers of their own labour-power... Free workers, in the double sense that they form neither part of the means of production as would be the case with slaves, serfs, etc., nor do they own the means of production...

39. Marx, *Economic and Philosophical Manuscripts of 1844*, trans. Martin Milligan (New York: International Publishers, 1982), p. 110.
40. Ibid., p. 116.
41. Marx, *Capital*, vol. 1, pp. 874–75.
42. Ibid., pp. 715–16.
43. Ibid., p. 1003.
44. Ibid., p. 953.
45. Ibid., p. 1020.
46. Ibid., p. 755.
47. Ibid., p. 174.
48. Ibid., p. 167, as cited by Georg Lukacs in his *History and Class Consciousness: Studies in Marxist Dialectics,* trans. Rodney Livingstone (Cambridge: MIT Press, 1971), p. 49.
49. In *Capital*, vol. 1, ch. 1, sec. 4, Marx compares the fetishism of commodities with the imaginary reifications of religion.
50. Ibid., p. 990.
51. Marx, *Economic and Philosophical Manuscripts of 1844*, p. 111.
52. Marx, "On James Mill," in *Karl Marx: The Early Texts*, ed. David McLellan (New York: Barnes and Noble, 1972), p. 189.
53. Marx, *Capital*, vol. 1, p. 173.
54. Marx, *Grundrisse*, cited by Roger Gottlieb in his "A Marx-

ian Concept of Ideology," *Philosophical Forum* (Boston) 6 (1974–75), p. 383.

55. Engels, *On the Origin of the State*, selections reprinted in *The Marx-Engels Reader*, ed. Robert C. Tucker (New York: W. W. Norton Co., 1972), p. 655.

56. Engels, *Socialism: Utopian and Scientific*, selections reprinted in *The Marx-Engels Reader*, p. 634.

57. Engels, *On the Origin of the State*, p. 655.

58. John Mepham, "Theory of Ideology in *Capital*," in *Issues in Marxist Philosophy*, vol. 3: *Epistemology, Science, Ideology*, ed. John Mepham and David-Hillel Ruben (Atlantic Highlands, N.J.: Humanities Press, 1979), p. 151.

59. Norman Geras, "Marx and the Critique of Political Economy," in *Ideology in Social Science: Readings in Critical Social Theory*, ed. Robin Blackburn (New York: Pantheon, 1972), p. 286.

60. Derek Sayer, *Marx's Method: Ideology, Science and Critique in "Capital"* (Atlantic Highlands, N.J.: Humanities Press, 1979), p. 8.

61. Norman Geras, "Marx and the Critique of Political Economy," p. 286.

62. However, not all commentators have overlooked the link between alienation, inversion and ideology in Marx's writings. For example, in Mihailo Markovic's essay "The Language of Ideology," *Synthese* 59 (1984), p.72, Markovic comments:

> Marx specifies the types of social situation in which ideological consciousness emerges: this is invariably a society that is governed by forces and mechanisms that man has created and over which he has lost control. He produces commodities, money, capital, states, churches, political parties, but loses control over them, and rather than regulating them consciously he becomes an object governed by them. Under those conditions man produces theories that have no chance of being adequate pictures of reality since he is not able to see correctly...Therefore he produces a false illusory consciousness in which all real social structures have been turned upside down.

The quote from Markovic is a good summary of Marx's view that when human beings lose control over their social creations, humas become subordinate to their own creations. And a result of the alienation of human beings from their own social creations, human beings come to view their social world in an upside-down fashion.

CONCLUSION

1. Joe McCarney, *The Real World of Ideology* (Atlantic Highlands, N.J.: Humanities Press, 1980), p. 95.

2. Ibid., p. 80.

3. V. Z. Kelle remarks in his "Ideology as a Phenomenon of Social Consciousness," in *Philosophy in the USSR: Problems of Dialectical Materialism* (Moscow: Progress Publishers, 1977), p. 261:

> the illusoriness of the ideology of the exploiting class is related to the fact that in expressing a special (selfish, mercernary) interest of a given class it endows it with the form of universality...

It might be argued that against feudalism bourgeois ideologies really did serve the interests of the majority, because it was in the interest of the majority to overthrow an obsolete social system. However, while it was prudent for the oppressed proletariat to ally themselves with the bourgeois leaders in the revolution against feudalism, it can't be the case that bourgeois ideology provided the oppressed proletariat with a true understanding of their real interests.

In essence, bourgeois ideologies cannot truly serve the oppressed proletariat at any time in history, because bourgeois ideologies idealize and legitimate a new form of class society. But as Marx often said, the real interests of the proletariat consists, firstly, in overthrowing the class system, and secondly, in avoiding being "seduced" and "confused" by the pseudoliberationist themes of bourgeois ideologies. See notes 5 and 9 *infra*.

4. Marx and Engels, *The Communist Manifesto* (Northbrook, Ill.: AHM Publishing Corp, 1955), p. 27:

> the selfish misconception that induces you to transform into eternal laws of nature and of reason, the

social forms springing from your present mode of production and form of property...this misconception you share with every ruling class that has preceded you.

5. In this respect, it is of interest to note how Marx and Engels in their *Address of the Central Committee to the Communist League* (1850) admonished the German workers not "to be seduced" by bourgeois liberal democratic ideology and to get clear in their own minds as to their revolutionary, not reformist, political interests.

6. Cf. Ehud Sprinzak's remarks in her essay "Marx's Historical Conception of Ideology and Science," *Politics and Society* (1975). See also the writings of Barry Hindess and Paul Q. Hirst, who reject all epistemological evaluations of ideology and advocate political evaluations instead. For a critique of Hirst and Hindess, see the works of Ted Benton, and essays by Tony Skillen in the journal *Radical Philosophy*.

7. An excellent illustration of Marx's rational and scientific critique of ideology can be found in his *Theories on Surplus Value*, in which Marx criticizes Thomas Malthus's theory of population as an ideology. According to Marx, Malthus's theory of population (cf. Malthus's work *An Essay on the Principle of Population, as it affects the Future Improvement of Society, with Remarks on the Speculations of Mr. Godwin, M. Condorcet, and other Writers* [1798]) was an ideological theory because: (1) it served the political-economic interests of the reactionary elements of the ruling class as a justification for opposing any social reforms and political changes which might improve the lot of the poor and society as a whole; (2) it was false; and (3) it was anti-scientific.

Malthus's theory functioned as an "apology" for the ruling class, according to Marx, because it

> had the practical purpose to provide 'economic' proof in the interests of the existing English government and the landed aristocracy, that the tendency of the French Revolution and its adherents in England to perfect matters was utopian. In other words, it was a panegyric pamphlet for the existing conditions, against historical development and, furthermore, a justification of the war against revolutionary France. (p. 119)

Malthus's theory was false, according to Marx, because it had been refuted by Charles Darwin's theory of evolution:

> In his splendid work, Darwin did not realise that by discovering the 'geometrical' progression in the animal and plant kingdom, he overthrew Malthus's theory. Malthus's theory is based on the fact that he set Wallace's geometrical progression of man against the chimerical 'arithmetical' progession of animals and plants. In Darwin's work [therefore] we...find...the detailed refutation, based on natural history, of the Malthusian theory. (p. 121)

Finally, Malthus's theory was antiscientific, according to Marx, because Malthus allowed his class perspective and interests to bias and falsify his theoretical findings.

> ...when a man seeks to accommodate science to a viewpoint which is derived not from science itself...but from outside, from alien, external interests, then I call him 'base'...Malthus does not sacrifice the particular interests to production but seeks...to sacrifice the demands of production to the particular interests of existing ruling classes or sections of classes. And to this end *he falsifies* his scientific conclusions. This is his scientific baseness...The scientific conclusions of Malthus are 'considerate' towards the ruling classes in general and towards the reactionary elements of the ruling classes in particular... (pp. 119–20)

For my discussion of Marx's own "proletariatn class standpoint," in science, see chapter 2 on Bacon and Marx.

8. In *Interpretations of Marx*, ed. Tom Bottomore (London: Basil Blackwell, 1988), p. 295, Leszek Kolakowski remarks on Marx's demarcation criterion:

> The social function of ideology is to consolidate belief in the values which are essential to the fruitful activity of the group. Thus, ideology is not, and cannot be, 'pure' theory, for the knowledge of reality as such cannot incite anyone to activity...The distinction between ideology and science is not a distinction between false-

hood and truth. They are distinguished by their social function and not by their degree of veracity. I am using the concept of ideology, therefore, roughly in the sense in which Marx used it...Since all political action needs an ideology, it is impossible to get rid of ideology as a social phenomenon.

9. Marx's letter to Sorge, 19 October 1877, printed in *Letters on "Capital"*, trans. Andrew Drummond (London: New Park Publications, 1983), p. 319, says,

> The compromise with the Lassalleans has led to compromise with the half-way elements in Berlin, with Dühring and his 'admirers'...who want to give socialism a 'higher ideal' orientation, that is to say, to *replace its materialistic basis* (which demands serious objective study...) by modern *mythology* with its goddess of Justice, Freedom, Equality and Fraternity.

In a similar vein, Engels in his letter to Bebel, 28 March 1875 (cited in the same work, p. 337) says,

> The notion of socialist society as the realm of equality is a *superficial* French idea resting upon the old 'liberty, equality, fraternity'—an idea which was justified as a stage of development in its own time and place but which, like all the superficial ideas of the earlier socialist schools, should now be overcome, for they only produce *confusion* in people's heads and *more precise forms of description* have been found.

What Marx and Engels imply is that the ideological categories of bourgeois liberalism and "utopian socialism" (e.g., liberty, equality, fraternity, justice) were inappropriate for the proletarian revolutionary movement because their superficial and abstract nature causes "confusion in people's minds" while diverting the proletariat from a "materialistic" and objective understanding of their political aims and social goals. Their rejection of an ideological perspective for the proletarian movement is evident, in addition, in their mutual letter to Bebel, Liebknecht, Bracke, et al., cited in Drummond, p. 375:

> When the class struggle is pushed to one side as a disagreeable 'crude' phenomenon, nothing remains as a

basis for socialism but 'true love of humanity' and empty phraseology about 'justice'.

Hence, what Marx and Engels imply is that ideological and epistemologically adequate class-conscious perspectives are mutually exclusive. The former utilizes vague and misleading categories which have a "populist" and "humanist-moralistic" appeal. But because such categories have a "universal" appeal, they can be utilized by ruling classes to manipulate the oppressed. Hence, in the French Revolution, the bourgeoisie utilized populist-sounding categories like "the rights of Man" (e.g., "human rights") and "equality" to mobilize the support of the proletariat in the creation of a bourgeois republican state.

In contrast, the class or "anti-moralist" and "anti-humanist" perspective is distinctive in the fact that as a political outlook it seeks to address some groups in society while criticizing other groups (e.g., ruling groups) in society. The class perspective is "materialistic" or concrete in the respect that as a political perspective it openly acknowledges the reality of antagonistic and irreconcilable class interests. Finally, this class-conscious perspective emphasizes the priority of class interest as the basis for political action as opposed to moralistic sentiments for "universal" human rights or "equal" political rights, which have the potential of deflecting the proletariat from their real aims, according to Marx and Engels.

Marx and Engels, then, denied the suitability of a "humanistic" and "universal Idealistic" political perspective for the proletariat (i.e., a proletarian "ideology"), and demanded members of the Communist Party to adopt a class political perspective. Their letter to Bebel, et al., quoted in Drummond, p. 376 makes this clear:

> If people...from other classes join the proletarian movement, the first condition is that they should not bring any remnants of bourgeois, petty-bourgeois... prejudices with them but should whole-heartedly adopt the proletarian point of view."

10. In various writings, Marx referred to the "bourgeois horizon of thought" which structures and limits the social consciousness of agents. Cf. Marx's "Critique of the Gotha Program," in *The Marx-Engels Reader*, p. 388:

> In a higher phase of communist society, after the enslaving subordination of the individual to the divi-

sion of labor...only then can the narrow horizon of bourgeois right be crossed in its entirety...

In this spirit, see the discussion by Kenneth Dolbeare and Linda Medcalf in their *American Ideologies Today: From Neo-Politics to New Ideas* (New York: Random House, 1988), pp. 5 and 14:

> ...the way of thinking characteristic of a society sets limits to what people can think about...[For example] in the United States, the individual serves as the self-evident starting point for thinking about the nature and purpose of social life. We have no image of society as an independent organism with a life of its own and the right to ask certain behavior from the individuals who happen to make it up...

Finally, see the classic work by Herbert Marcuse, *One Dimensional Man: Studies in the Ideology of Advanced Industrial Society* (Boston: Beacon Press, 1964).

11. Bacon, *The New Organon* (New York: Macmillan, 1985), p. 22.

12. Holbach, *System of Nature*, trans. H. D. Robinson (New York: Burt Franklin, 1970), pp. 11, 84.

13. Hegel, *Reason in History*, trans. Robert S. Hartman (Indianapolis, Ind.: Bobbs-Merrill, 1953), p. 94. In his *What Marx Really Said* (New York: Schocken Books, 1967), p. 76, H. B. Acton comments on Marx's concept of false consciousness and suggests this Hegelian conception of the historical unconsciousness:

> What men say about what they are doing and why they are doing it cannot be relied upon as an account of what they are really doing. This is not necessarily because they are lying, but because they do not understand the forces that are moving society, and with society themselves.

14. Hegel, *The Phenomenology of Spirit*, trans. A. V. Miller (Oxford: Clarendon Press, 1977), pp. 229, 294.

15. Feuerbach, *The Essence of Christianity*, trans. George Eliot (New York: Harper Torchbooks, 1957), p. 204.

16. For example, Marx seems to imply that the idea of democracy appeals to oppressed groups because it suggests in a "vague

way" freedom from class oppression as well as anticipates a future classless or socialist society. Cf. Marx, *The Civil War in France*, reprinted in *The Marx-Engels Reader*, ed. Robert C. Tucker (New York: W. W. Norton, 1972), p. 554:

> The cry of 'social republic' with which the revolution of February was ushered in by the Paris proletariat, did but express a vague aspiration after a Republic that was not only to supersede the monarchical form of class-rule, but class-rule itself.

17. Cf. Marx, "Theses on Feuerbach," thesis #7:

> Feuerbach...does not see that the 'religious sentiment' is itself a social product, and that the abstract individual whom he analyses belongs to a particular form of society.

18. Cf. Marx and Engels, *The German Ideology, Part One*, ed. C. J. Arthur (New York: International Publishers, 1978), p. 47:

> ...we do not set out from what men say, imagine, conceive...in order to arrive at men in the flesh. We set out from real, active men, and on the basis of their real life-process we demonstrate the development of the ideological reflexes and echoes of this life process. The phantoms formed in the human brain are...sublimates of their material life-process...

19. Marx, *Capital*, vol. 1, trans. Ben Fowkes (New York: Vintage Books, 1977), p. 1024.

20. Marx, *Capital*, vol. 3, trans. David Fernbach (New York: Vintage Books, 1981), p. 969 and ibid., p. 680.

21. In *The Poverty of Philosophy* (New York: International Publishers, 1982), p. 189, Marx remarks on the false consciousness of Proudhon:

> Proudhon does not state directly that bourgeois life is for him an eternal verity; he states it indirectly by deifying the categories which express bourgeois relations in the form of thought. He takes the products of bourgeois society for spontaneously arisen eternal

beings, endowed with a life of their own, as soon as they present themselves to his mind in the form of categories...

22. For this proposition, I am indebted to the discussion of Fernuccio Rossi-Landi in his *Marxism and Ideology*, trans. Roger Griffen (Oxford: Clarendon Press, 1990). Rossi-Landi distinguishes between two predominant conceptions of ideology—the pejorative conception of ideology as false thinking and the descriptive sense of ideology as worldview. After discussing the different senses of the pejorative view of ideology, Rossi-Landi asserts that the "common denominator" of all the various senses of the pejorative view is ideology as false thinking.

Bibliography

SELECTED WORKS OF KARL MARX AND FREDERICK ENGELS

Marx. *Critique of Hegel's "Philosophy of Right."* Trans. Annette Jolin and Joseph O'Malley. Cambridge: Cambridge University Press, 1978.

———. *The Economic and Philosophic Manuscripts of 1844.* Trans. Martin Milligan. New York: International Publishers, 1964.

———, and Engels. *The German Ideology:* Part One. Ed. C. J. Arthur. New York: International Publishers, 1978.

———. *The Poverty of Philosophy.* New York: International Publishers, 1963.

———. *Class Struggles in France, 1848–1850.* New York: International Publishers, 1980.

———, and Engels. *The Revolution of 1848–49: Articles from the "Neue rheinische Zeitung."* Trans. S. Ryazanskaya. New York: International Publishers, 1972.

———. *Capital.* Vol. 1. Trans. Ben Fowkes. New York: Vintage Books, 1977.

———. *Capital.* Vol. 2. Trans. David Fernbach. New York: Vintage Books, 1981.

———. *Capital.* Vol. 3. Trans. David Fernbach. New York: Vintage Books, 1981.

———. *Theories of Surplus Value, Part II.* Trans. S. Ryazanskaya. Moscow: Progress Publishers, 1968.

Engels. *The Peasant War in Germany.* In *The German Revolutions: "The Peasant War in Germany,"* and *"Germany: Revolution and Counter-Revolution."* Ed. Leonard Krieger. Chicago: University of Chicago Press, 1967.

———. *Ludwig Feuerbach and the End of Classical German Philosophy*. Moscow: Progress Publishers, 1969.

———. *Anti-Dühring: Herr Eugen Dühring's Revolution in Science*. Trans. Emile Burns. New York: International Publishers, 1976.

EDITED ANTHOLOGIES ON THE WRITINGS OF MARX AND ENGELS

Bottomore, T. B., and Maximilien Rubel, eds. *Karl Marx: Selected Writings in Sociology and Social Philosophy*. New York: McGraw-Hill, 1956.

Drummond, Andrew, trans. *Letters on "Capital."* London: New Park Publications, 1983.

Fernbach, David, ed. *Karl Marx, Political Writings*. Vol. 2: *Survey from Exile*. New York: Vintage Books, 1974.

Goldway, David, Howard Selsam, and Harry Martel, eds. *Dynamics of Social Change: A Reader in Marxist Social Science, from the Writings of Marx, Engels and Lenin*. New York: International Publishers, 1983.

Martel, Harry, and Howard Selsam. *Reader in Marxist Philosophy, from the Writings of Marx, Engels and Lenin*. New York: International Publishers, 1980.

Tucker, Robert C., ed. *The Marx-Engels Reader*. New York: W. W. Norton, 1972.

SELECTED WORKS AND ANTHOLOGIES OF FRANCIS BACON
AND THE FRENCH "PHILOSOPHES"

Bacon. *The New Organon*. New York: Macmillan, 1985.

Beck, Lewis White. *18th-Century Philosophy*. New York: Free Press, 1966.

Gay, Peter, ed. *The Enlightenment: A Comprehensive Anthology*. New York: Simon and Schuster, 1973.

Helvetius. *Treatise on Man*. Vols. 1 and 2. Trans. W. Hooper. New York: Burt Franklin, 1969.

———. *Essay on Mind*. New York: Burt Franklin, 1970.

Holbach. *The System of Nature*. Trans. H. D. Robinson. New York: Burt Franklin, 1970.
Manuel, Frank, ed. *The Enlightenment*. Englewoods Cliffs, N.J.: Prentice-Hall, 1965.
Popkin, Richard, ed. *The Philosophy of the 16th and 17th Centuries*. New York: Free Press, 1966.

SELECTED WORKS OF G. W. F. HEGEL

Hegel. *The Phenomenology of Spirit*. Trans. A. V. Miller. Oxford: Clarendon Press, 1977.
———. *Encyclopaedia of the Philosophical Sciences, Part One*. Trans. William Wallace. Oxford: Oxford University Press, 1975.
———. *The Philosophy of Right*. Trans. T. M. Knox. Oxford: Oxford University Press, 1967.
———. *Reason in History: A General Introduction to the Philosophy of History*. Trans. Robert S. Hartman. Indianapolis, Ind.: Bobbs-Merrill, 1953.

SELECTED WORKS OF LUDWIG FEUERBACH

Feuerbach. *Towards a Critique of Hegel*. In *The Young Hegelians*, edited by Lawrence Stepelevich. Cambridge: Cambridge University Press, 1983.
———. *The Essence of Christianity*. Trans. George Eliot. New York: Harper & Brothers, 1957.
———. *Provisional Theses for the Reformation of Philosophy*. In *The Young Hegelians*, edited by Lawrence Stepelevich. Cambridge: Cambridge University Press, 1983.

SECONDARY BOOKS

Abercrombie, Nicholas. *Class, Structure and Knowledge: Problems in the Sociology of Knowledge*. New York: New York University Press, 1980.
Acton, H. B. *What Marx Really Said*. New York: Schocken Books, 1967.

Althusser, Louis. *Lenin and Philosophy and Other Essays*. Trans. Ben Brewster. New York: Monthly Review Press, 1971.
———. *For Marx*. Trans. Ben Brewster. London: NLB Verso, 1977.
Barrett, Michelle A. *Ideology and Cultural Production*. New York: St. Martin's Press, 1979.
Barth, Hans. *Truth and Ideology*. Trans. Frederic Lilge. Berkeley: University of California Press, 1976.
Beechey, Veronica, and James Donald, eds. *Subjectivity and Social Relations*. Philadelphia: Open University Press, 1985.
Bennett, Tony, Graham Martin, Colin Mercer, and Janet Woollacott, eds. *Culture, Ideology and Social Process: A Reader*. London: Open University Press, 1981.
Bensman, Joseph, and Arthur Vidich. *Small Town in Mass Society: Class, Power and Religion in a Rural Community*. Princeton: Princeton University Press, 1958.
Berki, R. N., Robert Benewick, and Bhikkhu Parekh, eds. *Knowledge and Belief in Politics: The Problem of Ideology*. London: Allen & Unwin, 1973.
Blackburn, Robin. *Ideology in Social Science: Readings in Critical Social Theory*. New York: Pantheon, 1972.
Bober, M. M. *Karl Marx's Interpretation of History*. New York: W. W. Norton, 1956.
Callinicos, Alex. *Marxism and Philosophy*. Oxford: Oxford University Press, 1983.
———. *Making History: Agency, Structure and Changes in Social Theory*. Oxford: Basil Blackwell, 1987.
Carlsnaes, Walter. *The Concept of Ideology and Political Analysis: A Critical Examination of its Usage by Marx, Lenin and Mannheim*. Westport, Conn.: Greenwood Press, 1981.
Cohen, G. A. *Karl Marx's Theory of History: A Defence*. Princeton: Princeton University Press, 1980.
Cranston, Maurice, and Peter Mair, eds. *Ideology and Politics*. Sijthoff: European University Institutes, 1980.
Dallmayr, Fred, and Thomas A. McCarthy, eds. *Understanding and Social Inquiry*. Notre Dame: University of Notre Dame Press, 1977.
Domhoff, G. William. *The Powers That Be: Processes of Ruling-Class Domination in America*. New York: Vintage Books, 1979.

Drucker, H. M. *The Political Uses of Ideology.* New York: Harper and Row, 1974.
Eyerman, Ron. *False Consciousness and Ideology in Marxist Theory.* New Haven: Yale University Press, 1983.
Femia, Joseph. *Gramsci's Political Thought: Hegemony, Consciousness and the Revolutionary Process.* Oxford: Clarendon Press, 1981.
Finnegan, Ruth, and Robin Horton. *Modes of Thought: Essays on Thinking in Western and Non-Western Societies.* London: Faber and Faber, 1973.
Frisby, David. *The Alienated Mind: The Sociology of Knowledge in Germany 1919–1933.* Atlantic Highlands, N.J.: Humanities Press, 1983.
Fromm, Erich. *Beyond the Chains of Illusion.* New York: Touchstone Books, 1985.
Gay, Peter. *Freud for Historians.* Oxford: Oxford University Press, 1985.
Geuss, Raymond. *The Idea of a Critical Theory: Habermas and the Frankfort School.* Cambridge: Cambridge University Press, 1981.
Giddens, Anthony. *Central Problems in Social Theory: Action, Structure and Contradiction in Social Analysis.* London: Macmillan, 1979.
Gruner, Shirley. *Economic Materialism and Social Moralism: A Study of Ideas in France from the latter part of the 18th century to the Middle of the nineteenth century.* Hague: Mouton, 1973.
Halle, Louis J. *The Ideological Imagination.* Chicago: Quadrangle Books, 1972.
Harris, Kevin. *Teachers and Classes: A Marxist Analysis.* London: Routledge & Kegan Paul, 1982.
Harris, Nigel. *Beliefs in Society: The Problem of Ideology.* Harmondsworth: Penguin Books, 1968.
Heilbroner, Robert L. *The Nature and Logic of Capitalism.* New York: W. W. Norton, 1985.
Hibben, Sally, ed. *Politics, Ideology and the State.* London: Lawrence and Wishart, 1978.
Hirst, Paul. *On Law and Ideology.* Atlantic Highlands, N.J.: Humanities Press, 1979.

Jakubowski, Franz. *Ideology and Superstructure in Historical Materialism*. Trans. Anne Booth. New York: St. Martin's Press, 1976.
Kennedy, Emmet. *A Philosophe in the Age of Revolution: Destutt De Tracy and the Origins of Ideology*. Philadelphia: APA, 1978.
Kostas, Axelos. *Alienation, Praxis, and Techne in the Thought of Karl Marx*. Trans. Ronald Bruzina. Austin: University of Texas Press, 1976.
Laclau, Ernesto. *Politics and Ideology in Marxist Theory: Capitalism, Fascism, and Populism*. London: NLB, 1977.
Larrain, Jorge. *The Concept of Ideology*. Athens: University of Georgia Press, 1979.
———. *Marxism and Ideology*. London: Macmillan Press, 1983.
Lash, Nicholas. *A Matter of Hope: A Theologian's Reflections on the Thought of Karl Marx*. Notre Dame: University of Notre Dame Press, 1982.
Lobkowicz, Nicholas. *Theory and Practice: History of a Concept from Aristotle to Marx*. Notre Dame: University of Notre Dame Press, 1967.
Lukacs, Georg. *History and Class Consciousness: Studies in Marxist Dialectics*. Trans. Rodney Livingstone. Cambridge: MIT Press, 1971.
Mannheim, Karl. *Ideology and Utopia: An Introduction to the Sociology of Knowledge*. Trans. Louis Wirth and Edward Shils. New York: Harcourt Brace Jovanovich, 1936.
Marcuse, Herbert. *Reason and Revolution: Hegel and the Rise of Social Theory*. Boston: Beacon Press, 1960.
Mattick, Paul. *Social Knowledge: An Essay on the Nature and Limits of Social Science*. New York: M. E. Sharpe, 1986.
McCarney, Joe. *The Real World of Ideology*. Atlantic Highlands, N.J.: Humanities Press, 1980.
McLellan, David. *Karl Marx: His Life and Thought*. New York: Harper & Row, 1970.
———. *Ideology*. Minneapolis: University of Minnesota Press, 1986.
Mitchell, W. J. T. *Iconology: Image, Text, Ideology*. Chicago: University of Chicago Press, 1986.
McMurty, John. *The Structure of Marx's World-View*. Princeton: Princeton University Press, 1978.
Mepham, John, and David-Hillel Ruben, eds. *Issues in Marxist Phi-*

losophy. Vol. 3. *Epistemology, Science, Ideology*. Atlantic Highlands, N.J.: Humanities Press, 1979.
Merquior, J. G. *The Veil and the Mask: Essays on Culture and Ideology*. London: Routledge & Kegan Paul, 1979.
Meszaros, Istvan. *Philosophy, Ideology and Social Science: Essays in Negation and Affirmation*. New York: St. Martin's Press, 1986.
———, ed. *Aspects of Historical Consciousness*. Boston: Routledge & Kegan Paul, 1971.
Nielsen, Kai, and Steven Patten, eds. *Marx and Morality*. Guelph, Ont.: Canadian Journal of Philosophy supplementary volume 7, 1981.
Parekh, Bhikkhu. *Marx's Theory of Ideology*. Baltimore: Johns Hopkins University Press, 1982.
Parel, Anthony. *Ideology, Philosophy and Politics: Essays*. Waterloo, Ont.: Calgary Institute Press, 1983.
Plamenatz, John. *Ideology*. London: Macmillan, 1970.
Rader, Melvin. *Marx's Interpretation of History*. New York: Oxford University Press, 1979.
Ricoeur, Paul. *Freud and Philosophy: An Essay on Interpretation*. Trans. Denis Savage. New Haven: Yale University Press, 1970.
Rossi-Landi, Ferruccio. *Marxism and Ideology*. Trans. Roger Griffen Oxford: Clarendon Press, 1990.
Ruben, David-Hillel. *Marxism and Materialism: A Study in Marxist Theory of Knowledge*. Atlantic Highlands, N.J.: Humanities Press, 1979.
Rubinstein, David. *Marx and Wittgenstein: Social Praxis and Social Explanation*. Boston: Routledge & Kegan Paul, 1981.
Sharp, Rachel. *Knowledge, Ideology and Politics of Schooling: Towards A Marxist Analysis of Education*. Boston: Routledge & Kegan Paul, 1980.
Sayer, Derek. *Marx's Method: Ideology, Science and Critique in "Capital."* Atlantic Highlands, N.J.: Humanities Press, 1979.
Sayers, Sean. *Reality and Reason: Dialectic and the Theory of Knowledge*. New York: Basil Blackwell, 1985.
Seliger, Martin. *The Marxist Conception of Ideology: A Critical Essay*. Cambridge: Cambridge University Press, 1977.
———. *Ideology and Politics*. London: George Allen & Unwin, 1976.
Therborn, Goran. *The Ideology of Power and the Power of Ideology*. London: Verso, 1980.

———. *Science, Class and Society: On the Formation of Sociology and Historical Materialism*. London: Verso NLB, 1976.
Thompson, Kenneth. *Beliefs and Ideology*. London: Tavistock, 1986.
Thompson, John. *Studies in the Theory of Ideology*. Berkeley: University of California Press, 1984.
Timpanaro, Sebastiano. *On Materialism*. Trans. Lawrence Garner. London: Verso NLB, 1975.
Trigg, Roger. *Understanding Social Science: A Philosophical Introduction to the Social Sciences*. New York: Basil Blackwell, 1985.
Wells, David. *Marxism and the Modern State: An Analysis of Fetishism in Capitalist Society*. Atlantic Highlands, N.J.: Humanities Press, 1981.
Williams, Raymond. *Marxism and Literature*. Oxford: Oxford University Press, 1977.
———. *Problems in Materialism and Culture*. London: Verso NLB, 1980.
Wood, Allen. *Karl Marx*. London: Routledge & Kegan Paul, 1981.

JOURNAL ARTICLES AND ESSAYS

Avineri, Shlomo. "Consciousness and History: List der Vernunft in Hegel and Marx." In *New Studies in Hegel's Philosophy*, edited by Warren Steinkraus. New York: Holt, Rinehart and Winston, 1971.
Bergmann, Gustav. "Ideology." *Ethics* 61 (April 1951).
Birkstead, I. "Validity and Ideology." *Radical Philosophy* 2 (1972).
Braybrooke, David. *Encyclopedia of Philosophy*, S.V. "Ideology."
Drucker, H. M. "Marx's Concept of Ideology." *Philosophy* 47 (April 1972).
Dupre, Louis. "Religion, Ideology, and Utopia in Marx." *New Scholasticism* 50 (1976).
Elster, Jon. "Belief, Bias and Ideology." In *Sour Grapes: Studies in the Subversion of Rationality*. Cambridge: Cambridge University Press, 1983.
Gabel, Peter. "Reification in Legal Reasoning." In *Research in Law*, edited by Steven Spitzer.
Geertz, Clifford. "Ideology as a Cultural System." In *Ideology and Its Discontents*, edited by David Apter. New York: Free Press, 1964.

Giaquinto, M. "Science and Ideology." *Proceedings of the Aristotelian Society* 84 (Summer 1984).

Gottlieb, Roger. "A Marxian Concept of Ideology." *Philosophical Forum* (Boston) 6 (1974–75).

Hahn, Eric. "Ideology and Reflection." *Revolutionary World* 27 (1978).

Hippolite, Jean. "The 'Scientific' and the 'Ideological' in a Marxist Perspective." *Diogenes* 64 (1968).

Hoffman, John. "Ideology and the Question of Value-Free Science." *Dialectical Humanism* 7 (Winter 1980).

Hudelson, Richard. "Marxist Science as Ordinary Science." *Nous* 20 (1986).

"Ideology." *Great Soviet Encyclopedia*.

Jameson, Frederic. "Science vs. Ideology." *Human Society* 6 (Spring–Summer 1983).

Kelle, V. Z. "Ideology as a Phenomenon of Social Consciousness." In *Philosophy in the USSR: Problems of Dialectical Materialism*. Moscow: Progress Publishers, 1977.

Kennedy, E. "'Ideology' from Destutt De Tracy to Marx." *Journal of the History of Ideas* 40 (1979).

Larrain, Jorge. "Ideology." In *Dictionary of Marxist Thought*, edited by Tom Bottomore. Cambridge: Harvard University Press, 1983.

Lichtheim, George. "The Concept of Ideology." *History and Theory* 4 (1965).

———. "Freud and Marx." In *Freud: The Man, His World, His Influence*, edited by Jonathan Miller. Boston: Little, Brown, 1972.

Mackie, J. L. "Ideological Explanation." In *Explanation: Papers and Discussion*, edited by Stephen Korner. New York: Basil Blackwell, 1975.

MacQuire, J. "Marx on Ideology, Power, and Force." *Theory and Decision*. 7 (1976).

Marcus, Gyorgy. "Ideology and its Ideologies." *Philosophy and Social Criticism* 7–8 (Summer 1981).

Mepham, John. "The Theory of Ideology in *Capital*." In *Epistemology, Science, Ideology*, edited by David-Hillel Ruben and John Mepham. Vol. 3 of *Issues in Marxist Philosophy*.

Mihailo, Markovic. "The Language of Ideology." *Synthese* 59 (1984).

Miller, David. "Ideology and the Problem of False Consciousness." *Political Studies* 20 (1972).

Mills, Charles W. "'Ideology' in Marx and Engels." *The Philosophical Forum* (Boston) 16 (Summer 1985).
Minogue, K. R. "Epiphenomenalism in Politics: The Quest for Political Reality." *Political Studies* 20 (December 1972).
Murdock, Graham. "Mass Communication and the Construction of Meaning." In *Reconstructing Social Psychology*, edited by Nigel Armistead. London: Penguin Books, 1974.
Niebuhr, Reinhold. "Ideology and Scientific Method." In *Christian Realism and Political Problems*. New York: Kelly, 1953.
Nielsen, Kai. "Justice and Ideology: Justice as Ideology." *Windsor Yearbook of Access to Justice* 1 (1981).
Partridge, P. H. "Politics, Philosophy, Ideology." In *Political Philosophy*, edited by Anthony Quinton. Oxford: Oxford University Press, 1967.
Rosenberg, Harold. "Politics of Illusion." In *Discovering the Present: Three Decades in Art, Culture and Politics*. Chicago: University of Chicago Press, 1973.
Runciman, W. G. "False Consciousness." *Philosophy* 44 (October 1969).
Schumpeter, Joseph. "Is the History of Economics A History of Ideology?" In *The Philosophy of Economics: An Anthology*, edited by Daniel Hausman. Cambridge: Cambridge University Press, 1984.
Small, Robin. "Knowledge and Ideology in the Marxian Philosophy of Education." *Educational Theory* 15 (1983).
Sprinzak, Ehud. "Marx's Historical Conception of Ideology and Science." *Politics and Society* (1975).
Stevenson, J. "Marx's Theory of Ideology." *Radical Philosophical Newsletter* 9 (Fall 1977).
Urbanek, E. "Roles, Masks, and Character: A Contribution to Marx's Idea of the Social Role." *Social Research* 34 (1967).
Williamson, Colwyn. "Ideology and the Problem of Knowledge." *Inquiry* 10 (1967).

Index

A
Abercrombie, Nicolas, 13, 176
absolutism, monarchical, 18. *See also* divine right of kings
alienated mind, Bacon on, 21; difference between Bacon and Hegel, on 93; Feuerbach on, 94–96; difference between Feuerbach and Marx, 117–118, 123; Hegel on 93–94; difference between Marx and Hegel, 125; Marx on, 95, 150–151; *philosophes* on, 30–31
alienation: Engels on, 151–152; Hegel on, 94, 102, 207; Feuerbach on, 96–97, 117; Marx on 94–95, 105, 109–110, 113, 118, 120–121, 127, 143–147, 213
Althusser, Louis, 4, 107
ancien regime, 21
ancient political thought, 196
anti-moralism, 160, 185, 198, 221–222
appearances, 14, 59; acquiring alien, mystified form, 93–95, 123–124, 134, 145–146; as ideology, 60, 63–64, 127; commonsense, 108–109, 130–131, 133, 135, 138; reified, 130, 142; representing reality in inverted form, 108, 138
a priori ideas. *See also* ideological fallacies: mistaking socially-historically contingent thought as eternally valid a priori ideas; innate truths
Avineri, Shlomo, 75

B
Barth, Hans, 101
base/superstructure, 13, 58–59, 195–196. *See also* economic systems
Beard, Charles, 183
Bible, 17
Braybrooke, David, 2

C
Callinicos, Alex, 5, 12, 69, 187, 189–190
camera obscura model of ideology, 105, 107–109, 150, 208–211
Carlsnaes, Walter, 11
Christianity: Catholic Church, 56, 80, 82; doctrine of heavenly afterlife, 53. *See also* ideologies: religious
class analysis, Bensman and Vidich on, 182; Engels on 79; Marx on 25, 68, 84, 140
class consciousness, 51
common sense, 13, 59, 65, 108–109, 128, 135
communitarianism, 79
Condillac, 32, 35
consciousness. *See* idealist conception of mind; materialist conception of

consciousness *(continued)*
  mind; social determination of ideological thought; social determination of thought
conspiracy theory of ideology, 52, 54, 58, 164, 187, 189, 204
cunning of reason. *See* Hegel: cunning of reason and false consciousness

D
Darwin, Charles, 177–178
deception, 9, 57–58. *See also* self-deception
demarcation criterion. *See* science/ideology, demarcation between
democracy, appeal to proletariat, 223–224; social democracy, 67. *See also* liberal democracy
Descartes, Rene, 18
De Tracy, Destutt, 36
dialectical logic, Marx on 179; method of argumentation, 16. *See also* materialism: dialectical
dialectical materialism. *See* materialism: dialectical
divine right of kings, 18, 21, 53–54, 66
division of labor: capitalist and proletariat, 131, 142; commodity form of, 128, 142; intellectuals and, 43–44; mental and manual, 22, 191; natural vs. social institution, 132, 140–142; socially relative vs. universal elements of, 140
doctrine of heavenly afterlife. *See* Christianity: doctrine of heavenly afterlife
dominant ideology thesis, 50–51, 57, 65, 189–193. *See* ruling ideas
Durkheim, Emile, 180–181

E
economists, bourgeois 23, 140–142, 188, 194; vulgar vs. scientific, 135–139, 142, 214
empiricism: Baconian, 31–32; Lockean influence on *philosophes*, 175; Marx on naive, 135; verification criterion, 36, 51, 174
equality, 67, 177, 198–199, 221
Eyerman, Ron, 170

F
fallacies, ideological. *See* ideological fallacies
false consciousness: as alienated thought, 10–12, 46, 162–163 (*See also* alienated mind); as commonsense social thinking, 13–14, 59, 65, 108–109, 127–128; as deluded thinking in politics, 81–83, 87–89; as false thinking, 13, 161, 165; as idealist political thinking, 77, 85; as idealist thought, 41–43; as ignorance of the socially determined nature of thought, 23, 38–41; as manipulated thought, *philosophes* on, 12, 54–55, 162; as metaphysical thinking (*See* false consciousness: as alienated thought, as idealist thought); as self-deceived thought, 9, 86; as unconscious historical and social thought, 7–8, 73–77, 162; Bacon on, 13, 19, 161; Hegel on 8, 73–74, 162–163; Feuerbach on religious, 95–97; philosophical problems with, 10; psychological vs. sociological, 7–9, 52, 54; religious, 25, 95–97
Fay, Brian, 11
Federalist Papers, 116
feminism, 71, 202
fetish: capital, 134, 154; Feuerbach on religious, 97, 127. *See* ideological fallacies: fetishistic thinking
fetishism of commodities, 24, 129, 134, 146, 149. *See also* religion: fetishism of commodities
feudal society. *See* medieval society
Feuerbach, Ludwig: critique of Hegel's metaphysics, 101–103; difference between Feuerbach and *philosophes* on religion, 96, 99–100; Hegel's influence on, 94; influence on young

Marx, 103–104, 111, 116–117; on religious false consciousness, 95–97, 163–164. *See also* alienated mind; alienation; religion
French revolution of 1789, 21
French revolution of 1848, 83–85
Freud, Sigmund, 9, 33
Fromm, Erich, 8
functionalist conception of ideology. *See* ideology: functionalist views on

G

genetic analysis of ideas, 32–33, 37, 43
German political struggles, 90–91
Gramsci, 68

H

Hegel, G. W. F., cunning of reason and false consciousness, 8, 12, 73–75; on alienated mind, 93, 102; philosophy of history, 46–47; system builder, 34; theory of state, 112. *See also* alienated mind; alienation
Helvetius, 12, 55–56. *See also* conspiracy theory of ideology; dominant ideology thesis; false consciousness: as manipulated mind, *philosophes* on; ideological analysis, methods of; rationalization
hermeneutics, 47
historical materialism. *See* materialism: historical
Holbach, 29–31, 35, 51–54. *See also* alienated mind: philosophes on; conspiracy theory of ideology; dominant ideology thesis; false consciousness: as manipulated mind; religion; metaphysics

I

idealism: conception of mind, 34, 37; historical materialist critique of, 46; idealism vs. materialism, 181; idealistic interpretations of thought, 2; philosophical outlook, 39, 46; political, 222; theories of society and history, 46–50. *See also* false consciousness: as idealist thought; illusions of speculative philosophy; *verstehen* methodology
ideological fallacies: bias, 19, 23; false absolutization, 22–23; fetishistic thinking, 24; inverted thinking, 24, 46, 99, 102–103, 105, 125; misrepresenting particular interests as general interests, 22, 57, 158; mistaking appearances for reality, 19, 22; mistaking socially-historically contingent thought as eternally valid a priori ideas, 40–42, 59–60, 159; reification, 20, 22; viewing socially contingent institutions as naturally ordained, 23–24, 42
ideology: as symbolic beliefs, 96, 98–99, 116–117; cognitive vs. non-cognitive views, 4–5; descriptive vs. pejorative, 225; epistemological vs. functionalist, 4–5, 68, 157–160; functionalist views on, 5, 68–72, 157–160, 200; materialist approaches to, 100, 164; realist vs. non-realist views, 175. *See also* conspiracy theory of ideology; dominant ideology thesis; rationalization; ruling ideas; science and ideology, demarcation between; self-deception
ideological analysis, methods of: Feuerbach, 98, 103; Helvetius, 56; Marx, 43, 84–85; materialist, 31–33, 43
ideologies: commonsense, 40, 59–60, 127–128; German peasant, 80–81; liberal democratic, 71, 87–89; of capitalism, 60–61, 127–128; of French bourgeoise, 84–85; of individualism, 208–209; of the oppressed, 53, 70, 90; of social systems, 65–66; religious, 51–53, 79–81; ruling class, 57–58, 70. *See also* ancient political thought; dominant ideology thesis; medieval political thought; ruling ideas
illusions of speculative philosophy, 11, 43

individualism, 208–209
innate truths, doctrine of: Cartesian, 34; critique of, by *philosophes*, 35; Marx on, 42–43, 176
inversion. *See* appearances: representing reality in inverted form; camera obscura model of ideology; ideological fallacies: inverted thinking

J
juridical ideas, 41–42
juridical illusions, 24, 41, 209, 211
justice, 60–63, 127

L
labor theory of value, 139–140, 145
language: descriptive vs. instrumental views, 20
Larrain, Jorge, 4, 10, 101, 106
law. *See* juridical ideas
laws of supply and demand, 133, 148
legitimation crisis, 18
liberal democracy: bourgeois, 71; ideological effects of, 87–89, 198; Marx's critique of, 87–89; young Marx's critique of, 113–116. *See also* democracy
Lichtheim, George, 8, 106
Locke, John, epistemological influence on *philosophes*, 36, 175; on government, 115
Lukacs, Georg, 170
Luther, Martin, 80

M
Madison, James, 116
Malthus, Thomas, 26, 178, 194, 219–220
Mannheim, Karl, 33, 72, 201
Markovic, Mihailo, 217
master-slave mentality. *See* ancient political thought
materialism: conception of mind, 35, 44–45; critical philosophy, 31–32; dialectical, 39, 179; French 12; historical, 9, 38, 80; mechanistic, 39; method of ideological analysis, 31–33, 37, 43; philosophical outlook, 31, 39; structuralist, 13. *See also* reflection theory of ideas
McCarney, Joe, 2, 7, 68, 157, 167
McLellan, David, 4, 10
McMurty, John, 9
medieval political thought, 66, 196–197
medieval society, 17, 40, 66
Merquior, J. G., 169, 201
Meszaros, Istvan, 5, 68
metaphysics: Cartesian, 32, 34, materialist critique of, 30, 36; method of knowledge, 36, 45; Scholastic, 17, 21, 32. *See also* false consciousness: as metaphysical thinking
methodological individualism, 209
Mill, John Stuart, on factors of production, 136
millenarianism, 81
money, young Marx on, 121–122; as universal measure, 133–134
moral point of view, in class stuggle, 160, 186, 198, 218–219
Münzer, Thomas, 81–82

N
naive realism. *See* empiricism: Marx on naive; ideological fallacies: mistaking appearances for reality
natural laws of marketplace, 131–132. *See also* laws of supply and demand
necessary truths. *See* innate truths
Nietzsche, 33, 174

O
organic model of political relations. *See* medieval political thought
origins of ideas/ideologies. *See* genetic analysis of ideas; social determination of ideological thought; social determination of thought

P
Peasant Rebellion, 79–83
personification of things, 24, 130, 134. *See also* fetishism of commodities;

ideological fallacies: fetishistic thinking
phenomenology, 47
Plamenatz, John, 169
power elite political theory, 56
primitive accumulation, 144
propagandists, 12, 50
Protestant Reformation, 79–83
Proudhon, Joseph, 23, 40, 42
psychoanalytical views of ideology. *See* false consciousness: psychological vs. sociological; rationalization: Freudian vs. Marxist views on

R
rationalism. *See* metaphysics: Cartesian
rationalization: Engels and Marx on, 79; Freudian vs. Marxist on, 9, Helvetius on, 55–56; Marx on, 85–86
reflection theory of idea, Marx's, 179, 192–193
reification, 93–94, 97, 102, 123–124, 163, 118–119, 212. *See also* ideological fallacies: reification
religion: as chimera, Holbach on, 51, 96; as dream state of mind, Feuerbach on, 96–97; as irrational idea, Holbach on, 52; as symbol, Feuerbach on, 96, 98–99; harmfulness of religion, Feuerbach on 100; *philosophes* on, 30; *philosophes* explanation of origins of, 52; in class struggles, 67; religion and fetishism of commodities, 147–152. *See also* false consciousness: religious; ideologies: religious
Ricardo, David, 135. *See* economists
Ricoeur, Paul, 183
rights, young Marx on, 115
Rossi-Landi, Ferruccio, 225
Rubinstein, David, 13–14
ruling ideas, 22–23, 29–30, 40, 47, 50–51, 57–60, 65–67, 82, 90, 127–128. *See* common sense; dominant ideology thesis; ideological fallacies: mistaking socially-historically contingent thought as eternally valid a priori ideas

S
Schmitt, Richard, 13
scholasticism. *See* metaphysics
Schultz, Alfred, 47, 181
science and ideology, demarcation between: 4–7; appearance vs. essence, 138–139, 152–154; biased vs. unbiased thought, 20, 26; cognitive vs. non–cognitive, 160; disinterested thought vs. partisan thought, 20, 26–27; false vs. true, 71–72, 160; idealist vs. materialist, 36, 46–50; practical vs. theoretical, 4–5
self-deception, 2, 10, 85–87
Seliger, Martin, 2, 201
skepticism, 18; on social science, 71–72, 168
Smith, Adam. *See* economists
social contract theory, 53
social determination of ideological thought, 25, 43–44, 58–60, 86–87 165–166, 172, 177–178, 186, 188–193, 194–195, 199, 201
social determination of thought, 38–40, 176
social science: deductive vs. inductive, 139; economics, 135–139 188; history, 46; idealist vs. materialist methods, 46–50; structuralist tradition in sociology, 13–14. *See also* Beard, Charles; *verstehen* methodology
social self-conceptions, 40
sociology of knowledge, 72
soul, philosophes on, 30
Spinoza, 32
standpoint epistemology, 72
state, political: bourgeois state, 114; religious conceptions of the state, 116–117; as symbol, young Marx on, 111–112, 116–117. *See also* Hegel: theory of state; liberal democracy
symbolism. *See* ideology: as symbolic beliefs; state, political

T
Taylor, Charles, 47

Thomson, George, 170
trinity formula of capitalism, 130, 136–137, 148

U
Unconscious, social and historical thought, 8; Freudian and Marxist views, 8–9
Unconscious motivation, Engels on 75–76, 78–79; Hegel on, 74
U.S. Declaration of Independence, 66

V
Verstehen methodology, 47, 84, 181–182

W
Weber, Max 47
Williams, Bernard, 17
Wood, Allen, 10, 12

Y
young Marx, on alienation, 121; young vs. mature Marx, 106–111, 150. *See* alienated mind; alienation; money, young Marx on; state, political

Z
Zinn, Howard, 184